Torture and the Recognition of Psychological Suffering in International Law

Torture and the Recognition of Psychological Suffering in International Law

ERGÜN CAKAL

OXFORD
UNIVERSITY PRESS

OXFORD
UNIVERSITY PRESS

Great Clarendon Street, Oxford, OX2 6DP,
United Kingdom

Oxford University Press is a department of the University of Oxford.
It furthers the University's objective of excellence in research, scholarship,
and education by publishing worldwide. Oxford is a registered trade mark of
Oxford University Press in the UK and in certain other countries.

Published in the United States of America by Oxford University Press
546 Fifth Avenue, New York, NY 10036, United States of America

British Library Cataloguing in Publication Data
Data available

Library of Congress Control Number: 2026939755

ISBN 978–0–19–898949–3

DOI: 10.1093/oso/9780198989493.001.0001

Printed and bound by
CPI Group (UK) Ltd., Croydon, CR0 4YY

The manufacturer's authorized representative in the EU for product safety is
Oxford University Press España S.A. of Parque Empresarial San Fernando de Henares,
Avenida de Castilla, 2 – 28830 Madrid (www.oup.es/en or product.safety@oup.com).
OUP España S.A. also acts as importer into Spain of products made by the manufacturer.

MIX
Paper | Supporting responsible forestry
FSC® C013604

For Josie, Charlie, Sonia, Aynur, and Ayşe

Usage

Readers should note that I use the terms 'the prohibition' or 'torture's prohibition' to refer in short to the entire spectrum of state violence prohibited, namely 'torture' and 'inhuman' and 'degrading' treatment—unless where specified. As not all legal frameworks refer to 'cruelty', I take it to be covered under the categories of inhuman and degrading treatment. As shortly elaborated, I take the following couplets as effectively synonymous: 'pain' and 'suffering'; 'treatment' and 'punishment'; 'mental' and 'psychological'. I use 'advocates' to refer to legally trained practitioners representing victim-survivors and 'adjudicators' to refer to any decision-maker, whether a judge or a committee or a tribunal member. I refer to 'victim-survivors' variably as victims, applicants, complainants, and petitioners. I have generally used OSCOLA citations except where they proved cumbersome (e.g. multiple case numbers).

Preface

This book emerged from anti-torture practice at the Danish Institute Against Torture (DIGNITY) between August 2016 and August 2021, followed by doctoral research at the University of Copenhagen's Faculty of Law between September 2021 and November 2024. Although it bordered on an unhealthy obsession, this has been a thoroughly fun and enthralling project. It allowed me to meet a host of clever people who helped me with my 'homework'. It offered solace from the familiar grind, wall-to-wall meetings, and institutional demands. For recognizing and nurturing an academic inclination, I thank Andrew Jefferson and Tomas Max Martin. For the confidence, ample autonomy, steering the research at its crucial stages, and getting me over the line, I thank my PhD supervisors, Mikael Rask Madsen and Toby Kelly.

From January to August 2025, I briefly returned to DIGNITY—partly on whose time I transformed the research into this (hopefully more engaging) book. For letting me (back) in and reminding me of the ropes, I thank Elna Søndergaard, Therese Rytter, and Marie Brasholt. This book does not necessarily represent their views or the position of DIGNITY at large. In fact, some findings challenge assumptions underpinning some programmes. Others, at DIGNITY and beyond, without whom this work would not be what it is include (in loose order of appearance): Vicky Canning, Steffen Jensen, Henrik Rønsbo, Jens Elo Rytter, Amnon Lev, Natasa Mavronicola, Amin Parsa, Ida Nafstad, Hannah Russell, Annika Lindberg, Darius Rejali, Carmi Lecker, Elise Ramirez, Liv Gaborit, Pau Pérez-Sales, Nimisha Patel, Michelle Farrell, Frederik Rom Taxhjelm, Ula Aleksandra Kos, Anouk Lamé, Aysel Eybil Küçüksu, Karen McGregor Richmond, Ellen Aagaard Marquard, Sarah Haddad, Ezgi Yildiz, Marie Thøgersen, Anne Heinisch, Genaro Andrés Manrique Giacomán, Oana Ichim, Zuzanna Godzimirska, Yussef Al Tamimi, Martin Lolle Christensen, Silvia Steininger, Dilek Kurban, Uğur Erdal, Jakob Holtermann, Henrik Palme Olsen, Laura Blanco, Anne Lise Kjær, Mette Saks, Lilli Streymnes, Valentin Jeutner, Mikkel Jarle Christensen, Nele Schuldt, Will Byrne, Lutz Oette, Jenny Orlando Salling, Pernille Kloster, and Joseph Bernasol.

I also thank the Danish taxpayer who not only paid my salary for these years but also footed an exorbitant bill, under the auspices of the Eliteforsk travel grant, to allow me to visit SOAS and Oxford where much of the doctoral research was rethought and reworked. I also thank my many librarians at Det Kgl. Bibliotek and at the ECtHR for digging up obscure texts for me. Then there were the multitudes who enriched the research through trusting to be interviewed or freely providing input, gifting insights into my work. For the opportunity to turn the doctoral dissertation into a book, I am indebted to my steadfast editors at Oxford University Press, especially Alexander Hardie-Forsyth. I thank you (one and all).

For a once working-class kid (long turned middle class), dreaming of such lofty research (not simply as a learned pursuit of living around books but as a means to weaving a safety net in case of a hard fall), I see that it was more the personal that propelled and protected me than the professional. My sister Aynur, mum Ayşe, and late dad Lütfi all kept me going through it in their own way. Along the way, far from home (yes, I still call Australia home), doors and souls were opened in Turkey, the US, the Netherlands, Sweden, and Denmark. On this score, I remember: the Fergusons, Emmett Minor, Usman Ashraf, the Lords, Karin Sjögren, Taha and Mehmet Ali, Fredrick and Ida, Tina Juul Skou, Per Jakobsen, Simon Skou Jakobsen, Nanna Schrøder, Eva and Solvej, the Ahmxds, and Caroline Lantto. To my dearest Josefine, there has been no stronger support than yours. Throughout this project I became a father twice, to Charlie and Sonia. I love you (one and all).

My core professional care and concern has long been the prevailing silences and denials in law and torture practice and research. As with my earlier work, I have written out of angst—at the lack of articulation and admission of the field's failings. It takes time (learning and unlearning the field's habitus) to identify such failings; to confidently confront the resistance of those in power to relinquish their hard-won mastery, authority, and ensuing identity and 'sense of control'.[1] It has taken time and will take time yet to more fully understand its implications for research and practice. International human rights law, its institutions and actors, are essentially of and for states. The dominant paradigm, and the medico-legal duopoly underwriting it, will not singlehandedly lead to torture's eradication. Eradication is not simply a question of more evidence. I have elaborated on this in a companion book.[2] Recognition as eradication, as the book at hand argues, is as much a socio-political and sense-centric question as it is technical. If the book conveys a singular point to the reader, I hope that this is it.

[1] Pierre Schlag, *Enchantment of Reason* (Duke University Press 1998) 11, 15.
[2] Ergün Cakal, *Law and Torture* (CUP 2025).

Contents

Abbreviations

ACHR	American Convention on Human Rights
CAT	Committee Against Torture
CEJIL	Center for Justice and International Law
CIDT	cruel, inhuman, and degrading treatment
CoE	Council of Europe
CPT	European Committee for the Prevention of Torture
CUP	Cambridge University Press
ECHR	European Convention on Human Rights
ECmHR	European Commission of Human Rights
ECtHR	European Court of Human Rights
GC	Grand Chamber
HRC	Human Rights Committee
IACmHR	Inter-American Commission of Human Rights
IACPPT	Inter-American Convention to Prevent and Punish Torture
IACtHR	Inter-American Court of Human Rights
ICCPR	International Covenant on Civil and Political Rights
ICRC	International Committee of the Red Cross
ICTY	International Criminal Tribunal for the former Yugoslavia
IRA	Irish Republican Army
Istanbul Protocol	Manual on the Effective Investigation and Documentation of Torture and Other Cruel, Inhuman or Degrading Treatment or Punishment
NGO	non-governmental organization
OAS	Organization of American States
ors	others
OUP	Oxford University Press
para	paragraph
PCATI	Public Committee Against Torture in Israel
UN	United Nations
UNCAT	UN Convention Against Torture and Other Cruel, Inhuman or Degrading Treatment or Punishment
UN NMR	UN Nelson Mandela Rules (2015)
UN OHCHR	Office of the High Commissioner for Human Rights
UN SMR	UN Standard Minimum Rules
UN SRT	UN Special Rapporteur on Torture

1
Introduction

> Torturers have learnt to adapt. Gone are the wheels, knotted ropes, trestles bristling with steel points, together with other complex and ingenious mechanisms. In a sense torture has become more domestic and unpretentious. But no less painful.[1]

> [T]he Court concedes that there are certain difficulties involved in assessing claims relating to alleged mental suffering or humiliation in the absence of actual bodily injury.[2]

How torture is practised has changed. How society understands suffering has also changed. This change has meant that torture, and suffering more broadly, no longer necessarily requires the infliction of overt physical acts or impacts. Prolonged solitary confinement, irreducible life imprisonment, threats to life, and sleep deprivation have all come to enter the prohibition's purview. These practices are now presumed to inflict suffering beyond the inevitable and permissible. While social sensitivities around suffering and state practices have shifted, there remains a difficulty in how these are argued and adjudicated in legal contexts. Despite general recognition, the invisibility of psychological suffering has invoked notions of the trivial and inevitable and has invited doubt and dismissal by legal actors. States too have encouraged such doubt around the gravity and veracity of victim-survivors' psychological suffering in closely guarding their psychologically oriented coercive practices from entering the purview of torture's prohibition. The figure of 'psychological suffering' has, in short, faced 'certain difficulties' in being readily afforded recognition. The following four vignettes, from cases well known and less known, serve to illustrate

[1] Antonio Cassese, *Inhuman States: Imprisonment, Detention and Torture in Europe Today* (Polity 1996) 63.

[2] *Dzerkorashvili and others v Georgia* [2023] ECtHR 70572/16 [68] involved the verbal abuse of an LGBT group at a police station and a courthouse. This case was ultimately not successful because the applicants' evidence was not put before national authorities, therefore it was deemed not admissible by the ECtHR.

Torture and the Recognition of Psychological Suffering in International Law. Ergün Cakal, Oxford University Press.
 DOI: 10.1093/oso/9780198989493.003.0001

the contours of this contest over the last five decades across at least three authoritative institutions.

Vignette 1. *Ireland v UK*, European Commission of Human Rights (ECmHR) and European Court of Human Rights (ECtHR). The series of rulings in *Ireland* in 1976 by the ECmHR and in 1978 and 2018 by the ECtHR have cast a long shadow over how torture's prohibition has been understood. In its 1976 ruling, the ECmHR first adjudicated on practices intended not to leave physical marks, including wall-standing, hooding, subjection to noise, deprivation of sleep, and deprivation of food and drink. In brief, the ECmHR found that these 'five techniques', used against suspected IRA members, constituted 'a modern system of torture falling into the same category as [previous] systems' under Article 3 (prohibition of torture and inhuman and degrading treatment) of the European Convention on Human Rights (ECHR).[3] When it progressed to the ECtHR in 1978, however, the ECtHR disagreed and instead held that the facts only gave rise to a finding of inhuman and degrading treatment but not torture as the necessary severity of suffering (or 'special stigma') was not established.

Dissenting judges unsuccessfully insisted that 'modern techniques of oppression [...] no longer presupposed physical violence', differed 'markedly from the primitive, brutal methods employed in former times', and were not 'only present in a medieval dungeon where the appliances of rack and thumbscrew or similar devices were employed'. The majority nevertheless downgraded the ECmHR ruling despite not having heard witness evidence, construing torture to require 'a special stigma' which it failed to identify in the 'five techniques'.[4] In reasoning so, the majority recognized a wide evidentiary discretion for itself in 'being master of its own procedure and of its own rules [having] complete freedom in assessing not only the admissibility and the relevance but also the probative value of each item of evidence before it'.[5] The ECtHR used its discretion in a state-deferential manner then (and since).[6] It led to two decades (1976–96) where there was no specific finding of torture by the ECtHR. And, most notably, it has led to no finding of torture where psychological suffering predominated or stood on its own. In the 2018 review of *Ireland* upon disclosure of new evidence, the ECtHR decided not to change its 1978 conclusion

[3] *Ireland v UK* [1976] ECmHR 5310/71 [512].
[4] *Ireland v UK* [1978] ECtHR 5310/71 [167].
[5] ibid [209].
[6] Marie-Bénédicte Dembour, 'Beyond Reasonable Doubt at Its Worst—But Also at Its Potential Best: Dissecting *Ireland v the United Kingdom*'s No-Torture Finding' (2023) 4 European Convention on Human Rights Law Review 375–425.

primarily upon the principle of legal certainty[7]—failing to progress towards a torture finding.[8] A dissent characterized this as narrow and as displaying a 'remarkable degree of judicial acrobacy' to 'shelter itself behind' legal certainty.[9] So, what was meant by 'special stigma' after all? What, if not an association between torture and physical marks, can explain this result?

Vignette 2. *NA v Finland*, ECtHR. In November 2017, Finland deported NA's father to Iraq after rejecting her father's asylum claim. He was deemed not to deserve protection from Finland despite a history of holding politically sensitive positions, being subjected to death threats, and surviving assassination attempts in Iraq. NA's father was shot dead within weeks of his return to Iraq. NA brought Finland before the ECtHR to argue that Finland's rejection of her father's claim exposed him to violations of Articles 2 (right to life) and 3 under the ECHR. The Court agreed. She also argued, being his daughter, that the experience had violated her own Article 3 rights with the 'uncertainty as to his fate' upon deportation and his violent death having 'caused her considerable suffering'. Finland disagreed and argued that she had not 'experienced any period of uncertainty as to her father's fate, nor had she been a direct witness to the events in Iraq' so that 'there were no such special factors in place giving the applicant's suffering a dimension and character distinct from the emotional distress which inevitably stemmed from the alleged violation itself'.

The Court prefaced its reasoning by pronouncing that it had 'always been sensitive in its case-law to the profound psychological impact of a serious human rights violation on the victim's family members'.[10] It nevertheless went on to accept Finland's arguments. Although NA had 'a very close relationship with her father', the Court determined, they had not lived together, and being 'unaware of his whereabouts for about fifteen days' was 'not sufficient for her emotional suffering on those grounds to constitute inhuman treatment'. NA's own claim to victimhood was thus summarily rejected; she had no special psychological suffering to argue. Her suffering was to be expected and thus accepted as 'inevitable'. There is much that remains unexplained in this decision. How did the judges determine that NA's suffering was too 'short' or not sufficiently 'special'? How was NA's suffering differentiated from other psychological suffering to which the Court had 'been sensitive'? How was 'inevitable' suffering understood? On what was this reasoning grounded; was it evidence,

[7] *Ireland v UK* [2018] ECtHR 5310/71 [122].

[8] Nigel Rodley, 'The Definition(s) of Torture in International Law' (2002) 55 Current Legal Problems 477 had hypothesized along these lines after the *Selmouni* principle.

[9] *Ireland v UK* [2018] ECtHR 5310/71, dissent of Judge O'Leary [74, 77].

[10] *NA v Finland* [2019] ECtHR 25244/18 [94–95].

experiences, emotion, common knowledge? Could NA have done more to substantiate her suffering? Would it have been different if her suffering had been more physical, or somehow more visible?

Vignette 3. *Cardenas v Peru*, Inter-American Court of Human Rights (IACtHR). In 1994, Magistrate Luis Cardenas was detained incommunicado and in isolation for a month on the grounds of being associated with a terrorist organization. Upon release, he complained of having been subjected to 'psychological torture', and was ultimately heard before the IACtHR. The majority of judges there considered that the uncertainty he faced amounted to a violation of his and his family's right to humane treatment under Article 5 of the American Convention on Human Rights (ACHR).[11] In so doing, the IACtHR acted on the presumption, based on caselaw in the absence of evidence, that 'solitary confinement can generate a situation of extreme psychological and moral suffering'.

Challenging the flexibility that the majority of judges afforded itself, Judge Sierra Harbor dissented and argued that the finding that the applicant had suffered was too much of a presumption by the majority. He raised a range of questions: how was his uncertainty to be considered intense when he was visited by his relatives, the International Committee of the Red Cross (ICRC), and prosecutors; how did the Court exempt the applicant from proving his allegations beyond accepting 'vague statements', particularly in not requiring that expertise in making its finding as with other Article 5 cases? What moved the Court in this case to reason the way it did? When and where do presumptions prove sufficient for substantiating psychological suffering and when is evidence necessary? Although potentially restricting the protection on offer, these are also legitimate questions.

Vignette 4. *Coppin v Ireland*, UN Committee Against Torture (CAT). Between 1964 and 1968, Elizabeth Coppin was institutionalized in the Magdalene Laundries due to being born to a single mother in Ireland. As a teenager, separated from her family, she was subjected to 'arbitrary detention, servitude and forced labour without pay for six days a week [...] numerous times to deliberate and ritual humiliation; denial of identity, educational opportunity and privacy; neglect; and other forms of grave physical and psychological abuse'.[12] She lived (and continues to live) with the suffering since—significant psychological suffering. She pursued redress in Ireland since 1997 with minimal

[11] *Galindo Cardenas et al v Peru* [2015] IACtHR [241–48].
[12] *Coppin v Ireland* [2023] CAT-C-73-D-879-2018.

results.[13] In state reviews of Ireland, the CAT had concluded as much—urging stronger accountability efforts on the part of the authorities. Nothing changed. Taking encouragement from its criticisms, Elizabeth Coppin petitioned the CAT in 2018. Coppin argued that her experiences were at least a violation of Article 16 of the UN Convention Against Torture (UNCAT; cruel, inhuman, and degrading treatment) based on the notion of a continuous violation for being refused an official investigation into her ill-treatment. She submitted overwhelming corroborative evidence including a psychological report attesting to the ongoing suffering, as prepared by a renowned psychologist with expertise in anti-torture documentation. This expert opinion confirmed that Coppin 'continues to severely suffer from psychological difficulties, including anxiety, features of chronic post-trauma stress and depression [related to her] experiences' in the Laundries.[14]

Ireland, in response, rejected her claim on the basis that 'the acts complained of have neither the required level of intensity or cruelty nor the impermissible purpose to permit them to be defined as torture [nor] within the definition of cruel or inhuman or degrading treatment or punishment'.[15] The CAT rejected Coppin's claim without assessing the nature of her suffering or explaining reasons for departing from its previous positions. Compared to *NA*, there is even thinner reasoning. Why was the nature of the suffering not assessed on the face of the decision? Was it even deliberated? Was there something about the nature of this suffering, beyond it being historical, that enabled the members to dismiss it so boldly? That it was psychological in nature? What weight was the medico-legal report given?

These are some of the questions, upon reading these several cases and hundreds of others from international human rights adjudicatory bodies, which drew me to writing this book. While these accounts consider diverse practices and experiences from the routine to the spectacular, their commonality is the psychologically overt (and thus relatively invisible) nature of the suffering concerned. This book aims to examine these lines of reasoning through the use of systematic caselaw analysis and interviews with advocates (applicant lawyers) and adjudicators (judges and quasi-judicial decision-makers), as well as senior institutional lawyers (registry or secretariat). These are further supplemented by non-legal experts (medical doctors and psychologists). The discussions

[13] Natasa Mavronicola, 'Cruel Legacies: The CAT's Decision in Coppin v Ireland', 12 February 2023, *Opinio Juris*; Máiréad Enright, 'Coppin v. Ireland: Depressing Conservatism from the UN Committee Against Torture', 12 February 2023, *Opinio Juris*.

[14] Nimisha Patel, 'Medico-Legal Report for Elizabeth Coppin',16 August 2017, 2.

[15] Submission of the Government of Ireland, 31 July 2020 [96].

reveal numerous inter-related reasons for this: that socio-political standards recognizing the significance of psychological suffering are selectively applied or altogether overlooked by international adjudicators; that scientific expertise documenting health impacts of psychologically oriented practices has not compelled adjudicators in all cases; that procedural pragmatism encourages caution and conservatism regarding the categorization of torture; and that interpretation still depends on sense-centric reasoning (intuition–emotion–presumption), potentially undercutting scientific expertise and perpetuating associations of severe suffering with the physical.

Conceptualizing and contextualizing torture's prohibition

Prominent historical accounts of torture take states as increasingly resorting to inflicting psychological suffering without leaving overt physical marks.[16] While physically oriented practices remain most prevalent,[17] these accounts attribute this marked change to official imperatives to evade detection, challenge, and accountability.[18] Despite the wide acceptance of such accounts, interpreting cases involving such psychological suffering has proven difficult for international human rights advocates and adjudicators working on the prohibition of torture and inhuman and degrading treatment. A systematic survey of the relevant international caselaw, as will be presented in this book, reveals vast variation in how psychological suffering is found to violate the prohibition (or not). When singled out in cases brought before the ECtHR, the IACtHR, and the CAT, three key authorities in interpreting the prohibition, psychological suffering has never been *specifically* categorized as torture, but

[16] Pau Pérez-Sales, *Psychological Torture: Definition, Evaluation and Measurement* (Routledge 2016) xix. Recent reports from anti-torture NGOs report a high prevalence of non-physical methods: Crew Against Torture, 'Prohibited Methods of Psychological Influence: Analysis of Russian and International Law' (2022); and Public Committee Against Torture in Israel (PCATI), 'Torture in Israel 2019: Situation Report'.

[17] This book is not about torture's prevalence. For a long-time legal advisor at Amnesty, the most common method worldwide is 'beating, in its various forms': Yuval Ginbar, 'Making Human Rights Sense of the Torture Definition' in Metin Başoğlu (ed), *Torture and Its Definition in International Law: An Interdisciplinary Approach* (OUP 2017) 304. Andrew Milewski and others, 'Reported Methods, Distributions, and Frequencies of Torture Globally: A Systematic Review and Meta-analysis' (2023) 6 (10) JAMA Netw Open also points to beatings being most prevalent followed closely by psychological methods.

[18] I will leave the important question of whether it is the prevalence or the recognition that is increasing to others to debate. For Didier Fassin and Richard Rechtman, *The Empire of Trauma: An Inquiry into the Condition of Victimhood* (Princeton University Press 2009) 160, the 'reality of this suffering [trauma] is of course not new, but the recognition of it certainly is. And does recognition not make it a little more real?'

as inhuman and degrading treatment.[19] What is more, psychological suffering is often excluded altogether from the purview of the prohibition, categorized instead as 'lawful sanctions' or as falling below the 'minimum level of severity' threshold, and therefore not found to be a violation. The doctrinal scholarship offers scant explanations for this categorization and exclusion of psychological suffering from the prohibition of torture in practice.

The nature of suffering included or excluded and how that is categorized under the prohibition informs how states treat those in their care and custody. States, equally autocratic or democratic, have pushed for maintaining thresholds of recognition as high. Since the very first international cases, states have argued against an expansive recognition of psychological suffering when standing on its own, given its short duration, its subjective (and self-serving) nature, or that it needed to be more than inevitable, but exceptional, to be recognized—especially as torture. Torture, for prominent scholars too, has rather been characterized as requiring a 'physical act'[20] and 'physical torment'.[21] Others have been more forceful in their rejection of 'structural and psychological violence' which, for them, appear as 'excuses for an ideological argumentation rather than scholarly concepts'.[22] Psychological suffering, further to the point, is similarly discounted in other areas of law that concern injury, namely tort law,[23] international criminal law, and international humanitarian law.[24] These have all reduced the archetypal understanding of readily recognizable and redress-worthy violence to its physical manifestation.[25]

[19] I do recognize *near*-exceptions from other international human rights bodies: UN Committee on the Rights of Persons with Disabilities' decision in *X v Tanzania* (CRPD/C/18/D/22/2014) that 'psychological torture and/or ill-treatment' resulted from revictimization from non-prosecution of the victim's offenders comes close but remains imprecise; the Inter-American Commission on Human Rights held rape to be 'psychological torture' in *Raquel Martí de Mejía v Perú* (OEA/SerL/V/II.91 Doc 7 at 157) (1996); and the UN Human Rights Committee considered as 'psychological torture' the threat to cut off the victim's arms in *Miguel Angel Estrella v Uruguay* (1990) CCPR-C-OP-2 [8.3]. I deal with the few similar close calls in the rest of the book.

[20] Elaine Scarry, *The Body in Pain* (OUP 1985) 28.

[21] Darius Rejali, 'Torture and Democracy: What Now?' in Shampa Biswas and Zahi Zalloua (eds), *Torture: Power, Democracy and the Human Body* (University of Washington Press 2011) 26. Richard Posner, 'Torture, Terrorism and Interrogation' in Sanford Levinson, *Torture: A Collection* (2004) distinguishes 'the line that separates psychological from physical coercion, and permit[s] it to be crossed only *in extremis*', holding that the latter is worse than the former.

[22] Pieter Spierenburg, *Violence and Punishment: Civilizing the Body through Time* (Polity 2013) 2.

[23] Harvey Teff, *Causing Psychiatric and Emotional Harm: Reshaping the Boundaries of Legal Liability* (Bloomsbury 2008).

[24] Eliav Lieblich, 'Beyond Life and Limb: Exploring Incidental Mental Harm under International Humanitarian Law' in Derek Jink and others (eds), *Applying International Humanitarian Law in Judicial and Quasi-Judicial Bodies* (Asser Press 2014); Solon Solomon, 'Quasi-judicial Bodies and the Establishment of Standards and Principles for Assessing Mental Harm Sustained by Civilians Exposed to Hostilities' (2021) 12 (1) Journal of International Dispute Settlement 104–24.

[25] Yves Winter, 'Violence and Visibility' (2012) 34 (2) New Political Science 195–202.

Against this backdrop, international human rights adjudication remains tasked with answering two key questions in all cases brought under the prohibition: (i) is the suffering to be *recognized* as violating the prohibition of torture and inhuman and degrading treatment *at all* and (ii) if recognizable, how is this suffering then to be *categorized* (namely, as torture, inhuman, or degrading)? Adjudicators are thus entrusted with the power to name and identify what is 'torture', 'inhuman', and 'degrading' or that which is altogether excluded from the prohibition's purview. Given that torture and inhuman and degrading treatment are *equally* prohibited,[26] this categorization has been dismissed as purely academic.[27] Keeping all categories under the same prohibition could be said to have been 'precisely to erect a barricade against the contestation that we so often hear concerning what ought to count as "real" torture'.[28] There persists, nevertheless, a continued insistence that certain acts are specifically called 'torture' and not 'inhuman' or 'degrading' and vice versa, or that certain acts are altogether excluded—producing and perpetuating a discursive tension between *narrow* (exclusive and conservative) and *broad* (inclusive, expansive, and progressive) interpretations. Given this complexity, the three institutions in view, the ECtHR, IACtHR, and CAT (and their actors), have thus come to enjoy substantial discretion.

The principled consensus in anti-torture scholarship, at least, is that both physically or psychologically oriented acts can *equally* produce severe suffering. This is reflected in the authoritative legal[29] as well as the non-legal scholarship.[30] While accepting this in principle, the interpretive practice has evaded conceptual coherence at all three institutions. How psychological suffering is included, excluded, or categorized, or recognition of it expanded, is not consistent or clear upon reading the relevant caselaw. Distinctions, that is to say, do not consistently turn on any one definitional element (i.e. intention, purpose, gravity of suffering), although the gravity of the suffering is often foregrounded. How that gravity is understood and assessed remains problematically vague.

[26] CAT, 'General Comment No 2' (2008) CAT-C-GC-2; CAT-68-D-818-2017 [8.2].

[27] Nigel Rodley, 'Reflections on Committee Against Torture General Comment No 2' (2008) 11 (2) New York City Law Review 356: torture is not 'at the top end of a pyramid of pain'.

[28] Danielle Celermajer, *The Prevention of Torture: An Ecological Approach* (CUP 2018) 37.

[29] Manfred Nowak and others (eds), *The United Nations Convention Against Torture and Its Optional Protocol: A Commentary* (2nd edn, OUP 2019) 50.

[30] Nora Sveaass, 'Destroying Minds: Psychological Pain and the Crime of Torture' (2008) 11 (2) New York City Law Review 303–24; Pérez-Sales (n 16).

The interpretive practices at all three institutions around the prohibition are further complicated given the changing contexts (socio-political/institutional/scientific) in which the nature of psychological suffering is understood. As understandings around suffering change, perhaps towards greater sensitivity to (and inclusivity of) its psychological aspects, conventional legal understandings (or interpretations) under the prohibition might be expected to shift as well. The jurisprudential authority for this premise is attributed to *Tyrer v UK* where the ECtHR characterized the ECHR as 'a living document [to be] interpreted in the light of present-day conditions'[31] and to the latter case of *Selmouni v France* where, building on the 'living instrument' doctrine, the ECtHR elaborated that[32]

> certain acts which were classified in the past as 'inhuman and degrading treatment' as opposed to 'torture' could be classified differently in the future. […] the increasingly high standard being required in the area of the protection of human rights and fundamental liberties correspondingly and inevitably requires greater firmness in assessing breaches of the fundamental values of democratic societies.

This conceivably expects an expansion in the nature of the suffering covered by the prohibition. The two precedents, in *Tyrer* and *Selmouni*, have been adopted by the CAT and IACtHR, meaning that all three institutions have interpreted their guiding instruments as 'living instruments'—influenced by contextual considerations as deduced by dynamic interpretation.[33] Related UN organs such as the Human Rights Committee (HRC) and the Special Rapporteur on Torture (UN SRT) have too adopted dynamic interpretation in their work—with the latter urging that it be directed to emergent technologies and techniques not needing direct physical interaction with the victim.[34] Yet

[31] *Tyrer v UK* [1978] ECtHR 5856/72 [31].

[32] *Selmouni v France* [1999] ECtHR 25803/94 [101].

[33] *Right to Information on Consular Assistance in the Framework of the Guarantees of the Due Process of Law, Mexico v United States* [1999] IACtHR Advisory Opinion OC-16/99 [114]; CAT, 'General Comment No 2' (2008) A/63/44 [1]. The UN HRC has held that the International Covenant on Civil and Political Rights (ICCPR) 'should be interpreted as a living instrument and […] applied in context and in the light of present-day conditions' (CCPR-C-78-D-829-1998 [10.3]). The UN SRT has also explicitly connected the prohibition of torture to 'present-day conditions and the changing values of democratic societies' (A/HRC/22/53 [14–15]).

[34] UN SRT, Report (2020) A/HRC/43/49 [12]. See also *Trop v Dulles* (1958) 356 US 86, p 101, connecting cruel and unusual punishment to 'evolving standards of decency that mark the progress of a maturing society [and] judged not by the standards that prevailed in 1685 [or] when the Bill of Rights was adopted, but rather by those that currently prevail'.

how these emerging socio-political understandings influence legal interpretation too remains unclear.

Three inter-related questions are begged as arising from all this lack of clarity: (i) why has psychological suffering never been categorized as torture under international human rights adjudication? (ii) Why has psychological suffering often been categorized as degrading treatment or often 'lawful' or falling below the minimum level of severity under international human rights adjudication? (iii) How are these questions answered in practice? This book clarifies these points through combining two tracks, analysing the *precedents* and *practices* of the primary actors of three international institutions examined. Using the doctrinal material, the first track initially reviews and analyses caselaw (their precedents) to identify the bounds of recognition, namely how these institutions have respectively included, excluded, expanded, and categorized psychological suffering. The material here consists of decisions as well as related press releases and guiding documents articulating institutional positions on the interpretation of the prohibition.

Through the use of semi-structured interviews, the second track then identifies and systematizes the different perspectives and positions pertaining to how relevant actors have undertaken their interpretive tasks (practices) with respect to cases where psychological suffering was predominant (and was singled out in reasoning). The actors in focus are respectively the advocates, adjudicators, senior institutional lawyers, and non-legal experts involved in litigation. Actors' perspectives on their *practices* relate to how they are influenced by socio-political standards (invocation and selection of evidence of social change with respect to psychological suffering), scientific expertise (having the capacity to understand and receive expert evidence of psychological suffering), and sense-centric reasoning (through intuition, emotion, and presumption) pertaining to assessing the gravity of psychological suffering. These different analytic angles (in Figure 1.1) will shortly be introduced.

Contesting psychological suffering

It is worth addressing three central terms used in this book from its outset: 'psychological suffering', its 'recognition', and its 'categorization'. To take the most fraught term first: although commonly invoked, 'psychological suffering' is questioned in terms of its scientific utility and accuracy—namely, whether it aids in accurately conceptualizing the reality of severe suffering. Despite its prevalent use, it draws a false dichotomy between the mind and the body. It

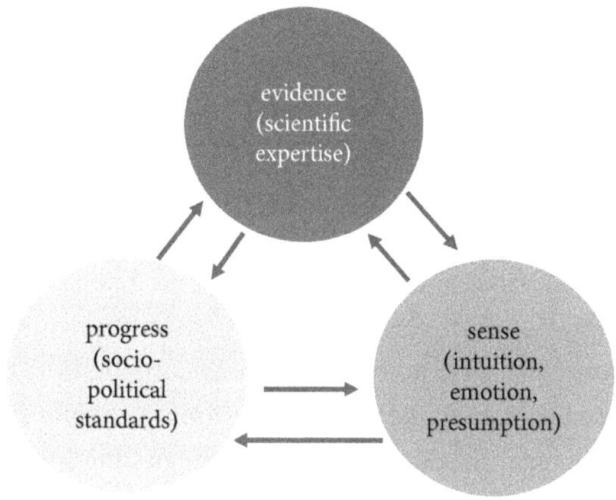

Figure 1.1 Three notions explicating the discursive conditionalities for recognition.

is not scientifically or philosophically sound, and thus stands to be readily rejected. I too accept this.

As early as 1973, Amnesty International held that, although 'the concept of a mind–body dichotomy may appear to be in the development of moral and behavioural norms, it poses severe obstacles to a proper understanding' of suffering and is as such unacceptable. What was promoted instead was to situate suffering more on a 'physical-psychological continuum'.[35] Medical and historical scholarship,[36] denoting the 'psychological' more broadly, is also not without contestation or controversy. It invokes a generally rejected Cartesian dualism—assuming a workable distinction between mind and body. Conventionally, this distinction has attributed 'real' pain as biomedical, physical, and 'anchored in visible tissue damage'—leading to the dominance of medicine in its study and response and the exclusion of cultural, cognitive, and affective dimensions.[37]

For those rejecting this distinction, the increasing focus on psychological suffering has fragmented the anti-torture field and as not being psychiatrically,[38]

[35] Amnesty International, *Report on Torture* (Duckworth 1973) 35.

[36] Mark Sullivan, 'Finding Pain between Minds and Bodies' (2001) 17 (2) The Clinical Journal of Pain 146–56.

[37] Simon J Williams and Gillian Bendelow, *The Lived Body: Sociological Themes, Embodied Issues* (Routledge 1998) 157.

[38] Metin Başoğlu and others, 'Torture vs Other Cruel, Inhuman, and Degrading Treatment: Is the Distinction Real or Apparent?' (2007) 64 Archives of General Psychiatry 277 concludes that stress indicators of psychological methods can be as severe as physical methods.

psychologically,[39] culturally,[40] or philosophically[41] sound. While emphasizing the importance of psychological suffering, for instance, the UN *Manual on the Effective Investigation and Documentation of Torture and Other Cruel, Inhuman or Degrading Treatment or Punishment* (the *Istanbul Protocol*, the IP) too underlines that the 'distinction between physical and psychological methods of torture is artificial'.[42] The IP urges that suffering be understood holistically instead—that, from a holistic, evidence-based perspective, both physical and psychological suffering need to be anticipated from any harmful act.

Numerous prominent experts involved in documentation have nevertheless urged a revision and refinement of conceptions, particularly with a view to psychological suffering, and that just because 'the distinction is artificial (i.e., made for epistemological purposes), it does not mean that we shouldn't keep in mind that the ultimate target of torture is the conscious self, and that we should reflect on contemporary torture and the complex ways in which this conscious self is attacked and controlled'.[43] Despite the issues with the mind–body dichotomy and the consensus to approach suffering more holistically, experts continue therefore to focus specifically on documenting psychologically oriented practices, namely threats, solitary confinement, and sleep deprivation.[44] From an epistemological, pragmatic, and pedagogical perspective, they work towards better informing perception and practice that psychological suffering is equally harmful. Ultimately, the physical–psychological distinction continues to both facilitate and hinder the discussion. I too accept this position.

To be clear, although some victims call their experience 'psychological torture', this term is not in general use in all three institutions. Reductively put, 'psychological torture' is the use of psychological suffering with intent and purpose. 'Psychological torture', as proposed by the UN SRT, 'include[s] all methods, techniques and circumstances which are intended or designed to purposefully inflict severe mental pain or suffering without using the conduit or effect of severe physical pain or suffering.'[45] The added notion of intent

[39] Nimisha Patel, 'Psychological Torture' (2020) 29 Torture 79; Sveaass (n 30) 315; Rob Boddice, *Pain: A Very Short Introduction* (OUP 2017) 77: 'distinct notions of emotional and physical pain perpetuates the dualism that denies [their] interrelation and interdependence'.

[40] Mary-Jo DelVecchio Good (ed), *Pain as Human Experience: An Anthropological Perspective* (University of California Press 1994) 11: 'The dichotomy between mind and body upheld by both medical and psychological research is invalid and unavailing'; Talal Asad, 'Agency and Pain: An Exploration' (2000) 1 (1) Culture and Religion 43.

[41] Michael Davis, 'Torture and the Inhumane' (2007) 26 (2) Criminal Justice Ethics 29–43.

[42] Istanbul Protocol I (1999) [145], Istanbul Protocol II (2022) [372].

[43] Pérez-Sales (n 16) 308.

[44] Elna Søndergaard and others (eds), *Three Protocols for the Medico-Legal Documentation of Psychological Torture* (DIGNITY 2024).

[45] UN SRT (n 34) [19–25].

brings it closer to torture and away from the related categories. The SRT has drawn a strict distinction between 'practices', 'rationale', and 'effects' and, in opting for 'practices', has excluded 'no marks' practices such as solitary confinement, sleep deprivation, and stress positions. With my focus on evidentiary invisibility and difficulty, opting with practices or rationale (inputs) would have narrowly focussed on the nature of the act, though that too is important, and would have excluded invisible impact occasioned by physical force. After trying 'psychological torture' as a guiding concept, I found 'psychological suffering' as more conducive to discuss all forms of violence which do not leave *overt* physical evidence.

'Psychological suffering', which I opt for, on the other hand, is a term all three bodies commonly use. Unlike 'psychological torture', 'psychological suffering' is also a term that enables exploration not only of the category of torture but also inhuman and degrading treatment, as well as what is rendered to fall outside of the prohibition. Cognizant of tensions, I have chosen to cautiously utilize the concept given its wide legal use in adjudication, in drawing attention to acts and impacts, experiences and practices that produce suffering without leaving overt physical marks. Psychological suffering here is thus used to attend to all *invisible* harms—or more precisely to the difficulties of imagining and evidencing them. To overcome this complexity, the book opts for an open-ended conceptual orientation, refraining from seeking to conclusively define psychological suffering. There has been a contestation in anti-torture discourse over what it includes and excludes, which this book avoids by using it as broadly as possible. Unlike the UN SRT, I also take it to include both 'no touch' practices (solitary confinement or threats) and physical practices that may not leave visible marks (slaps). I have, therefore, accepted as relevant such cases which (i) explicitly mentioned and assessed 'psychological suffering' (or adjacent concepts for example 'mental damage') and (ii) implied or inferred 'psychological suffering' from the nature of the practices in question, such as solitary confinement or life imprisonment, or the invisibility of the suffering.

As for the inclusion criteria, I looked for cases concerning (a) physical acts with non-physical impacts (e.g. slaps) and (b) non-physical acts with non-physical impacts (e.g. threats). I included physical exertion such as forced standing (given the relative invisibility of impact) but excluded physical spectacles such as force-feeding. There were inherent difficulties that led me to use an inferential method, an inductive approximation in drawing the boundaries between inclusion and exclusion. The primary difficulty was that not all cases on their face adequately detailed whether there were indeed no marks—so selection had to be inferred from the practice in question. The alternative would have required me to talk to all the victims and their lawyers to further investigate, which I could not due to ethical issues and the scope of the research. In aiming for broad capture and in my hesitation to not impose rigid brackets, I intentionally avoided too detailed a working definition as I was looking not for a *definition* but an *imagination*. The overtly physical was there as a comparator—in the finding that only physical spectacles such as police beatings, electrocution, and falanka have been categorized as torture.

Another aspect of inclusion was the possibility of singling out the act and impact. That is, knowing full well that torture and inhuman and degrading treatment target the mind as well as the body, the secondary difficulty was differentiating between acts and impacts in any given case. There is, put differently, a seeming fluidity (or permeability) between physical and psychological suffering which required careful consideration. This meant that my inclusion was limited to cases where this could be done with relative ease. Much was left out on this score. My justification, in light of the otherwise scientifically shaky grounds to 'single' out psychological suffering, has been pedagogical. I am by no means the first to have done so. As such, I have followed other scholars and the practice-oriented documentation project based at DIGNITY who also identify a need to single out certain practices—especially threats, sleep deprivation, and solitary confinement. There not being a simple solution or position here, I anticipate the conceptual discussion to continue beyond this book.

I now turn to the remainder of my definitional and conceptual choices. I also do not take there to be a material difference between the terms 'pain' and 'suffering', using both interchangeably.[46] Similarly, I take 'treatment' to be synonymous with 'punishment'. Cursory reading of the caselaw confirmed the position that the distinction between 'treatment' and 'punishment' is not normally made or 'subject to separate analysis, since in many cases punishment must involve treatment'.[47] Others too have pointed out that punishment is a 'narrower idea' and that 'treatment seems able to capture the idea of punishment within it, which is not the case from the opposite perspective' and that punishment 'invokes an immediate association with individuals in detention'.[48] A more critical position would be to argue, as has Elaine Webster, that the conflation between 'treatment' and 'punishment' has problematically overlooked the conceptual complexities inhering in each term, possibly because they are

[46] Boddice (n 39) 6 differentiates: 'Modern English has separated out pain (a physical feeling of hurt) from suffering, with all the latter's emotional connotations.'

[47] Bernadette Rainey and Pamela McCormick, *Clare, White and Ovey's The European Convention on Human Rights* (8th edn, OUP 2021) 185–86.

[48] Elaine Webster, 'Exploring the Prohibition of Degrading Treatment within Article 3 of the European Convention on Human Rights', doctoral thesis, University of Edinburgh (2009) 23–24.

'difficult to decipher' as used in the caselaw.[49] I have chosen not to decipher the reasoning on this front.

By 'recognize', I mean how actors have variably come to *generally* 'include' in the prohibition a specific instance of psychological suffering, thereby deciding that it constitutes a violation—or not, which is what I mean by 'exclude'. 'Expansion' refers to extending recognition to additional experiences not previously included or categorized as 'less' than torture. By 'categorize', I refer to how adjudicators *specifically* configure, differentiate, and grade the phenomenon of psychological suffering in question under the prohibition either as 'torture', 'inhuman', 'degrading', or not a violation at all. These terms are not used in the scholarship with conformity and are often interchanged with, among other terms, 'interpretation', 'specification', 'definition', 'conceptualization', or 'qualification'. I have sought to use 'recognition' and its constitutive terms, 'inclusion', 'exclusion', 'expansion', and 'categorization', with regularity to avoid confusion. I have reproduced related terms and by-words when used in official documents or interviews. I also use 'substantiation' to refer to the practices in how the three institutions *establish* that alleged acts have occurred through admitting and assessing evidence, particularly in proving the gravity of the suffering.

Methodological choices

An explanation of the methodological choices used in generating the material presented in this book is also warranted. I selected the institutions based on their prominence and influence regarding relevant cases and assuming that they could be compared given important similarities in form, purpose, and context. Their jurisprudence is publicly (and electronically) accessible in English. They are relatively transparent and receptive to researchers. Although its rulings on the prohibition of torture (under Article 7 of the ICCPR and general comments) are also important, the UN HRC was not included as much of its reasoning is shorter and not susceptible to similar analysis to the other selected institutions. National jurisdictions were largely excluded to maintain an international keel.

As I was interested in how psychological suffering and adjacent concepts featured in the caselaw, I started the research for this book with systematic searches in the authoritative databases connected to the three

[49] ibid 173–74.

institutions.[50] I downloaded and proceeded to read all final judgments (under which I include individual communications from the CAT but exclude admissibility decisions) and related documents generated by the searches. I read all the material with a view to any argumentation and discussion around psychological suffering. I chose to use material that addressed the nature of suffering beyond merely identifying it. With 'psychological suffering' as a guiding concept, I excluded cases where physical force had both a physical and psychological impact and was not differentiated in legal reasoning. The searches were conducted on 14 May 2025. In compiling relevant IACtHR cases, I relied on the Center for Justice and International Law's (CEJIL's) database. I included all Article 5 (1) and 5 (2) cases.

I also systematically reviewed the secondary doctrinal literature, textbooks, and academic commentary, with probative and pertinent insights regarding the objects of inquiry. I then used the interview method in order to gain access to individual accounts and articulations which are not found elsewhere (specifically not revealed in court documents) in all their 'depth, nuance, contingency, complexity, ambivalence'[51]—advancing the research through first-hand, experience-based accounts of implicated actors about psychological suffering. Anticipating a wide variation in responses, I used interviews in an exploratory manner, so as not to unduly theorize possible explanations for unreflected practices. I have instead systematized and thematized the material as much as possible (see Annex 2 for sample interview questions).

I proceeded on the premise that the broader discourse of torture's legal interpretation is global, circulating, and dialectic, with the three institutions drawing on (at least normatively importing/exporting) each other's jurisprudence. Both the ECtHR and the IACtHR have at least nominally accepted the UNCAT as the universally and operationally authoritative instrument in relation to the definition of torture.[52] This (complex) normative mobility is identified but not precisely traced here. The plurality and circularity here lend themselves to comparative methods, which is concerned with 'identifying, analysing, and explaining similarities and differences in how actors in different legal systems understand, interpret, apply and approach international law'.[53]

[50] CAT and other relevant UN bodies: documents.un.org; juris.ohchr.org; ECtHR: hudoc.echr.coe.int; IACtHR: summa.cejil.org.

[51] Jennifer Mason, *Qualitative Researching* (3rd edn, Sage 2017) 111–14.

[52] *Selmouni v France* (n 32) [100]; *Bueno-Alvez v Argentina* [2007] IACtHR [77]; see further on this point, Magdalena Forowicz, *The Reception of International Law in the European Court of Human Rights* (OUP 2010) 195–202.

[53] Anthea Roberts and others, 'Comparative International Law: Framing the Field' (2015) 109 American Journal of International Law 467, 469.

Comparative aims were admittedly limited given the disparity between the volume of cases between the three institutions. Despite strong yet sparse parallels, there was a dearth of conceptual depth at the IACtHR and the CAT primarily given their volume of cases compared to that of the ECtHR. Focus on the ECtHR, therefore, proved to be the most extensive whereas the other two are more limited. Given that the central aim was to study the parallel interpretive practices at the three institutions (representing three case studies), comparison became primarily a means of broadening the data set and examining the variability in practices. The choice of three institutions offered a broader sample size and the ability to compare, contrast, and confirm. My comparisons have also been cautiously framed given the three institutions exude complex differences in terms of constitutional, normative, and procedural frameworks, operational language(s), and institutional history, not to mention the legal cultures of their actors (most particularly victims, advocates, and adjudicators but also experts). The comparative framework adopted by the book has therefore been open-ended to flex with these difficulties. Further to this point, sensitivity to temporal, linguistic, cultural, and political points of differentiation was closely attended to—with certain decisions as to what has been included or excluded explained throughout the text.

Structure of the book

Across seven chapters, the book offers explanatory insights with respect to the configuration and contestation of psychological suffering under torture's prohibition in international human rights law. Chapters 2 and 3 are more squarely focussed on psychological suffering as recognized in the work of the three institutions, whereas Chapters 4–6 more broadly examine the conditions shaping that recognition.

Chapter 2: Between inclusion and exclusion

The nature of the suffering to be legally recognized as torture and inhuman and degrading treatment has long been the concern of scholars—a 'perennial point of academic labour' of the 'law and torture' scholarship.[54] Perennial perhaps

[54] Ergun Cakal, 'Law and Torture: Contemporary Legal Scholarship on Torture, from the Doctrinal to the Critical' (2023) 25 (5) International Community Law Review 407; Manfred Nowak and Elizabeth McArthur, 'The Distinction between Torture and Cruel, Inhuman or Degrading Treatment' (2006)

because these exercises are arguably 'intended to measure what are often incommensurable standards of behaviour'.[55] Since the very first case, namely *The Greek Case*, activists, advocates, and adjudicators have 'been concerned with the difficult question of how to separate torture from other painful acts', with the politics around it so 'fierce' and 'contentious' and with no state wanting to be branded as having committed torture.[56]

Recent scholarship has offered some insights as to the broader normative developments of torture's prohibition in the ECtHR jurisprudence, accounting for institutional conditions across time for this interpretation.[57] While drawing many useful connections between the ECtHR and its socio-political context, these scholars have not extensively trained attention on psychological suffering. Scholarship on the CAT, empirical or otherwise, has focussed mostly on its state review process.[58] There is no comparable scholarship on the IACtHR, focussing on its interpretation of the prohibition of torture. My own previous research offers doctrinal reviews on certain methods as threats, solitary confinement, and sleep deprivation.[59] Scholarly accounts on national experiences are similarly sparse. Where available, stark parallels to the international experience are present.[60] The Italian experience, for instance, attests to the contestation over psychological suffering not in its adjudication but in its criminalization.[61]

16 (3) Torture 147–51; Manfred Nowak, 'What Practices Constitute Torture? US and UN Standards' (2006) 28 (4) Human Rights Quarterly 809–41.

[55] Talal Asad, 'On Torture, or Cruel, Inhuman, and Degrading Treatment' in Arthur Kleinman and others (eds), *Social Suffering* (University of California Press 1997) 286.

[56] Jamal Barnes, *A Genealogy of the Torture Taboo* (Routledge 2017) 120–21.

[57] Ezgi Yildiz, *Between Forbearance and Audacity: The European Court of Human Rights and the Norm against Torture* (CUP 2023); Corina Heri, *Responsive Human Rights: Vulnerability Ill-Treatment and the ECtHR* (Hart 2021) 194.

[58] Ronagh McQuigg, 'How Effective Is the United Nations Committee Against Torture?' (2011) 22 (3) European Journal of International Law 813–28; Tobias Kelly, 'The UN Committee Against Torture: Human Rights Monitoring and the Legal Recognition of Cruelty' (2009) 31 Human Rights Quarterly 777.

[59] Ergun Cakal, 'Perception, Practice and Proximity: Qualifying Threats as Psychological Torture in International Law' (2021) 31 (1) Torture 19–36; Ergun Cakal, 'Befogging Reason, Undermining Will: Understanding Sleep Deprivation as Torture and Other Ill-Treatment in International Law' (2019) 29 (2) Torture 11–22. See also Ergun Cakal, 'Debility, Dependency and Dread: On the Conceptual and Evidentiary Dimensions of Psychological Torture' (2018) 28 (2) Torture 15–37.

[60] Others have widely discussed Israel's rationalization of 'moderate pressure'; *Report of the Commission of Inquiry in the Matter of Interrogation Methods of the General Security Service Regarding Hostile Terrorist Activity* (1987) 61, commonly known as 'the Landau Report', recommended a model of combining 'non-violent psychological pressure of an intense and prolonged interrogation [. . .] with a moderate measure of physical pressure' without ever reaching 'the level of physical torture'.

[61] Antonio Marchesi, 'Implementing the UN Convention Definition of Torture in National Criminal Law (with Reference to the Special Case of Italy)' (2008) 6 (2) Journal of International Criminal Justice 195, 208, 213 details the 'issue of determinacy' over psychological torture; that it was 'too loose a concept' and the possibility that it could 'result in unacceptable limitations to the state's authority in areas

The empirical research exists but has looked elsewhere.[62] These scholars have explicated the implicit considerations informing naming practices in specific instances in specific settings, particularly in asylum claims or sexual violence cases, underscoring the forms of suffering that are often excluded. What these critical scholars argue generally is that the category of torture, and the prohibition framework as a whole, has served a particular nature of suffering, that which is spectacular, exceptional, and physical—downgrading the more invisible and psychologically oriented. This scholarship, importantly, has not directly examined international adjudication.[63] It therefore informs the book in two primary ways: (i) it foregrounds and frames the interpretive practices through the notions of 'inclusion', 'exclusion', 'expansion', and 'categorization'; and (ii) it identifies 'psychological suffering' as playing a significant role in these practices.

Chapter 2 presents how (and how much) the respective institutions have recognized psychological suffering to date (not strictly limited to cases using the term 'psychological suffering' but also the diverse iterations and references to adjacent concepts). Based on a systematic review, the chapter presents the precedent-setting moments in how the three institutions have approached interpreting the prohibition in including or excluding psychological suffering. I start with the European institutions before I turn to their counterpoints—identifying a counter-history of how that recognition came with important state resistance and institutional delimitations, particularly on temporal (e.g. combination, length, and intensity of suffering) and political considerations (e.g. necessity of certain practices for states).

These are historical institutional accounts in overall tone to start with but end up more complicated, revealing problematic nuances and dubious grounds in legal reasoning missed by previous scholarship. That psychologically oriented practices, the chapter highlights, faced difficulty in being categorized as torture was apparent shortly after the contemporary legal frameworks

such as interrogation procedures or conditions of detention', engendering 'a special mistrust' on the part of numerous parliamentarians.

[62] Tobias Kelly, 'Sympathy and Suspicion: Torture, Asylum, and Humanity' (2012) 18 (4) The Journal of the Royal Anthropological Institute 753–68; Victoria Canning, *Torture and Torturous Violence* (Bristol University Press 2022); Michelle Farrell, 'The Marks of Civilisation: The Special Stigma of Torture' (2022) 22 (1) Human Rights Law Review 1–26; Tobias Kelly, 'Recognizing Torture: Credibility and the Unstable Codification of Victimhood' in Steffen Jensen and Henrik Rønsbo (eds), *Histories of Victimhood* (University of Pennsylvania Press 2014) 144–60; Kelly (n 58) 781.

[63] Canning (n 62) 24–28: 'How survivors of violence—whether subjected to legally recognized forms of torture or not—discuss torture themselves varies. There is no monolithic experience, and no monolithic interpretation.'

were established. Beyond these findings, the chapter identifies that the 'how' and 'how much' of recognition have been subject to close configuration and contestation since institutional inception—leading to a vast variation and lack of precision in legal reasoning. The questions of 'how' and 'how much' recognition, posed here, are built on in the discussion on categorization.

Chapter 3: Categorization and its discontents

That the protection extended by the prohibition is contingent on interpretation in specific cases is generally accepted in the anti-torture field as self-evident.[64] Once a particular practice is *included*, therefore prohibited, it becomes easier to advocate against the use of the practice more generally. Scholarly attention to *categorization* works on a similar premise—drawing attention to the strength of the protection on offer by the specific category of torture relative to the categories of inhuman and degrading treatment. The preponderance of the current 'law and torture' research and practice ascribes approximately to this model (see Table 1.1).

As all categories are equally prohibited, however, some scholars emphasize that they should not be viewed vertically (hierarchically) but horizontally (or in a 'branched manner';[65] see Table 1.2). Another position identified in the scholarship is 'constructive ambiguity', namely the avoidance of clear delineations which states can then side-step.[66] Nevertheless, there are strong indications that categorization matters, especially for scholars and states.[67] The position that the element of 'severe suffering' is, or ought to be, the predominant differentiator in categorization has played out among scholars and

[64] Natasa Mavronicola, *Torture, Inhumanity, and Degradation under Article 3 of the ECHR: Absolute Rights and Absolute Wrongs* (Hart 2021) 17.

[65] Rod Morgan and Malcolm Evans, *Combating Torture in Europe: The Work and Standards of the European Committee for the Prevention of Torture* (Council of Europe 2001) 66; Mavronicola (n 64) 90 finds that all three categories 'encompass distinct qualities'—all three boxes should thus be situated side by side as qualitatively different, not hierarchically; Malcolm Evans, 'Getting to Grips with Torture' (2002) 51 International and Comparative Law Quarterly 365, 382; Pérez-Sales (n 16) 261.

[66] Kelly (n 58) 790; John Parry, '"Just for Fun": Understanding Torture and Understanding Abu Ghraib' (2005) 1 Journal of National Security Law & Policy 253, 258: 'a separate category for an intentionally narrow set of practices labelled and banned as "torture" only functions to normalise and legitimate the remaining practices that are "not-torture"'.

[67] Lutz Oette, *The Transformation of the Prohibition of Torture in International Law* (OUP 2024) 53 finds the differences to 'still matter' despite principled downplaying; Hans Danelius, 'The International Protection against Torture and Inhuman or Degrading Treatment or Punishment' in Frank Emmert (ed), *Collected Courses of the Academy of European Law/Recueil des cours de l'Académie de droit européen* (1993) 179: 'many Governments would consider it to be a much more serious stigma if they are found guilty of torture than if the finding is one of inhuman or degrading treatment'.

Table 1.1 Vertical/hierarchical/severe-plus model

Torture	'Severity-plus', official, purpose, intent, 'special stigma'
Inhuman	'Simply severe', official
Degrading	Severity not necessary
Lawful sanctions	Below minimum level of severity, inherent

Table 1.2 Horizontal/qualitative model

Torture as ('simply') severe, purposeful, intentional, official, 'special stigma'	Inhuman treatment as severe, official No purpose/intent ('torture-minus'*)
Degrading treatment: above minimum level of severity but not as severe as torture/inhumanity	
Lawful sanctions: below minimum level of severity and not torture/inhumanity/degradation	

Note: There is clearly a partial hierarchy here between 'torture/inhumanity' and 'degradation'. Like Mavronicola (n 64) 90, I hold that if we are to appreciate all three categories as 'encompass[ing] distinct qualities', all three boxes should be situated side by side as qualitatively different, not hierarchically.

* Ginbar (n 17) 274.

continues to do so, with some defending its doctrinal coherence and force[68] and others deeming it rigid and outdated.[69]

More importantly for the present discussion, how the nature of psychological suffering impacts that categorization becomes significant. Do adjudicators, for example, search for a particular form of suffering in categorization? One study, at least, has found the ECtHR to privilege 'tangible injuries' as a shortcut to finding violations.[70] Another study found the notion of 'special stigma', a vague element required for the categorization of torture, to closely link the category to physical suffering—unduly to the exclusion of practices that predominantly produce psychological suffering.[71] As no study has examined these systematically or empirically (through engaging the relevant actors), I have done so in this book.

[68] Andrea Carcano and Tullio Scovazzi, *Upholding the Prohibition of Torture: The Contribution of the European Court of Human Rights* (Brill 2023); Danelius (n 67) 169. Before drafting the UNCAT, Danelius was also a member of the ECmHR secretariat.

[69] Ergun Cakal, 'Assessing (and Making Sense of) Severity: Conceptualising and Contextualising Torture's Core' (2022) 91 (2) Nordic Journal of International Law 284–309; Nowak (n 54) 818; Rodley (n 8) 491; Nigel Rodley and Matt Pollard, *The Treatment of Prisoners under International Law* (3rd edn, OUP 2011) 123; A/HRC/13/39 [60].

[70] Mavronicola (n 64) 64, 199.

[71] Farrell (n 62).

How, Chapter 3 asks, has psychological suffering been *categorized* in the broader recognition as canvassed in Chapter 2? As mentioned from the outset, no case categorized as torture has included psychological suffering standing on its own: no case of solitary confinement, irreducible life imprisonment, or threats, however serious. What then is typical torture precisely? What practices and experiences have been associated with the category? What about for the categories of inhuman and degrading treatment? This chapter corresponds to chapter 4 ('Exceptionalising suffering') of my companion text, *Law and Torture*.

Chapter 4: Recognition and the socio-political

Activists, academics, advocates, and adjudicators have occasionally underscored the evolving understanding of torturous practices and experiences in arguing for expanded recognition.[72] In tending to emerging forms or understandings of suffering, they have identified that states 'put a premium on methods which cause suffering and intimidation without leaving much in the way of embarrassing long-term visible evidence of brutality'[73] and that state practices have 'become more domestic and unpretentious [b]ut no less painful'.[74] Expansionist interpretations of the prohibition have grounded their arguments in social change and what I broadly refer to as 'socio-political standards'.[75]

I include under this concept all collective (social, cultural, political, legal) expressions of recognition of forms of suffering, whether codified or not. Given the complexity in defining social, cultural, and political values, I adopt a composite definition one scholar offers as:

> a collection of ideas, values, practices, and material objects that are meaningful to a group of people or the entire society, and which allows them to carry out their collective lives in relative order and harmony [or] broad

[72] Rejali (n 21) 35–39, 562: 'Jurists have always preferred to define torture narrowly, while activists have favored definitions that are quite broad. The latter can be so inclusive as to make the term useless, while the former can be so narrow as to miss important features of modern torture.'

[73] ibid 2–3.

[74] Cassese (n 1) 63; see also Pérez-Sales (n 16) xix.

[75] John Vorhaus, 'Bringing People Down: Degrading Treatment and Punishment' (2021) 24 (3) New Criminal Law Review 436, 449: 'Since cultural practices vary over time, a decision on whether any particular violation meets the threshold required under Article 3 will require some acknowledgement of contemporary cultural sensibility.'

> guidelines defining what a group considers good, desirable, right, or important [as] express[ing] the ideals of society, as well as of groups of every size.[76]

These shape collective expectations of how states ought to care for those in their care and custody.[77] Where codified, these standards work to define, regulate, prevent, and redress suffering—informing how individuals make sense of (identify and are impacted by) the suffering experienced or observed.[78] This does not simply pertain to how victim-survivors make sense of what they experience but also to how those external to an experience, namely advocates and adjudicators, argue and assess the suffering. The question of psychological suffering at the hands of the state after all, and what to do about it, is very much evident in social movements and standard setting efforts more broadly (in treaties, declarations, guidelines, and civil society reports).

In contrast to the vast and diverse scholarship on how pain and punishment have been connected to 'socio-political standards',[79] reflection on the relationship between the law and its socio-political context is surprisingly not common. A rare account sources this at the implicit and incommensurable nature of the relationship, speculating that prohibition's constitutive categories:[80]

> elicit some shared sense of positive morality, some 'common conscience' we already share, some code that already exists or resonates among us. I believe that these provisions, these standards, make an appeal to social facts and not just to individual moral judgment; they evoke positive morality not critical morality or the philosophers' moral reality. They appeal to what is supposed to be a more-or-less shared sense among us of how one person responds as a human to another human, a more-or-less shared sense of what humans can and should be expected to endure, a more or less shared sense of basic human dignity, a more-or-less shared sense of what it is to respond appropriately to

[76] Mosche Hirsch, *Invitation to the Sociology of International Law* (OUP 2017) 6.

[77] Jeremy Waldron, *Torture, Terror, and Trade-Offs: Philosophy for the White House* (OUP 2010) 300: 'What makes a certain attitude towards suffering or distress appropriate or inappropriate? Sometimes the answer is to be found in the background norms of a certain institution.'

[78] Anne Bloom, David M Engel, and Michael McCann (eds), *Injury and Injustice: The Cultural Politics of Harm and Redress* (CUP 2018), 'Introduction', 4–5.

[79] Rob Boddice, *Pain and Emotion in Modern History* (Palgrave 2014); Javier Moscoso, *Pain: A Cultural History* (Palgrave 2012); DelVecchio Good (n 40); Ian Wilkinson, *Suffering: A Sociological Introduction* (Polity 2005); Pieter Spierenburg, *The Spectacle of Suffering: Executions and the Evolution of Repression—From a Preindustrial Metropolis to the European Experience* (CUP 1984); David Garland, *Punishment and Modern Society: A Study in Social Theory* (Clarendon Press 1993).

[80] Waldron (n 77) 315.

> the elementary exigencies of human life. […] to some sort of shared conscience, ('con-science' in the etymological sense of 'knowing together').

Histories on the pre- and early modern abolition explicitly point to the role of socio-political standards in not only leading to torture's abolition but also in how understandings of torture have expanded from judicial torture (physically overt interrogational torture) to now also including psychological suffering.[81] That adjudicators recognize (i) broader socio-political standards around suffering generally and (ii) the changes in torturous techniques and contexts necessitate a constant (re)evaluation is widely accepted in 'law and torture' scholarship.[82] Through the doctrine of 'evolutive' or 'dynamic' interpretation,[83] as articulated in *Tyrer* and *Selmouni*, state practices that were historically viewed as legitimate and left unquestioned have increasingly (although variably) come into view as falling afoul of the prohibition. Prolonged solitary confinement, reproductive rights, irreducible life imprisonment, rape, sleep deprivation, threats, lengthy prisoner transportation, enforced disappearances, human trafficking, conversion therapy, and forced psychiatric treatment, among other illustrations, are normally advanced as evidence.[84] How and when these socio-political standards impact adjudication matters to all users of the institutions to better understand the processes which will ultimately affect state coercive practices. The influence of socio-political standards on the recognition of psychological suffering, despite the extensive experience, is doctrinally accepted but not empirically studied.

International law scholars too have begun marking the complexities and ambiguities of the law's relationship to its context more broadly.[85] Despite frequent references to doctrines of dynamic interpretation or state practice,

[81] Page duBois, *Torture and Truth* (Routledge 1991); Lisa Silverman, *Tortured Subjects: Pain, Truth, and the Body in Early Modern France* (University of Chicago Press 2001).

[82] Rodley and Pollard (n 69) 82; Juan Méndez and Andra Nicolescu, 'Evolving Standards for Torture in International Law' in Metin Başoğlu (ed), *Torture and Its Definition in International Law: An Interdisciplinary Approach* (OUP 2017) 215–45; Chris Ingelse, *United Nations Committee Against Torture: An Assessment* (Nijhoff 2001) 23, 61: 'Attitudes about man, about what is deemed cruel, and, therefore, about torture, have changed. Such attitudes have influenced practice.'

[83] I use 'dynamic' and 'evolutive' interpretation interchangeably.

[84] Ronli Sifris, *Reproductive Freedom, Torture and International Human Rights: Challenging the Masculinisation of Torture* (Routledge 2016); Clare McGlynn, 'Rape, Torture and the European Convention on Human Rights' (2009) 58 International and Comparative Law Quarterly 565; Ilias Trispiotis and Craig Purshouse, '"Conversion Therapy" as Degrading Treatment' (2022) 42 (1) Oxford Journal of Legal Studies 104.

[85] Georges Abi-Saab and others (eds), *Evolutionary Interpretation and International Law* (Hart 2019); Georg Nolte (ed), *Treaties and Subsequent Practice* (OUP 2013); Kathryn McNeilly, 'Are Rights Out of Time? International Human Rights Law, Temporality, and Radical Social Change' (2019) 28 Social & Legal Studies 817; Bloom and others (n 78) 1–24.

these scholars have found thin official conceptualization, with reasoning left implicit and unreflected.[86] Building on and beyond this scholarship, Chapter 4 systematically examines how and when 'socio-political standards' are invoked (or not) at the three institutions, particularly in cases relating to psychological suffering. The chapter traces the contours of how advocates and adjudicators have negotiated regressive (narrow) and progressive (broad) socio-political considerations under dynamic interpretation of the prohibition. This is a more expansive chapter than earlier chapters, examining the broader institutional conditions which determine the invoking, weighing up, or altogether overlooking of socio-political standards pertaining to psychological suffering. This chapter corresponds to chapter 3 ('Progressive impulses') of my companion text, *Law and Torture*.

Chapter 5: Scientific expertise

The recognition of psychological suffering under the prohibition is commonly characterized as a 'problem of evidence', evidence which is difficult to obtain primarily due to state denial.[87] When available, however, the effective use of scientific evidence has proven problematic for a range of reasons and questioned in national[88] and international contexts.[89] Despite the amplified significance of evidence, including in cases related to prohibition, scholarly attention here has also been relatively rare, understudied,[90] and normally 'taken for granted by both outsiders and insiders'.[91] What is established, however, is that advocates and adjudicators working on such cases face evidentiary issues in substantiating the veracity of the suffering before them.

Scholars have found, for instance, the CAT and ECtHR's reasoning to fall silent and fail in providing clarity and specificity on assessing medical

[86] Daniel Moeckli and Nigel White, 'Treaties as "Living Instruments"' in Dino Kritsiotis and Michael Bowman (eds), *Conceptual and Contextual Perspectives on the Modern Law of Treaties* (CUP 2018) 157.

[87] IRCT, *Shedding Light on a Dark Practice – Using the Istanbul Protocol to Document Torture* (IRCT 2009) 10; Metin Başoğlu (ed), *Torture and Its Definition in International Law: An Interdisciplinary Approach* (OUP 2017) 397.

[88] Efrat Shir, 'How Do You Say Istanbul Protocol in Hebrew? The Curious Case of Mr Firas Tbeish' (2019) 29 (2) Torture 90–95. See also the Torture Documentation Project, www.torturedocumentationproject.wordpress.com.

[89] Rembrandt Aarts and others, 'Expert Medico-Legal Reports: The Relationship between Levels of Consistency and Judicial Outcomes in Asylum Seekers in The Netherlands' (2019) 29 (1) Torture 36–38.

[90] Marie-Bénédicte Dembour, 'Introduction: The Evidentiary System of the European Court of Human Rights in Critical Perspective' (2023) 4 European Convention on Human Rights Law Review 1.

[91] Mariana Valverde, *Law's Dream of a Common Knowledge* (Princeton University Press 2003) 5.

evidence.[92] The UN Istanbul Protocol, representing widely accepted medico-legal standards internationally, is found not to be 'uniformly applied within international human rights bodies'.[93] In other words, scholarship generally identifies the problem but is less attentive to or agreed about its causes or solutions. It variably points to issues around values or visibility in how adjudicators might overlook or override scientific expertise, including through adjudicators simply substituting scientific expertise with their own opinion.[94] These are not currently understood with sufficient precision. This provides the operative background to the doctrinal and empirical exploration of evidentiary practices at the institutions.

The discussion on scientific expertise presented in Chapter 5 departs from the assumption that the nature of psychological suffering, namely that it is relatively invisible, renders corroborative evidence to be of some importance—amplifying the difficulties of the substantiation of torture more broadly. I follow three inter-related issues as identified from the scholarship: (i) the availability of evidence and expertise; (ii) the competence of advocates and adjudicators to understand that evidence; and (iii) the failure of adjudicators to give due attention to that evidence in adjudication. This chapter corresponds to chapter 5 ('Substantiating suffering') of my companion text, *Law and Torture.*

Chapter 6: Sense-centric reasoning

Socio-political standards and scientific expertise do not stand alone in guiding advocates or adjudicators in recognizing psychological suffering. An adjudicator might simply not ('feel' the) need, or have the time, to require scientific expertise to assess the gravity of the psychological suffering in question. These 'non-expert knowledges of right and wrong' can be more instrumental than 'expert knowledges' in determining recognition, yet have been rarely researched despite being 'the everyday currency of legal discussions and adjudications'.[95]

Much, therefore, can also be left to sense-centric reasoning, which refers to three inter-locking dimensions inhering in reasoning (Figure 1.2). The first is

[92] Marcel Reneman, 'Forensic Medical Reports in Asylum Cases: The View of the European Court of Human Rights and the Committee Against Torture' (2020) 38 (3) Netherlands Quarterly of Human Rights 206–28.

[93] Vincent Iacopino, 'The Istanbul Protocol: Development, Practical Applications, and Future Directions' in James Payne-James and others (eds), *Monitoring Detention, Custody, Torture, and Ill-Treatment: A Practical Approach to Prevention and Documentation* (2018) 262.

[94] David Rhys-Jones and Sally Verity Smith, 'Medical Evidence in Asylum and Human Rights Appeals' (2004) 16 (3) International Journal of Refugee Law 381–410, 396.

[95] Valverde (n 91) 2.

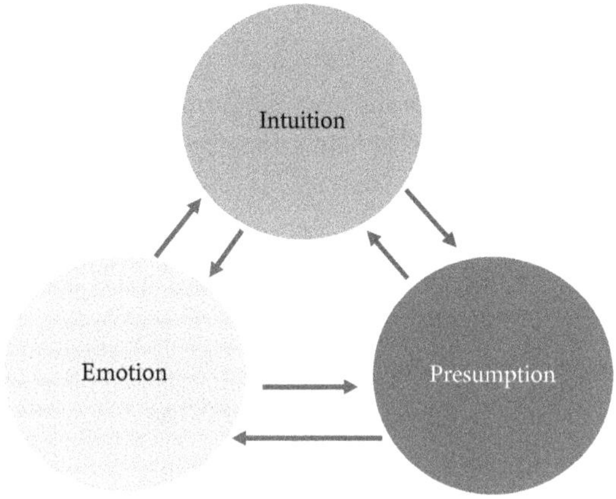

Figure 1.2 Sense-centric reasoning, registers, and purposes.

intuition, by which I refer to the more unarticulated registers of sensing that some injustice was committed. This includes impressionistic, inferential, and associational reasoning, the use of gut feeling, guesswork, and *sana critica*. The second is emotion, by which I refer to a relatively more articulated register. This can include much as anger and regret, but I have chosen to focus this on empathy (and alternatively sympathy), sadness, and visceral reactions through witnessing and hearing suffering. The third inter-locking dimension of sense-centric reasoning is presumption. This includes a range of related notions that serve to presume the nature of an instance of suffering. Here I focus on: 'must have felt' reasoning, rules of logic, personal experience, common sense, common and contextual knowledge, vulnerability, and temporal proxies. These are not represented as mutually exclusive or exhaustive. These deal with evidentiary absence, complexity, proximity, and expedience.

Chapter 6 continues to argue that, contrary to the prevailing premium placed on evidence in the anti-torture field, scientific evidence is not always deemed necessary by advocates and adjudicators. Sense-centric reasoning, I find, appears to serve four broad purposes: to address the absence of evidence; to manage the complexity of evidence; to get closer to the facts of the case and the victim's experience; and for the timely disposition of the case. Indicating an interplay between standards, science, and sense (or sensibility), these dynamics raise central questions that merit special attention: when do adjudicators *not* feel the need for evidence? When is a practice *presumed* to be harmful? There is an unreflecting nature in how commonly held associations, between physical marks and the categorization of torture, for example, have gone 'barely noticed' given how 'intuitive' they seem.[96] It is possible, therefore, that not closely reasoning on a rigorous socio-political and scientific register might allow for the entry of adjudicators' personal values, inferences, experiences, and need for expedience. So what considerations inform these devices in how and when they are used? Do these explain the thin reasoning, or an implicit privileging of certain perceptions of suffering? This chapter corresponds to chapter 6 ('Sensing suffering') of my companion text, *Law and Torture.*

Chapter 7: Conclusions

The final chapter consolidates six key cross-cutting conclusions. The first is that cases focussing prominently on psychological suffering have been broadly recognized under the respective frameworks of all three institutions—from institutional inception to date. The second is that recognition has been delimited based on exceptionality, temporality, and necessity. The third is that the torture categorization has not been afforded to psychological suffering in all three institutions in individual cases. The fourth is that, despite a general acceptance, there has been a selective and cautious use of socio-political standards regarding psychological suffering and more broadly. The fifth is that evidentiary practices at all institutions have recognized the importance of scientific evidence in principle but have been hampered by a lack of competence to assess as well as an undue emphasis on causal certainty, feeding a propensity to undermine the recognition of psychological suffering. The sixth is that sense-centric reasoning has predominated in creating and preserving associations with certain experiences; the physical spectacle with the torture categorization and prolonged psychological suffering with 'lesser' categories. The chapter ends by relating these findings to broader 'law and torture' research and practice.

[96] Farrell (n 62) 2, 5–6.

2
Between inclusion and exclusion

> 'Severe pain and suffering' relates to physical and mental suffering equally, with psychological torture and other forms of ill-treatment being 'by no means less severe than physical abuse'. This is very important, as mental suffering of the same intensity than physical pain and suffering can be inflicted without actual physical contact.[1]

The terms 'psychological suffering' or 'psychological torture' do not appear in the UN Convention Against Torture (UNCAT),[2] the American Convention on Human Rights (ACHR),[3] the Inter-American Convention to Prevent and Punish Torture (IACPPT),[4] or the European Convention on Human Rights (ECHR)[5]—though the phenomenon has come to be variably named and recognized by academics, advocates, and adjudicators. What emerges upon a more panoramic view within and across the three institutions is a terminological variability that evades clarity when referring to the 'psychological' and to 'suffering'. There has been no uniformity whatsoever in how what I call 'psychological suffering' has been grasped at the three institutions. In bringing some clarity, at least to what can be said on the question of psychological suffering, this chapter systematically presents the precedent-setting moments in how the three institutions have approached interpreting the prohibition in including or excluding psychological suffering since their inception. I start with the European institutions before I turn to counterpoints.

[1] Manfred Nowak and others (eds), *The United Nations Convention Against Torture and Its Optional Protocol: A Commentary* (2nd edn, OUP 2019) 50.

[2] UN General Assembly, Convention Against Torture and Other Cruel, Inhuman or Degrading Treatment or Punishment, 10 December 1984, UN Treaty Series, 1465, 85.

[3] Organization of American States (OAS), American Convention on Human Rights, 'Pact of San Jose', Costa Rica, 22 November 1969.

[4] OAS, Inter-American Convention to Prevent and Punish Torture, 9 December 1985, Treaty Series, no 67.

[5] Council of Europe (CoE), European Convention for the Protection of Human Rights and Fundamental Freedoms, as amended by Protocol Nos 11 and 14, 4 November 1950, ETS 5.

Torture and the Recognition of Psychological Suffering in International Law. Ergün Cakal, Oxford University Press.
 DOI: 10.1093/oso/9780198989493.003.0002

European Commission—Court of Human Rights

Article 3 of the ECHR, predating the UNCAT, ACHR, and IACPPT, does not include a *definition* but a simple *prohibition* that '[n]o one shall be subjected to torture or to inhuman or degrading treatment or punishment'. As with the UNCAT, ACHR, and IACPPT, Article 3 recognizes a plurality of categories: torture, inhuman treatment, and degrading treatment (though *immaterially* not cruel treatment). Unlike the UNCAT and IACPPT, Article 3 does not *explicitly* refer to psychological suffering. This, however, has not meant that interpretation has been impervious to it.

When looking to the linguistic labelling of what I have called 'psychological suffering', listing all relevant terms apparent on the face of decisions indicates that none of the institutions has *uniformly* referred to psychological aspects pertaining to the prohibition. In fact, combinations of terms have occasionally been used in the same paragraph without apparent reason.[6] The ECtHR has used: 'psychological suffering' (one of the most frequently used terms),[7] 'mental condition',[8] 'mental damage',[9] 'mental distress',[10] 'mental integrity',[11] 'mental scars',[12] 'mental fatigue',[13] 'mental violence',[14] 'mental well-being',[15] 'moral suffering',[16] 'mental injuries',[17] 'mental suffering',[18] 'mental pain or suffering',[19] 'psychological abuse',[20] 'psychological ill-treatment',[21] 'psychological integrity',[22] 'psychological ordeal',[23] 'psychological influence/attack/impact/condition',[24] 'psychological trauma',[25] 'psychological pressure',[26] 'moral resistance', 'emotional resistance',[27] 'psychological effects',[28] 'moral

[6] *Jalloh v Germany* [2006] ECtHR 54810/00 [82]; *Gäfgen v Germany* [2010] ECtHR 22978/05 [108].
[7] *Gutsanovi v Bulgaria* [2014] ECtHR 34529/10 [125].
[8] *Ismaaciil and Warsame v Malta* [2016] ECtHR 52160/13 [83].
[9] *Shyti v Romania* [2013] ECtHR 39756/07 [24].
[10] *Kurt v Turkey* [1998] ECtHR 15/1997/799/1002 [131].
[11] *Bati and others v Turkey* [2004] ECtHR 33097/96 [114]; *Jalloh* (n 6) [82].
[12] *RS v Hungary* [2019] ECtHR 65290/14 [72].
[13] *Denisenko and Bogdanchikov v Russia* [2009] ECtHR 3811/02 [109].
[14] *Iljina and Saruliene v Lithuania* [2011] ECtHR 32293/05 [53].
[15] *A and others v UK* [2009] ECtHR 3455/05 [128].
[16] *Gurepka v Ukraine* [2005] ECtHR 61406/00 [37].
[17] *Badalyan v Azerbaijan* [2021] ECtHR 51295/11 [48].
[18] *Acar v Turkey* [2004] ECtHR 26307/95 [239].
[19] *Dikme v Turkey* [2000] ECtHR 20869/92 [91].
[20] *Bati and others v Turkey* [2004] ECtHR 33097/96 [115].
[21] *Labita v Italy* [2000] ECtHR 26772/95, dissent of Judge Ridruejo and others [2].
[22] *Premininy v Russia* [2011] ECtHR 44973/04 [90].
[23] *Gutsanovi v Bulgaria* [2014] ECtHR 34529/10 [137].
[24] *AV v Ukraine* [2015] ECtHR 65032/09 [51–52].
[25] *Kovacevic v Croatia* [2018] ECtHR 34804/14 [41].
[26] *Boyle v UK* [2001] ECtHR 26269/07, p 3.
[27] *Premininy v Russia* [2011] ECtHR 44973/04 [81].
[28] *Tyrer v UK* [1978] ECtHR 5856/72 [33].

effects',[29] 'prolonged uncertainty', 'inducing desperation',[30] 'feelings of fear, anxiety and powerlessness',[31] 'very great anguish, mental torment, stress and suffering',[32] 'afraid, depressed and hopeless',[33] defeating 'hope',[34] 'intense fear and apprehension',[35] 'constant mental anxiety',[36] 'fear and helplessness',[37] and 'feeling of arbitrariness and the feeling of inferiority and anxiety often associated with it'.[38] Most often, the ECtHR has used the term 'mental anguish' in connection with and contrast to 'physical pain or suffering'.[39]

I find, through a close analysis as supported by interviews, that the diversity in the terms used reflects, at best, an organic process of creatively capturing the suffering in question and, at worst, an unthinking reflex not adequately informed by science. Interviewees, particularly senior registry lawyers, point to how some terms are simply (and unreflectingly) lifted from the case material (applicants' submissions) and continue to be used in subsequent comparable cases.

The ECtHR has, in all, come to freely draw on the language of emotion and affect in assessing an act's affective context, often in terms of the 'sense of vulnerability' it causes the victim[40] as well as 'the atmosphere of heightened tension and emotions'.[41] These devices, it has been argued by others, serve the ECtHR's 'avoidance of analysing psychological suffering or in general of providing more elaborate analyses but it has also served the applicants who do not submit evidence of psychological harm'.[42] While it might be assumed that all suffering is at least partly psychological and it might be expected for adjudicators to follow such a logic, there seems to be a shortage of consistently reasoning through the science of pain—which will be returned in Chapters 5 and 6.

[29] *Makaratzis v Greece* [2004] ECtHR 50385/99, dissent of Judges Tsatsa-Nikolovska and Straznicka.
[30] *MSS v Belgium and Greece* [2011] ECtHR [GC] 30696/09 [263].
[31] *Volodina v Russia (no 2)* [2019] ECtHR 41261/17 [75].
[32] *Ulku Ekinci v Turkey* [2002] ECtHR 27602/95 [147].
[33] *Premininy v Russia* [2011] ECtHR 44973/04 [81].
[34] *Vinter and ors v UK* [2013] ECtHR [GC] 66069/09, opinion of Judge Power-Forde.
[35] *Akkoc v Turkey* [2000] ECtHR 22947/93 [116].
[36] *Rodić v Bosnia and Herzegovina* [2006] ECtHR 22893/05 [73].
[37] *Milanovic v Serbia* [2011] ECtHR 44614/07 [87].
[38] *MSS v Belgium and Greece* [2011] ECtHR [GC] 30696/09 [233].
[39] *Tyrer* (n 28) [33]; *Soering v UK* [1989] ECtHR 1/1989/161/217 [100]; *Aydin v Turkey* [1997] ECtHR 57/1996/676/866 [84]; *Korneykova and Korneykov v Ukraine* [2016] ECtHR 56660/12 [47].
[40] *Rachwalski and Ferenc v Poland* [2009] ECtHR 47709/99 [58–63]; *Aydin* (n 39) [84].
[41] *Selmouni v France* [1999] ECtHR 25803/94; *Bouyid v Belgium* [2015] ECtHR [GC] 23380/09 [86].
[42] Liana Morica Muntean, 'Determining Torture in Interrogation Cases: Comparative Analysis of the Case Law of the European Court of Human Rights, the UN Bodies and the US Courts', doctoral thesis, Central European University (2017) 147–48.

Laying the foundations

The psychological dimensions of torture and related ill-treatment were promptly recognized in the first case to deal with European torture since World War II. The *Greek Case*, brought before the ECmHR in 1969, concerning the interrogational torture of political prisoners in Greece, was instrumental in this respect. There, Article 3 was interpreted 'to cover the infliction of mental suffering by creating a state of anguish and stress by means other than bodily assault'[43]—ultimately finding that a combination of physical and psychological ill-treatment (including intimidation, humiliation, and threats to family and friends) to have constituted torture. It is difficult here to assess the significance of the combination or whether the psychological ill-treatment could have in itself amounted to torture in the absence of the physical. The ECmHR's reasoning is also credited with informing the UN Declaration on Torture in 1975, the direct precursor to the UNCAT, wherein, as observed by Amnesty International, for 'the first time the concept of causing severe mental suffering was explicitly accepted as part of the international prohibition of state torture'.[44]

The *Greek Case* stands as a foundational precedent with respect to psychological suffering. It was followed in the 1973 case of *East African Asians v UK*, where the applicants successfully claimed that racial discrimination amounted to degrading treatment. Again, there, the ECmHR reiterated the *Greek Case* in its recognition of 'non-physical' degrading treatment but not torture. It found the applicants to have been rendered stateless and 'left throughout in a state of complete uncertainty as to where they might live'. Responding to and rejecting the UK's arguments that 'degrading treatment' be interpreted as referring to physical acts only, the ECmHR reasoned that this interpretation was unnecessary as it would be 'too restrictive'.[45] The contents of torture's prohibition were being challenged at the infancy of the European protection against torture, notably by a Western liberal democracy at that. While the *East African Asians* case is relatively ignored in contemporary discourse, the *Greek Case* remains a historical way-marker for 'law and torture' research.

This ready recognition might not be surprising in light of the *travaux preparatoires* of the ECHR. These record propositions, made by a UK

[43] *Denmark, Norway, Sweden and Netherlands v Greece* [*The Greek Case*] [1969] ECmHR 3321/67, 3322/67, 3323/67, 3344/67 [186].

[44] Amnesty International, *Torture in the Eighties* (1984) 14; Magdalena Forowicz, *The Reception of International Law in the European Court of Human Rights* (OUP 2010) 195.

[45] *East African Asians v UK* [1973] ECmHR 4403/70 [190].

representative, that Article 3 be amended to expressly prohibit additional forms of harm including forceful pharmacological interventions and 'imprisonment with such an excess of light, darkness, noise or silence as to cause mental suffering'.[46] The ECHR *travaux*, albeit incomplete, also reveal a discussion among the drafters on the historicity of torture, with overt tones of civilization and morality through the use of phrases including: 'inconsistent with civilised society'; 'incompatible with civilisation'; 'offences against Heaven and Humanity'; 'relic of barbarism'; 'terrible wave of barbarism and bestialism which has broken over our world'; and 'wholly evil'.[47] The Nazi atrocities were also amply and explicitly invoked to fuel the discussion. There was also a casual association made between the physical and torture where the same representative proposed to condemn that 'all forms of physical torture […] must be prohibited'.[48]

With the aim of keeping the treaty text as short as possible, the *travaux* note that proposed amendments were discussed at some length and ultimately rejected. It was style then more than substance that defeated the proposal. While this doesn't all speak directly to psychological suffering, it does depict the imagination at play which associated the prohibition at the point in time, and since, with extreme suffering. Although not discernible upon reading the final minimalist formulation of the prohibition, previous research has concluded that '[h]aving the Nazi atrocities as frame of reference, the drafters set the bar high'—a point which is returned to in discussing torture's exceptionality.[49]

Largely overlooked in the 'law and torture' scholarship, there were also arguments made during the drafting of the ECHR as to practices that ought to be excluded from the prohibition's purview. The *travaux* reveal that objections were raised, by Denmark and Sweden, to the express mention of forced sterilization, then practised lawfully in those states. Ultimately defeating the inclusion, the Danish representation argued that 'the same may be the case in other civilised countries' and that it was not 'the business of the Council of Europe to prohibit individual countries from having such Acts'.[50] The final (minimalist) formulation of Article 3 does not include any reference to methods or a 'lawful sanctions' delimitation.

[46] ECmHR, 'Preparatory Work on Article 3 of the European Convention of Human Rights' (CoE 1956) DH (56) 6 2–3, per Seymour Cocks.

[47] ibid.

[48] ibid 5, 3.

[49] Ezgi Yildiz, 'A Court with Many Faces: Institutional Identities and Interpretive Preferences: The Case of the European Court of Human Rights and the Norm against Torture', PhD thesis, IHEID Geneva (2016) 214.

[50] ECmHR (n 46) 5, 3.

State arguments to limit the prohibition's breadth, as in *East African Asians*, are also identifiable in other foundational cases at the ECmHR and ECtHR. *Tyrer v UK*, a case which explicitly invoked socio-political considerations in recognizing suffering, concerned the imposition of corporal punishment (birching) on a fifteen-year-old boy on the Isle of Man. While this involved physically overt suffering, it remains instructive on a number of fronts beyond giving name to the 'living instrument' doctrine. It included an important dissent by Judge Gerald Fitzmaurice who accepted that the suffering fell below the 'minimum level of severity' also as based on his own experiences as a child. It also involved arguments from the UK and Isle of Man authorities as to the temporality (or temporariness) of the suffering. The Isle of Man, that is, described the treatment as 'a short, sharp punishment' which involved the infliction of physical pain as an alternative to another form of punishment 'such as some time in prison'.[51] While these arguments were not accepted by the majority, their logics germinated in later cases—picked up below on 'timing suffering'.

A species of argument related to that identified in *Tyrer* was made (and rejected) by the UK government in another case involving the threat of corporal punishment, *Campbell and Cosans v UK*. There, the applicants argued 'that the threat of (corporal) punishment or the attempt to inflict it contravened Article 3 just as much as the actual infliction of the same'.[52] Before the ECmHR, the UK government rejected psychological suffering in anticipation of the physical punishment, arguing that 'neither of the children could be considered to be a victim since corporal punishment had never been inflicted upon them'.[53] Although it accepted the concept of anticipatory harm in principle, the ECmHR ultimately found that there was no violation because the punishment was not realized.[54] Commissioner Klecker emphasized in dissent that:[55]

> we have here that mixture of fear and hope, that anguished anticipation which not only degrades human beings but seriously threatens their equilibrium, particularly in the case of those who, like Gordon Campbell, are still at the that tender age when they need confidence and affection at least

[51] *Tyrer* (n 28), Mr Corrin, verbatim report of the public hearings of 17 January 1978, p 70.

[52] *Campbell and Cosans v UK* [1980] ECmHR [1982] ECtHR 7511/76.

[53] ibid (ECmHR) 61; in its memorial, the UK government [4.17] argued that 'the element of mental anguish involved in anticipating the punishment to which the Court drew attention is wholly or very largely lacking'.

[54] ibid (ECmHR) 123: 'measuring the severity of a punishment in the light of Article 3 cannot, in principle, be made in cases like the present ones where there has been no concrete act of physical chastisement. It makes no difference in this respect that there was a decision to punish Jeffrey Cosans: since the decision was never executed, the test for measuring the severity equally cannot be made'.

[55] ibid (ECmHR), dissenting opinion of Mr Klecker [4–5].

> as much as a firm hand to guide them and help them to form their personality. […] Until the beginning of the twentieth century, coercion by means of actual or threatened punishment was generally regarded as essential both to school discipline and to academic progress […]. Modern pedagogy holds, on the other hand, that man is not naturally or innately bad or depraved. […] Pedagogical research has established that, where punishment is severe and accompanied by intense fear, it wholly absorbs the attention and causes pain and mental confusion.

The majority nevertheless decided to dismiss arguments relating to the threatening nature of the punishment. Yet, the arguments made by the UK and in the dissent reflect the narrow and expansive impulses in adjudication more generally. These articulate two temporal registers: the macro which urges a historical assessment, to situate suffering in its social history, while the micro urges a narrow temporal frame for what ought to count as real suffering. The Court also followed in rendering 'apprehension or disquiet', 'group tension', and 'a sense of alienation' to not be serious enough to violate the prohibition.[56] The point of trivializing here is also found in the cases to follow.

Similar state resistance is also found in other early cases focussing on psychological suffering. One such overlooked case is that of *Zeidler-Kornmann v Germany* where the ECmHR held that the applicant being 'severely and roughly handled' during a prison transfer and being placed in a straitjacket in an isolation cell had not amounted to any violation under Article 3. The ECmHR reached this conclusion on the grounds that there was 'no evidence of any substantial physical injury' and the straitjacket had been necessitated by the applicant's behaviour.[57] There was no further articulation offered as to how this conclusion was reached beyond a gesture to necessity, a notion returned to time and again by states as an explanation for excluding certain practices—first in drafting and later (as here) in defending cases.

Another early case to set the tone with psychological suffering was the 1978 case of *Ensslin, Baader and Raspe v Germany*,[58] which concerned the simultaneous use of sensory isolation and complete social isolation on Red Army Faction members. The three applicants were subjected to a strict regime and were ultimately found dead in their cells (officially recorded as suicides). The ECmHR, in this case, prefaced the reasoning with the recognition that

[56] ibid (ECtHR) [30].

[57] *Zeidler-Kornmann v Germany (Merits)* [1967] ECmHR 2686/65 [59–61].

[58] *Ensslin, Baader and Raspe v Germany* [1978] ECmHR 7572/76.

'complete sensory isolation coupled with complete social isolation can no doubt ultimately destroy the personality' and would conceivably be a violation. However, it went on to qualify this with the point that the 'segregation of a prisoner from the prison community did not in itself constitute a form of inhuman treatment'.

The ECmHR's assessment entailed regard to 'the particular conditions, the stringency of the measure, its duration, the objective pursued and its effects on the person concerned'—and in so doing recognized the need for 'stringent security arrangements [...] for dangerous prisoners'.[59] Given that the sensory and social isolation was 'partial', as access to books and news and contact with each other, families, and lawyers were allowed, the ECmHR found there to have been no violation of Article 3. This approach, especially the distinction between 'total' and 'partial', a device of the ECmHR's own invention, has been instrumental in the subsequent caselaw on solitary confinement—setting a particularly high threshold to reach the specific finding of torture. Beyond this, the judgment does not offer anything further on how psychological suffering was conceptualized. Although *Ensslin* looks to be disfavoured, with some cases avoiding its citation, its logics flow freely in both early[60] and more contemporary jurisprudence—which will be returned to in the next chapter.

Reviewing more recent precedent

The ECtHR has since maintained the position, at least in principle, that psychological suffering is an integral dimension of torture's prohibition—understanding that the absence of visible marks is not conclusive of the absence of suffering[61] and underscoring the need for national criminal codes 'to take into account psychological suffering'.[62] Beyond this important rhetoric,

[59] ibid, p 111.

[60] ECmHR similarly reasoned and rejected *McFeeley v UK* [1984] ECmHR 8317/78.

[61] *Boicenco v Moldova* [2006] ECtHR 41088/05 [109]: 'that the applicant did not have bruises and other visible signs of ill-treatment on his body is not conclusive [...] there are methods of applying force which do not leave any traces on a victim's body'. *Suslov and Batikyan v Ukraine* [2022] ECtHR 56540/14 [98]: 'the absence of injuries alone is not enough to undermine the credibility of an allegation of ill-treatment, given that certain methods of applying force do not leave any traces on a victim's body. And, of course, the consequences of any intimidation, or indeed any other form of non-physical abuse, would in any event have left no visible trace'. I note here that the 'constant psychological pressure' during police investigation as alleged in this case was ultimately not proven.

[62] *Myumyun v Bulgaria* [2015] ECtHR 67258/13 [74]: stressing that 'one of the distinguishing characteristics of torture is that it not only—and not always—seriously damages the physical health of the person subjected to it but also affects in a very serious way that person's dignity and psychological well-being'.

the caselaw between 1978 and 2018 is otherwise varied in how psychological suffering has been recognized. Offering a useful review starting with *Ireland* (1978), as detailed at the book's outset, Liana Muntean views the ECtHR's consideration of psychological suffering as having 'gone through several paradigm shifts', finding that as with the *Ireland* majority the 1990s caselaw[63]

> was also not particularly anxious about psychological suffering. In 1992 in *Tomasi* and then in 1995 in *Ribitsch*, both applicants had invoked mental ill-treatment and suffering resulting from beatings and insults. The Court however did not make any comment on these allegations. It merely focused on the physical acts and injuries in order to conclude that inhuman treatment had taken place. The exception in this period is the case of *Aydin*.

So it was in findings of torture against Turkey between 1996 and 2000 where the ECtHR more meaningfully considered notions of 'mental anguish', 'mental violence',[64] and 'psychological pressure'.[65] Although these cases included both physical and psychological suffering, the ECtHR ventured to explain that the psychological elements would have been torture in their own right (or, in the ECtHR's own words, if 'taken separately').[66] Yet, this remains hypothetical as there was also extreme physical suffering in these cases, very much emphasized by judges in reasoning towards a categorization of torture.

It was also in *Aydin v Turkey* that the ECtHR came to accept rape as unequivocally 'leav[ing] deep psychological scars on the victim which do not respond to the passage of time as quickly as other forms of physical and mental violence'.[67] Although rape has eventually come to be categorized as torture, that it was not always thus had attracted critique from feminist scholars as being discriminatorily downgraded or dismissed. How the ECtHR differentiated between torture and inhuman and degrading treatment on this front, on one account, evidenced a 'we know it when we see it' reasoning, reliant on 'visceral impressions of primarily male decisionmakers' ignoring 'the very real pain experienced by female survivors of gender-specific abuses', as opposed to a more principled approach.[68]

[63] Muntean (n 42) 143.
[64] *Aydin* (n 39) [84, 86].
[65] *Akkoc v Turkey* [2000] ECtHR 22947/93 [116].
[66] *Aydin* (n 39) [86]; *Akkoc* (n 65) [117].
[67] *Aydin* (n 39) [83].
[68] Evelyn Aswad, 'Torture by Means of Rape' (1996) 84 Georgetown Law Journal 1913–43.

Around the same time, expanded recognition of the psychological suffering of families also found its way into the jurisprudence through novel articulations. Whereas once only the person who was disappeared would be counted as a victim, now their families could be too. Judges increasingly established that a lack of information or providing false or misleading information to relatives of persons detained or disappeared produced severe emotional suffering that violated Article 3. In framing the degree of proximity to the disappeared to presume harm in *Orhan v Turkey*, the Court identified and instituted an emotional regime related to the acceptable and affordable empathy (specifically the proximity of the family tie, the particular circumstances of the relationship, the extent to which the family member witnessed the events in question, the involvement of the family member in the attempts to obtain information about the disappeared person, and how the authorities responded to those enquiries).[69] An important delimitation followed this inclusion, however: that the suffering of a family member needed to have a 'dimension and character distinct from the emotional distress inevitably stemming' from the situation.[70]

The next noteworthy case to single out psychological suffering was *Gäfgen v Germany*. There, the ECtHR similarly speculated that 'the real and immediate threats of deliberate and imminent ill-treatment [as having caused] considerable fear, anguish and mental suffering' could in principle be considered torture.[71] Importantly, the ECtHR was also attentive to the state of 'particular vulnerability and constraint' (the applicant was handcuffed in the interrogation room) and the 'atmosphere of heightened tension and emotions' (the police were under pressure to locate the whereabouts of a kidnapped child) in which the threat took place.[72] The delimitation here was that threats had to be immediate or imminent to be considered sufficiently serious. The ECtHR ultimately prescribed that whether any threat of physical torture amounted to a violation depended on the individual circumstances of a case, primarily

[69] *Orhan v Turkey* [2002] ECtHR 25656/94 [358].

[70] *Akkum and ors v Turkey* [2005] ECtHR 21894/93 [258–59]; *Orhan* (n 69) [358]; *Çakıcı v Turkey* [1999] ECtHR 23657/94 [98]; *NA and others v Russia* [2023] ECtHR 48523/19; *Khojoyan and Vardazaryan v Azerbaijan* [2022] ECtHR 62161/14 [74]; *Acar v Turkey* [2003] ECtHR 26307/95 [239]; *Esmukhambetov and others v Russia* [2011] ECtHR 23445/03 [189–90]; *Janowiec and ors v Russia* [2013] ECtHR [GC] 55508/07 [188]; *Nesibe Haran v Turkey* [2006] ECtHR 28299/95 [84]. Following a similar logic, the suffering of family members of those killed in violation of Article 2 (right to life) has never been recognized as a rule: *Boboc and others v Moldova* [2022] ECtHR 44582/16 [61]; *Vyacheslavova and others v Ukraine* [2025] ECtHR 39553/16 [435–36]: 'The Court has never questioned in its case-law the profound psychological impact of a serious human rights violation on the victim's family members [but] it does not consider that it had a dimension and character which went beyond the suffering inflicted by grief following the wrongful death of a close family member and stemming from the absence of an effective investigation into the circumstances of that death.'

[71] *Tyrer* (n 28) [33].

[72] *Gäfgen* (n 6) [80–81, 106].

'the severity of the pressure exerted and the intensity of the mental suffering caused'.[73] Equally important, the ECtHR explicitly ruled that there was no requirement for psychological suffering be coupled with physical suffering in order to be recognized. Again, there was no finding here of torture but of inhuman treatment. Importantly, cases to follow involving threats have also not amounted to torture.[74] Numerous instances where applicants felt intimidated or coerced at a police station have also been dismissed outright.[75] Such recognition around threats was also extended to what can be called 'anticipatory harm' in awaiting before corporal[76] or capital[77] punishment or simply uncertainty as to what treatment would come next.[78]

Threats serve to illustrate not only the contested categorization well but also what in a case is foregrounded or backgrounded in assessments. Threats, for instance, have often been identified but merely feature as part of a combination of ill-treatment without much emphasis.[79] In a case of incommunicado detention, the ECtHR agreed that the applicant 'was left entirely vulnerable […] to the reprehensible conduct of his custodians and the police officers responsible for questioning him, and even more seriously, to acts of physical torture'.[80] The 'even more seriously' can be interpreted as spelling out a hierarchy between the physical and psychological. It has also not been uncommon for adjudicators to identify psychological suffering as 'aggravating' the physical.[81] Relatedly, certain cases concerning a combination of physical and psychological indicate that, where having found a violation on the physical allegations, adjudicators explicitly overlook the non-physical, to 'not consider it necessary to go on to

[73] ibid [108].

[74] *Rodic and ors v Bosnia and Herzegovina* [2008] ECtHR 22893/05 [73]; *Kramarenko and ors v Russia* [2021] ECtHR 21840/13 [62–63]; *El-Masri v Macedonia* [2012] ECtHR 39630/09 [202]; *Zamferesko v Ukraine* [2013] ECtHR 30075/06 [53]; *Bogulak v Poland* [2001] ECtHR 33866/96; *Chumakov v Russia* [2012] ECtHR 41794/04 [102]; *RB v Hungary* [2016] ECtHR 64602/12; *Oganezova v Armenia* [2022] ECtHR 71367/12 72961/12 [96]; *Khachatryan v Armenia* [2024] ECtHR 11829/26 [161]; *D v Latvia* [2024] ECtHR 76680/17 [47–50]; *SP and others v Russia* [2023] ECtHR 36463/11 [92–96].

[75] *Foka v Turkey* [2008] ECtHR 28940/95 [61]; *Protopapa v Turkey* [2009] ECtHR 16084/90 [49]; *Berktay v Turkey* [2001] ECtHR 22493/93 [176]; *Nechiporuk and Yonkalo v Ukraine* [2011] ECtHR 42310/04 [285–88].

[76] *Tyrer* (n 28) [33].

[77] *Soering* (n 39) [100]: 'account is to be taken not only of the physical pain experienced but also, where there is a considerable delay before execution of the punishment, of the sentenced person's mental anguish of anticipating the violence he is to have inflicted'.

[78] *Aydin* (n 39) [84]: 'in a constant state of physical pain and mental anguish brought on by the beatings administered to her during questioning and by the apprehension of what would happen to her next'; *Kurt v Turkey* [1998] ECtHR 15/1997/799/1002 [131]: 'the uncertainty, doubt and apprehension suffered by the applicant over a prolonged and continuing period of time caused her severe mental distress and anguish'; *Korneykova and Korneykov v Ukraine* [2016] ECtHR 56660/12 [47].

[79] *Süheyla Aydın v Turkey* [2005] ECtHR 25660/94 [187]; *Elçi and ors v Turkey* [2003] ECtHR 23145/93 [21].

[80] *Dikme* (n 19) [82].

[81] *Lapunov v Russia* [2023] ECtHR 28834/19 [108].

assess whether the other allegations of physical or psychological abuses are true, particularly in view of the difficulty of proving such treatment'.[82] Psychological suffering, albeit present, is thus backgrounded, indicating a lack of attention to the full spectrum of suffering born out of practical considerations.

Notwithstanding the nuances, a review of the ECtHR caselaw reveals a long (and growing) list of practices to being included under the prohibition,[83] particularly those that have inflicted psychological suffering alone. Some have initially required relatively more consideration than police beatings as with: forced nudity;[84] destruction of home;[85] denial of ongoing treatment (including drug substitution);[86] cells with no division between eating, sleeping, and toileting facilities;[87] cages and glass-boxes;[88] poor (crowded or lengthy) transportation;[89] forced sterilization;[90] living conditions due to home destruction and racial discrimination;[91] serious overcrowding;[92] detainee's spectacles taken away for five months;[93] detention of a person with a disability in a car;[94] prisoner transportation;[95] insults and extortion during military service;[96] secondary victimization;[97] separation of mother and child;[98] humiliation of student by teacher;[99] immigration detention, particularly of children;[100] forced urine sample;[101] legal implications of conscientious objection;[102] discriminatory remarks against minority;[103] life imprisonment;[104] psychologically

[82] *Bati* (n 20) [115]; *Dikme* (n 19) [83]; *Yavuz v Turkey* [2006] ECtHR 67137/01 [39].
[83] *RB v Hungary* [2016] ECtHR 64602/12 [34].
[84] *Musayeva v Russia* [2008] ECtHR 12703/02; *Hellig v Germany* [2011] ECtHR 20999/05; *Lyalyakin v Russia* [2015] ECtHR 31305/09.
[85] *Ilhan v Turkey* [2005] ECtHR 22494/93; *Dulas v Turkey* [2001] ECtHR 25801/94.
[86] *Wenner v Germany* [2016] ECtHR 62303/13.
[87] *Mironov v Russia* [2008] ECtHR 22625/02; *Chudun v Russia* [2011] ECtHR 20641/04.
[88] *Svinarenko and Slyadnev* [2014] ECtHR [GC] 32541/08 [53–76].
[89] *Petrov v Russia* [2013] ECtHR 23185/03.
[90] *IG and others v Slovakia* [2013] ECtHR 15966/04; *NB v Slovakia* [2012] ECtHR 29518/10.
[91] *Moldovan and others v Romania* [2005] ECtHR 41138/98.
[92] *Kondratishko and others v Russia* [2012] ECtHR 3937/03.
[93] *TK v Lithuania* [2018] ECtHR 14000/12.
[94] *Shalyavski and others v Bulgaria* [2017] ECtHR 67608/11.
[95] *Kavkazskiy v Russia* [2018] ECtHR 19327/13.
[96] *Filippovy v Russia* [2022] ECtHR 19355/09 [99].
[97] *B v Russia* [2023] ECtHR 36328/20; *JI v Croatia* [2023] ECtHR 35898/16 [98].
[98] *Mayeka and Mitunga v Belgium* [2007] ECtHR 13178/03 [69]: the separation and deportation of a five-year-old's mother caused the child 'extreme anxiety' and showed a 'total lack of humanity', causing the mother 'deep anxiety'.
[99] *VK v Russia* [2017] ECtHR 68059/13 [172].
[100] *Darboe and Camara v Italy* [2022] ECtHR 5797/17; *GB and others v Turkey* [2020] ECtHR 4633/15; *AB and others v France* [2016] ECtHR 11593/12.
[101] *RS v Hungary* [2019] ECtHR 65290/14.
[102] *Ülke v Turkey* [2006] ECtHR 39437/98 [59] 'amounting almost to "civil death"'.
[103] *Women's Initiatives Supporting Group and others v Georgia* [2022] ECtHR 73204/13 74959/13; *Oganezova v Armenia* [2022] ECtHR 71367/12.
[104] *Karpenko v Ukraine* [2006] ECtHR 10559/03.

coercive police interrogation;[105] threatening nature of an informal prisoner hierarchy;[106] hate speech against LGBTI people;[107] and the forced shaving of a prisoner's hair. While some instances had been rejected in the past as inherent, trivial, or otherwise not meeting the 'minimum', these are now understood to produce the sufficient level of psychological suffering to reach the threshold. Others, such as prolonged solitary confinement and irreducible life imprisonment, straddle the threshold, which are elaborated in the next chapter.

Timing suffering

Although there is no rigid durational requirement in torture's definition, one implicit factor gleaned from the review is how time (or temporal frames) works as a device of exclusion.[108] There is nothing on the face of the formal frameworks in the three institutions that require that suffering be lengthy. States have, however, regularly emphasized the short duration of suffering in their responses[109] or the absence of long-health consequences to downgrade the severity assessment.[110] Adjudicators have responded variably to such arguments, at times accepting (as in *NA*) and others rejecting,[111] sometimes without much clarity. Violations have not been found, for instance, where the period of disappearance, uncertainty, and subsequent death 'do not as such appear long',[112] where the applicant was young and didn't suffer long enough,[113] or where the family did not witness the disappearance and learned of it on the same day through the media.[114] Ten months,[115] two

[105] *Suslv and Batikyan v Ukraine* [2023] ECtHR 56540/14; *Dokukiny v Russia* [2022] ECtHR 1223/12.

[106] *D v Latvia* [2024] ECtHR 76680/17 [50–51]; *SP and others v Russia* [2023] ECtHR 36463/11 [92–96].

[107] *Romanov and others v Russia* [2023] ECtHR 58358/14 [67].

[108] I note that the French 'aiguës' (or acute) in the UNCAT definition as compared with the English 'severe' is indicative here that torture involves 'acute', not 'chronic', pain.

[109] *Adam v Slovakia* [2016] ECtHR 68066/12 [43]; *Lecomte v Germany* [2016] ECtHR 80442/12 [83]; *Hinderberger v Germany* [2010] ECtHR 28183/06, p 8; *Gavrilovici v Moldova* [2010] ECtHR 25464/05; *Staszewska v Poland* [2010] ECtHR 10049/04 [57]: 'the applicant's injuries were not very serious and, as reported by the domestic authorities, the impairment of the applicant's health lasted for a period shorter than seven days [. . .]. The applicant did not need hospitalisation'.

[110] *Barakhoyev v Russia* [2017] ECtHR 8516/08 [43]: 'the Court observes that the applicant sustained multiple injuries to his body, which must have caused him mental and physical suffering. Contrary to the Government's assertion, the absence of long-term health consequences cannot exclude a finding that the treatment is serious enough to be considered inhuman or degrading'.

[111] *Corley and others v Russia* [2021] ECtHR 292/06 [103]: 'the relative brevity of a period of detention does not automatically exclude the treatment complained of from the scope of Article 3'.

[112] *Saribekyan and Balyan v Azerbaijan* [2020] ECtHR 35746/11 [90–91].

[113] *Khachukayevy v Russia* [2020] ECtHR 34576/08 [74].

[114] *Khojoyan and Vardazaryan v Azerbaijan* [2022] ECtHR 62161/14 [73].

[115] *Luluyev and others v Russia* [2007] ECtHR 69480/01 [115–18].

years,[116] and fifteen years[117] conversely have been considered 'long enough'. Adjudicators, on the whole, look to prefer longer durations of suffering, emphasizing a 'long period of uncertainty, doubt and apprehension'[118] and pointing out that the suffering was inflicted over 'hours at a stretch',[119] remained with 'the passage of time',[120] or was otherwise prolonged.[121]

Beyond duration, time has also featured in anticipation, accumulation, and imminence. The gravity of suffering as induced by threats[122] or health consequences arising from deportation,[123] for instance, have been linked directly to the notion of anticipation and imminence (or temporal distance). Cumulative assessments, to elaborate, have been key in emphasizing the gravity of certain (particularly psychologically oriented) practices in combination,[124] and against viewing them in isolation from each other.[125] The significance of cumulative reasoning is evident particularly when it is not used, engendering strong dissents decrying how splitting up the 'treatment' into 'separate phases', for instance, can 'lose sight' of the total impact of the treatment.[126] Circumstantial

[116] *Khachukayevy v Russia* [2020] ECtHR 34576/08 [74].

[117] *Adzhigitova and others v Russia* [2021] ECtHR 40165/07 [227]. See also *Janowiec* (Chamber) (n 70) [143, ten-year test] here.

[118] *Çakıcı v Turkey* [1999] ECtHR 23657/94 [96].

[119] *Ireland v UK* [1978] ECtHR 5310/71 [167].

[120] *Cyprus v Turkey* [2001] ECtHR 25781/94 [155]; *AB and ors v France* [2016] ECtHR 11593/12 [114], eighteen-day detention of a four-year-old: 'the passage of time is of primary significance in this connection [with Article 3]'.

[121] *Arapkhanovy v Russia* [2014] ECtHR 2215/05 [152]: 'there was no distinct long-lasting period during which the applicants sustained uncertainty, anguish and distress characteristic to the specific phenomenon of disappearances [...] the mental suffering endured by the applicants has not reached a dimension and character distinct from the emotional distress which may be regarded as inevitably caused to relatives of a victim of a serious human-rights violation'. In a death-row case against Bulgaria, the ECtHR conversely considered that similar 'feelings of fear and anxiety must have diminished as time went on and as the moratorium continued in force': *Iorgov v Bulgaria* [2004] ECtHR 40653/98 [79].

[122] *El-Masri v Macedonia* [2012] ECtHR 39630/09 [202]: 'the threat that he would be shot if he left the hotel room was sufficiently real and immediate which, in itself, may be in conflict with Article 3' (violation: inhuman and degrading).

[123] *D v UK* [1997] ECtHR 30240/96; *N v UK* [2008] ECtHR 26565/05 [22]; *Paposhvili v Belgium* [2016] ECtHR 41738/10 [183].

[124] UN SRT, Report (2016) A/71/298 [44]: while legitimate uses of some psychological pressure are recognized, accusatorial, protracted, or suggestive interviews overlayed with threats, manipulation, and coercion are underscored as problematic, and depending on their 'degree, severity, chronicity and type, undue psychological pressure and manipulative practices' have been understood to amount to ill-treatment; UN SRT, Report (1997) E/CN.4/1997/7 [121]: '[e]ach of these measures on its own may not provoke severe pain or suffering' but may do so in combination when 'applied on a protracted basis of, say, several hours'; UN Commission on Human Rights, Situation of Detainees at Guantánamo Bay; E/CN.4/2006/120 (2006) [52]: 'the simultaneous use of these techniques is even more likely to amount to torture'; see also Hernan Reyes, 'The Worst Scars Are in the Mind: Psychological Torture' (2007) 89 (867) International Review of the Red Cross 591, 616.

[125] *Levchuk v Ukraine* [2020] ECtHR 17496/19 [80]: 'however trivial the isolated incidents might be'.

[126] *T v UK* [1999] ECtHR 24724/94, joint partly dissenting opinion of Judges Ridruejo and others; *Pinon and ors v Malta* [2018] ECtHR 71645/13.

findings of intent have also proven contingent on longer temporal frames—with acts needing to be 'premeditated' and 'applied for hours at a stretch',[127] not 'spontaneous [but] calculated'.[128]

Conversely, the search for accumulation has served downplaying the gravity of short but otherwise harmful experiences. Blindfolding, despite all evidence against its use, however long, was on one occasion deemed a violation only after several days and in combination with other ill-treatment.[129] In other cases where the treatment was deemed short, for a violation to be found, additional significant factors were needed such as the presence of a particularly vulnerable individual, such as a sick or mentally ill detainee,[130] exceptionally egregious conditions, such as overnight stays in confined areas with no place to lie down or lack of access to sanitary facilities,[131] or confinement in a locked cell unsuited for habitation or otherwise dangerous.[132]

Dominant approaches have thus discretely deployed temporal logics in selecting and reconstructing facts—in delineating the contextual and historical dimensions of an experience which are taken to count. Although the principled stance is not to require physical, prolonged, or permanent damage, adjudicators continue to take these as core considerations (or 'as a proxy for the intensity of suffering experienced'[133]) in conducting their assessments. This potentially leaves more difficult facts ill-considered or overlooked—'distorting the specification of torture' away from more expansive recognition of psychological suffering.

[127] *Kudla v Poland* [2000] ECtHR 30210/96 [92].

[128] *Gäfgen* (n 6) [104].

[129] *Öcalan v Turkey (no 1)* [2005] ECtHR 46221/99 [183]: 'Artificially depriving prisoners of their sight by blindfolding them for lengthy periods spread over several days may, when combined with other ill-treatment, subject them to strong psychological and physical pressure. The Court must examine the effect of such treatment in the special circumstances of each case.'

[130] *Brega v Moldova* [2010] ECtHR 52100/08 [42–43]; *Parascineti v Romania* [2012] ECtHR 32060/05 [53–55]; *Dzhambekova and others v Russia* [2009] ECtHR 27238/03.

[131] *T and A v Turkey* [2014] ECtHR 47146/11 [95–99]; *Gavrilovici v Moldova* [2009] ECtHR 25464/05 [42–44]; *Aliev v Turkey* [2014] ECtHR 30518/11 [81]; and *Burzo v Romania* [2008] ECtHR 75240/01 [99–100].

[132] *Koktysh v Ukraine* [2009] ECtHR 43707/07 [93–95]; *Căşuneanu v Romania* [2013] ECtHR 22018/10 [61–62]; *Ciupercescu v Romania (no 2)* [2012] ECtHR 64930/09; *Tadevosyan v Armenia* [2008] ECtHR 41698/04 [55]; and *Neshkov and Others v Bulgaria* [2015] ECtHR 36925/10 [198].

[133] Natasa Mavronicola, *Torture, Inhumanity, and Degradation under Article 3 of the ECHR: Absolute Rights and Absolute Wrongs* (Hart 2021) 65.

Altogether out

Exclusions have come to be viewed through the black box of reasoning represented by the 'minimum level of severity' threshold, a conceptual aid to adjudicators in assessing whether suffering falls within the scope of Article 3 at all, or are altogether out as being 'inherent', 'incidental', and 'lawful'. For the ECtHR, this 'minimum' has served a role analogous to Article 1 of UNCAT's 'lawful sanctions' clause[134] in that it seeks to exclude altogether treatment that is taken as lawfully inherent to law enforcement—or, in other words, 'legitimate' suffering. No definitive guidance is provided as to how 'inherent', 'incidental', and 'lawful' are to be defined. In tracing the evolving nature of the minimum, the ECtHR has connected its expansion to the recognition of psychological suffering.[135] In more candid moments, the ECtHR has admitted that it 'is extremely difficult to trace the dividing line between what is "inhuman and degrading" within the meaning of Article 3 and what is not'.[136] My review of how the 'minimum level of severity' has been applied confirms this and finds that it has been used, particularly through the notion of 'inevitability', to downgrade and dismiss practices not leaving physical marks.

Determinations of what reaches this threshold, in principle, draw on considerations of the 'duration of the treatment, its physical or mental effects and, in some cases, the sex, age and state of health of the victim'.[137] While this seems sufficiently open-ended and receptive, my caselaw review indicates that this line has effectively been drawn in a way that sees psychological suffering as legitimate (incidental) and permissible. There is a tendency for prevalent and protected state (law enforcement) practices, such as interrogations, imprisonment, and isolation, to generally be accepted as lawful but for police beatings to be taken as unnecessary and unlawful. Necessity, a corollary device here, also enters the equation to dismiss or downgrade practices that are more psychologically oriented than physical.

[134] Despite the nominal alignment of Article 1 of the UNCAT with Article 3 of the ECHR, the ECtHR has made merely one pointed reference to the 'lawful sanctions' clause in its entire caselaw (*Korobov v Ukraine* [2011] ECtHR 29598/03 [10]).

[135] *D v Latvia* [2024] ECtHR 76680/17 [47]: on the 'minimum level of severity, the Court's approach has evolved. Initially, the Court held that "the mere feeling of stress of a detained person" or "the mere fear of reprisals from the [applicant's] cellmates" were not of themselves sufficient to bring the situation within the ambit of Article 3. However, when this fear of reprisals was accompanied by other factors, the Court has found that "the cumulative effect of overcrowding and the intentional placement of a person in a cell with persons who may present a danger to him may in principle raise an issue under Article 3 of the Convention"' (references omitted).

[136] *T v UK* [1999] ECtHR 24724/94, partly dissenting opinion of Judges Rozakis and Costa.

[137] *Ireland* (n 119) [162].

Practice has led to no violations being found in cases involving (see Annex 3 with citations): lack of a window in detention cell; destruction of property; difficulty in obtaining gender reassignment surgery; imprisonment of a blind man; threatened with criminal sanction for wearing a burqa; vaginal examination; mental impact of court and related official/administrative processes; adequacy of medical assistance; surveillance; less than six hours of sleep deprivation; lengthy prison sentences; forcible examinations and searches; uncertainty and fear caused by state authorities; psychologically pressured interrogation techniques; therapeutic intervention; suspension of a driver's licence; insufficient social security payments; limited access to toilet while detained; homelessness, eviction, and dispossession; witnessing injuries on others; immigration detention; low age of criminal responsibility; public display of criminal conviction; defamation; forced to travel for an abortion; military discharge; storage of dead bodies; and a number written by pen on the hands of applicants in the process of being expelled. Again, these are all psychological in nature. In articulating its 'minimum', the ECtHR has deployed distinct heuristic devices to downgrade and dismiss psychological suffering as *inevitable* (and necessary) or as *trivial*. It is the fear of the *psychological* violation that is front and centre here, not a *bloody lip*.

In sum, a systematic reading of the caselaw reveals that the two institutions, the ECmHR and ECtHR, were called to conceptualize and recognize psychological suffering from their first cases on Article 3. States, it is also shown, have also almost always argued against an expansive inclusion of psychological suffering, characterizing it as 'lesser', necessary, temporary, or trivial suffering as compared to physical suffering. To be clear, this is not to say that state arguments have always been rejected and that there have been no exclusions of psychological suffering.

Inter-American Court of Human Rights

There are two operative provisions pertaining to the prohibition of torture and inhuman and degrading treatment at the IACtHR: Article 2 of the IACPPT read in conjunction with the earlier Article 5 of the ACHR. Importantly for the recognition of psychological suffering, in the drafting of Article 5, a number of states proposed that the initial draft of 'physical integrity' be widened to include 'mental well-being'. An authoritative commentary recounts that states considered how the earlier proposal,[138]

[138] Ludovic Hennebel and Hélène Tigroudja, *The American Convention on Human Rights: A Commentary* (OUP 2021) 201.

> which referred exclusively to physical integrity, did not reflect the duality of the human person, so that its mental dimension had to be added to physical integrity. In Venezuela's view, the term 'moral' was to be preferred to 'psychic,' the former having a broader and therefore more protective meaning. Nicaragua, for its part, proposed that the three terms 'physical,' 'mental,' and 'moral' be retained.

The resulting legal formulations demonstrate an unreflecting variance and vagueness in terminology. Article 5 is broadly titled 'right to humane treatment'. This then consists of Article 5 (1) which protects the right to 'physical, mental, and moral integrity' and 5 (2) which prohibits torture and cruel, inhuman, and degrading treatment. None of these terms are defined or elaborated. Addressing this absence, Article 2 of the IACPPT defines torture, including 'mental' aspects as it variably refers to 'mental pain or suffering', 'mental capacities', and 'mental anguish'.[139]

Article 6 of the IACPPT, like Article 16 of the UNCAT, refers to 'other cruel, inhuman, or degrading treatment or punishment'. Again, there is no further illustration or guidance provided as to what specific techniques or practices are envisaged—except, as with Article 1 (1) of UNCAT, to specify that torture is not taken to 'include physical or mental pain or suffering that is inherent in or solely the consequence of lawful measures'. Similar to the ECHR, though fleeting, the IACPPT *travaux*, where the Organization of American States aimed to define torture in what became Article 2, depict a similar discussion about thresholds and imaginaries. Discussions, for instance, readily repeat the symbolism that torture 'constitutes a crime that is repulsive of the conscience of all nations' and that protected practices such as 'judge-ordered isolation' be excluded.[140] Nothing more is revealed.[141]

139 Article 2 of the IACPPT: 'torture shall be understood to be any act intentionally performed whereby physical or mental pain or suffering is inflicted on a person for purposes of criminal investigation, as a means of intimidation, as personal punishment, as a preventive measure, as a penalty, or for any other purpose. Torture shall also be understood to be the use of methods upon a person intended to obliterate the personality of the victim or to diminish his physical or mental capacities, even if they do not cause physical pain or mental anguish'.

140 OAS, 'Report of the Committee on Juridical and Political Affairs on the Draft Convention Defining Torture as an International Crime', OEA/Ser.G. CP/doc.1524/84, 1984, 9, 57.

141 Cecilia Medina Quiroga, *The American Convention on Human Rights: Crucial Rights and Their Theory and Practice* (2nd edn, Intersentia 2016) 153. As an aside, it is also instructive to consider how the IACtHR has reconciled (or evaded) the interplay between the ACHR and IACPPT. In extra-legal work, former Judge Quiroga argued that the IACPPT 'does not replace Article 5 of the American Convention but rather complements it' and that 'the Court applies the obligations of the [IACPPT] in earnest, but is reticent to apply the definition of torture in Article 2 of that Convention'. She continued to characterize the definition as inefficient and argued the need for IACtHR to preserve the discretion afforded by the ACHR.

In a *broad* sense, there is nothing entirely novel in the IACtHR's recognition of the non-physical nature of torture, particularly in view of the close alignment to developments in the ECtHR caselaw in articulating its own approach.[142] In *Cantoral-Benavides*, as a seeming result of such normative receptivity, the IACtHR observed that '[i]nternational jurisprudence has been developing the notion of psychological torture'.[143] While there is a conceptual differentiation, as at the other two institutions, a *formal* hierarchy between *physical* and *psychological* is absent here. The IACtHR has also broadly adopted the ECtHR's approach that 'even in the absence of physical injuries, psychological and moral suffering, accompanied by psychic disturbance during questioning, may be deemed inhuman treatment'.[144] Noting the 'inhuman' here, a similar contestation pertaining to categorization is revealed as at the two other institutions.

In line with normative developments elsewhere, Article 5 has come to cover a broad range of harms, informed both objectively and subjectively.[145] Specifically engaging with the invisible nature of pain, the IACtHR has on one occasion accepted an expert opinion that 'pain [. . .] is a subjective piece of information that cannot be seen'.[146] On another occasion, Judge Trindade wrote that torture 'in all its perversion is not limited to the physical injuries' but also aimed[147]

> to annihilate the victim's identity and integrity. It causes chronic psychological disturbances that continue indefinitely, making the victim unable to continue living normally as before. It worsens the victim's vulnerability, causes nightmares, generates a loss of trust in others, hypertension, and depression. Several expert opinions rendered before this Court in various cases in recent years have asserted this unanimously. A person tortured in prison loses the spatial dimension and even that of time itself.

Elaborating on the complexity of pain, on another occasion, the IACtHR has also read there to be 'a connection between personal autonomy, reproductive

[142] IACtHR observed that the definition of torture needed to consider a wide range of sources: *Bueno-Alves v Argentina* [78]: 'This concept is particularly relevant for International Human Rights Law, which has shown substantial progress through the evolution in the interpretation of international protection instruments.'

[143] *Cantoral-Benavides v Peru* [2000] IACtHR [102] citing *Campbell and Cosans* [1983] ECtHR.

[144] *Loayza Tamayo v Peru* [1997] IACtHR [57].

[145] ibid; *Maritza Urrutia v Guatemala* [2003] IACtHR, separate opinion of ReRoux Rengifo: 'let us admit that the conducts capable of entailing a violation of the right to humane treatment can assume the most diverse forms and means'.

[146] *Cabrera García and Montiel Flores v Mexico* [2010] IACtHR [129].

[147] *Gómez-Paquiyauri Brothers v Peru* [2004] IACtHR, separate opinion [21].

freedom and personal and psychological integrity'.[148] These explorative moments are notable in how they are grounded, at least in appearance, in expertise. It was this concept of 'psychological integrity' that the IACtHR developed before 'psychological torture' first in *Loayza Tamayo*, a case involving threats of torture, repeated rape, and solitary confinement.[149] This was followed by its ruling in *Moiwana Community v Suriname*, which concerned an indigenous land rights claim, where the IACtHR found the community members to have 'endured significant emotional, psychological, spiritual and economic hardship'.[150] Moreover, as at the ECtHR, the IACtHR has also characterized rape as inherently causing serious psychological and social suffering beyond the physical.[151] As with *Gäfgen* at the ECtHR, in *'Street Children' (Villagran-Morales et al) v Guatemala*, the IACtHR also required threats to be 'sufficiently real and imminent'—surveying the context and the events to have preceded the threats in ruling that they were indeed imminent.[152] This was also coupled with the requirement of proximity (namely, the physical possibility of the authorities to act to achieve the threatened consequences).[153]

The IACtHR too has employed a plurality of terms including 'psychological distress',[154] 'emotional suffering',[155] 'psychological damage',[156] 'psychic and moral integrity',[157] 'psychological and emotional effects', 'mental, spiritual, moral, psychological',[158] and 'psychological and emotional suffering,

[148] *Artavia Murillo et al v Costa Rica* [2012] IACtHR [147].

[149] *Loayza Tamayo* (n 144).

[150] *Moiwana Community v Suriname* [2005] IACtHR [103].

[151] *Miguel Castro-Castro Prison v Peru* [2006] IACtHR [311]: 'an extremely traumatic experience that may have serious consequences and it causes great physical and psychological damage that leaves the victim "physically and emotionally humiliated," situation difficult to overcome with time, contrary to what happens with other traumatic experiences'; *Rosendo Cantú and others v Mexico* [2010] IACtHR [114]: 'the after-effects of rape will not always be physical injuries or disease. Women victims of rape also experience complex consequences of a psychological and social nature [...] [it] means dishonor, stigmatization, blame, and the disgrace it somehow causes within the family, [and ...] the neighborhood'; *Río Negro Massacres v Guatemala* [2012] IACtHR [134]; *Women Victims of Sexual Torture in Attenco v Mexico* [2018] IACtHR [152]: 'the severity of the effects is considered to be inherent'; *Azul Rojas Marín et al v Perú* [2021] [162, 164]: 'rape is an extremely traumatic experience that has severe consequences and causes great physical and psychological harm'.

[152] *'Street Children' (Villagran-Morales et al) v Guatemala* [1999] IACtHR.

[153] *Rochela Massacre v Colombia* [2007] IACtHR [136]: 'the passage of time'; *Caesar v Trinidad and Tobago* [2005] IACtHR [99]; *Miguel Castro-Castro Prison* (n 151) [333]; *Tibi v Ecuador* [2004] IACtHR [148].

[154] *Raxcacó-Reyes v Guatemala* [2005] IACtHR [101].

[155] *Cantoral-Benavides* (n 143) [91].

[156] *Miguel Castro-Castro Prison* (n 151) [311].

[157] *Acosta-Calderón v Ecuador* [2005] IACtHR [143].

[158] *'Juvenile Reeducation Institute' v Paraguay* [2004] IACtHR [134]: victims' relatives 'have also suffered psychological and emotional effects as a result of the deaths of the inmates and/or the injuries they sustained' [172]; 'the children are at a critical stage in their physical, mental, spiritual, moral, psychological and social development that will impact, in one way or another, their life plan'.

constitut[ing] a psychological torture'.[159] The IACtHR has also at times referred to the 'emotional integrity' interchangeably with mental and moral.[160] That is, the IACtHR has not strictly distinguished between emotional, psychological, mental, and moral integrity,[161] with the 'moral' conceivably applying to any diminishment of dignity.[162]

The first IACtHR case to use and elaborate on the notion of 'psychological torture' (as opposed to 'psychological integrity') was *Cantoral-Benavides* in 2000.[163] 'Psychological torture', at the IACtHR, has come to stand for purposeful psychologically oriented practices producing psychological effects and was freely linked and interchanged with 'moral anguish', 'mental or moral suffering', 'mental resistance', and 'mental torture'.[164] There was also an appreciation, although implicit in the reasoning there, that this had *only now* (meaning at that time) come to be prohibited, as physical practices did not attract the same need for conceptualization in comparison. What is distinct in the IACtHR caselaw is how psychological suffering is translated into 'psychological torture'—the latter is used relatively rarely by the ECtHR and the CAT except where it is a reference to an applicant's own wording. There is no apparent explanation for this preference on the face of decisions.

The notion of 'psychological suffering' has also been used by the IACtHR to expand recognition to various experiences such as people in fear of their life or the lives of their family members.[165] For instance, in *Rochela Massacre v Colombia*, three survivors of a massacre 'felt the possibility that they might die

[159] *Miguel Castro-Castro Prison* (n 151) [293].

[160] *VRP, VPC et al v Nicaragua* [2018] IACtHR [333].

[161] Laurence Burgorgue-Larsen and Amaya Úbeda de Torres, *The Inter-American Court of Human Rights: Case-Law and Commentary* (OUP 2011) 379: '[t]he criteria necessary to identify forms of treatment other than torture that are prohibited under Article 5(2) have not been (and maybe never will be) developed with [...] analytical rigour'; 'the conclusions [that the Court] reaches are always all-encompassing rather than precise'; *Tineo Family v Bolivia* [2013] IACtHR [206–08].

[162] Trindade criticized the ambiguity in *Acosta-Calderón* (n 157) [143], separate opinion [7]: 'the Court lost a valuable opportunity to consider possible violations to Article 5 of the Convention and, specifically psychic and moral integrity, to determine the differences between the violation to humane treatment and the type of evidence required for its determination regarding violations to psychic and moral integrity'. Victor Madrigal-Borloz, 'Damage and Redress in the Jurisprudence of the Inter-American Court of Human Rights (1979–2001)' (2001) Human Rights and Development Yearbook 211, 230 (references omitted): finds that 'moral damage' pertains to the 'psyche of the individual' and that 'associated with the experience of various forms, to varying degrees, of fear and suffering: anxiety, humiliation, degradation and the inculcation of feelings of inferiority, insecurity, frustration, and impotence. [...] associated with hindrance to cultural values that are particularly significant to the injured parties, and has generally been equated with the violation of personal integrity'.

[163] *Cantoral-Benavides* (n 143) [100–02]; the term 'psychological torture' was first used by the IACmHR in *Gobardhan v Suriname* [1985] IACmHR [6], a case which involved death threats and mock executions.

[164] *Maritza Urrutia* (n 145) [91–93], followed in *Tibi* (n 153) [147], *Miguel Castro-Castro Prison* (n 151) [288].

[165] *Mapiripán Massacre v Colombia* [2005] IACtHR [136, 284].

in those moments as well […] knowing that the paramilitaries could return at any moment'.[166] There, the IACtHR underscored the 'intense psychological suffering of the survivors' and the 'profound fear that they would be deprived of their lives in a violent and arbitrary manner' arising from witnessing torture and execution.[167] While coming close to a specific finding of torture where psychological suffering was prominent, the rest of the facts of physical suffering provided the IACtHR with an important context which enabled the strong condemnation of the psychological suffering.

Furthermore, the IACtHR has recognized the suffering of family members beyond the context of enforced disappearances (although not as torture), having found that the personal integrity of the mother of a man who was restrained in psychiatric care and died was also violated.[168] The IACtHR has ruled similarly in finding violations as arising from witnessing torture and execution,[169] also finding that disappearances created 'a general state of anguish, insecurity and fear'.[170] Again, as with the ECtHR, the model of family used here only includes 'close' family, with a 'special' connection, leading to the exclusion of those not understood to be sufficiently 'close' or 'special' such as friends. Similar recognition was afforded to the suffering of a family who witnessed the death of their family member on death row due to diabetes,[171] family members of an isolated prisoner not allowed visitation rights,[172] re-traumatization during a judicial process,[173] and the death of a child at the hands of the state.[174] None of these instances was qualified as torture. In all, the institutional narrative depicts the IACtHR as readily recognizing the psychological suffering to have been brought before it but not as torture.

Unlike the ECtHR, there is not much by way of exclusion in IACtHR caselaw. The 'lawful sanctions' logic is exceptionally discerned in cases involving the

[166] *Rochela Massacre* (n 153) [135].
[167] ibid 136.
[168] *Ximenes-Lopes v Brazil* [2005] IACtHR [157]: 'three days after his admission, she found him in extremely bad conditions, but was unable to do anything for him. She learnt about his death when she arrived home after leaving him in said institution. This made her very sad and caused her great pain. After [his] death, she has suffered from deep depression and health problems'.
[169] *Rochela Massacre* (n 153) [136]; *Baldeón-García v Perú* [2006] IACtHR [128]; *González et al v Mexico* ('Cotton Field') [2019] IACtHR [419, 424]; *Godínez-Cruz* [1989] IACtHR [197]; *Velásquez-Rodríguez v Honduras* [1988] IACtHR [187]; *Álvarez and ors v Guatemala* [2012] IACtHR [204].
[170] *Velásquez-Rodríguez* (n 169) [149].
[171] *Revolorio and ors v Guatemala* [2019] IACtHR; *Bedregal and ors v Bolivia* [2024] IACtHR.
[172] *García-Asto and Ramírez-Rojas v Peru* [2005] IACtHR [234].
[173] *Angulo Losada v Bolivia* [2022] IACtHR [83, 124].
[174] *Vargas-Areco v Paraguay* [2006] IACtHR [95–96]: relatives 'suffered large psychological impact and endured a great deal of pain and anguish as a direct consequence of the death of the minor Vargas-Areco [they] have long lived, and still today, feeling uncertainty, frustration, anguish and powerlessness due to the lack of an adequate investigation […] seriously impairing the lifestyle of the family as a group and of each member individually'.

life imprisonment of children,[175] death penalty methods (by hanging),[176] incommunicado detention (after three days),[177] visitation restrictions,[178] and the death-row phenomenon.[179] Notably, these were complex cases which saw strong state responses. While there has been no extended discussion, invocations of necessity[180] and inevitability[181] provide useful entry-points into how the Court has approached the question of inclusion and exclusion. In one case, the Court has held the restrictions of the rights of privacy and intimacy to be 'unavoidable consequences' of detention, but was quick to subject this position to a rigorous test of necessity.[182] In another case, it used UN *Standard Minimum Rules on the Treatment of Prisoners* in ruling that whipping was not legitimate punishment.[183] Elsewhere, it has explained that its assessments could not be 'left to the whim of the authority or of public opinion',[184] or the 'socially tolerable'.[185]

In sum, Article 5 of the ACHR has afforded the IACtHR with wide room to manoeuvre in the recognition of psychological suffering offering expansive recognition. Psychological suffering was included in its drafting, with terms as 'psychological', 'mental', and 'moral' suffering used variably and without rigid

[175] *Mendoza and ors v Argentina* [2013] IACtHR [174]: 'punishments considered radically disproportionate, such as those that can be described as atrocious fall within the sphere of application of the articles that contain the prohibition of torture and [CIDT]'.

[176] *Boyce et al v Barbados* [2007] IACtHR [102].

[177] *Chaparro Álvarez and Lapo Íñiguez v Ecuador* [2007] IACtHR.

[178] *García-Asto and Ramírez-Rojas v Peru* [2005] IACtHR [229].

[179] *Fuentes and ors v Guatemala* [2019] IACtHR; *Avila v Guatemala* [2019] IACtHR [183].

[180] *Barrios Family v Peru* [2001] IACtHR [52]: 'any use of force that is not strictly necessary to ensure the appropriate behavior of detainee constitutes an attack against human dignity'.

[181] *Sandoval v Guatemala* [2016] IACtHR [169]: 'state to ensure that the manner and method of deprivation of liberty does not exceed the inevitable level of suffering inherent in detention' [174]; 'many decisions adopted by international bodies invoke the [SMR] to interpret the content of the right of persons deprived of liberty to dignified and humane treatment'.

[182] *Lopez and others v Argentina* [2019] IACtHR [92]: 'this restriction of rights, a consequence of the deprivation of liberty or a collateral effect thereof, must be rigorously limited, since any restriction on a human right is only justifiable under international law when it is necessary in a democratic society'; *Garcia Asto and Ramirez Rojas v Peru* [2005] IACtHR [223]: 'The situations described above are contrary to the "essential aim" of imprisonment sanctions.'

[183] *Caesar* (n 153) [2005] IACtHR [31]; see also [66]: it 'represents a form of punishment no longer acceptable in a democratic society', rejecting that mere national legislation could be looked upon as justification. Marijke De Pauw finds that, for the IACtHR, soft law has been 'an interpretive tool' allowing it 'to read the ACHR's provisions in the context of modern-day circumstances and in light of changing human rights perceptions', 'The Inter-American Court of Human Rights and the Interpretative Method of External Referencing' in Yves Haeck and others (eds), *The Inter-American Court of Human Rights: Theory and Practice, Present and Future* (Intersentia 2015) 12.

[184] *Bayarri v Argentina* [2008] IACtHR, per Garcia Ramirez [11]: 'being necessary or "essential" is not left to the whim of the authority or of public opinion, which could characterize as necessary or essential a measure that, in reality, is unnecessary or can be substituted'.

[185] *Almonacid-Arellano et al v Chile* [2006] IACtHR [105] citing ICTY, *Prosecutor v Erdemovic*, IT-96-22: 'Crimes against humanity [are] inhumane acts that by their extent and gravity go beyond the limits tolerable to the international community.'

distinction since. Cases where psychological suffering was argued before the IACtHR involved systematic abuses and were often argued together with grave physical suffering and state silence, which has conceivably allowed the IACtHR to more freely recognize the nature of psychological suffering. The exclusion (or non-recognition) of practices centred on psychological suffering has not been a pressing concern for the IACtHR, a point which is brought into stark relief through comparison with the ECmHR–ECtHR caselaw over the years.

UN Committee Against Torture

Article 1 (1) of the UNCAT, the authoritative definition of torture for the CAT as well as universally, defines torture as being constituted by 'severe pain or suffering, whether physical or *mental*' (emphasis added). To distil its paragraph-long definition, for an act to amount to torture it needs to be (i) intentional, (ii) purposeful, and (iii) official, and (iv) to inflict severe physical or mental suffering.[186] Although differentiated, there is no formal hierarchy drawn here between *physical* and *psychological* suffering. Beyond this definition, the UNCAT does not provide any practical illustrations of what is to be recognized as torture, or psychological suffering for that matter, but an additional principle is pronounced that torture 'does not include pain or suffering arising only from, inherent in or incidental to lawful sanctions'. Article 1 of the UNCAT opts for an open-ended approach, being inclusive and indicative[187] and not offering categories of methods or illustrations.[188]

The *travaux* to the UNCAT reveals that the concept of 'mental suffering' was not extensively discussed by the Working Group drafting Article 1, except that delegates from the UK and Germany pointed out the difficulty of its interpretation and adjudication.[189] The UK representative already then noted that 'the

[186] Article 1 of the UNCAT reads: 'the term "torture" means any act by which severe pain or suffering, whether physical or mental, is intentionally inflicted on a person for such purposes as obtaining from him or a third person information or a confession, punishing him for an act he or a third person has committed or is suspected of having committed, or intimidating or coercing him or a third person, or for any reason based on discrimination of any kind, when such pain or suffering is inflicted by or at the instigation of or with the consent or acquiescence of a public official or other person acting in an official capacity. It does not include pain or suffering arising only from, inherent in or incidental to lawful sanctions'.

[187] Manfred Nowak and Elizabeth McArthur, *The United Nations Convention Against Torture: A Commentary* (OUP 2008) 40.

[188] While pedagogically helpful, categorization runs the risk of reducing complexity.

[189] Ahcene Boulesbaa, *The UN Convention on Torture and the Prospects for Enforcement* (Brill 1999) 18; Nowak and McArthur (n 187) 38; UN Commission on Human Rights Draft Convention Against Torture and Other Cruel, Inhuman or Degrading Treatment or Punishment, 'Report of the Working Group' E/CN.4/11367 (1980) 19 (3) International Legal Materials 647.

essentially subjective concept of mental pain or suffering created some difficulties, particularly if it was linked to motives based on discrimination' and that 'to prevent the provisions of the convention from being bypassed, it should not exclude pain and suffering deriving from the use of lawful sanctions'.[190] Despite these misgivings, psychological suffering was incorporated into the definition of torture.

The UNCAT drafting history offers limited clues in understanding the final formulation of its 'lawful sanctions' clause which qualifies the definition of torture to *exclude* harms that are deemed 'inherent in or incidental to lawful sanctions'. The definition in the UN Declaration on Torture (1975), a direct textual antecedent to the UNCAT, expressly incorporated the 'lawful sanctions' clause which also qualified it 'to the extent consistent with the Standard Minimum Rules for the Treatment of Prisoners' (UN SMR). The UN SMR, now revised as the UN Nelson Mandela Rules (UN NMR, 2015), regulate detention practices known to be harmful—importantly including solitary confinement.[191] The Swedish Draft Convention unsuccessfully proposed to keep the UN SMR as the measure of lawful sanctions for the UNCAT[192]—with its eventual deletion described in one account as 'complex'.

Early accounts speculate that 'some members favouring strong universal standards might have accepted the deletion because of prisoners, as being only of marginal relevance to the whole problem of sanctions'.[193] Yet, proposals to refer to international law and to explicitly (and somewhat circularly) state that lawful sanctions could not themselves constitute inhuman and degrading treatment were not adopted. The latter was subsequently the approach taken in the IACPPT which holds that 'the concept of torture shall not include physical or mental pain or suffering that is inherent in or solely the consequence of lawful measures, provided that they do not include the performance of the acts or use of the methods referred to in this article'. As at the other institutions, state resistance to whether certain practices were 'lawful' or not was also documented.[194]

190 E/CN.4/1984/SR.33 (5 March 1984) [25].

191 UN NMR 2015 (A/RES/70/175); UN SRT, Report (2020) A/HRC/43/49 [41–42, 84].

192 Boulesbaa (n 189) 28–30.

193 Maxime E Tardu, 'The United Nations Convention Against Torture and Other Cruel, Inhuman or Degrading Treatment or Punishment' (1987) 56 Nordic Journal of International Law 303, 309.

194 J Herman Burgers and Hans Danelius, *The United Nations Convention Against Torture: A Handbook on the Convention Against Torture and Other Cruel, Inhuman, or Degrading Treatment or Punishment* (Nijhoff 1988) 103; objections by Libya and Saudi Arabia to the UN's criticism on their flogging practices soon after UNCAT came into effect have fuelled this imagination: see E/CN.4/1987/13, p 18 [57], E/CN.4/1989/15, p 18.

From its very outset, the 'lawful sanctions' clause has attracted criticism and caution as a 'monstrosity',[195] being 'rather vague and open',[196] and as presenting potentially a 'bypass'[197] or 'a serious loophole for governments'.[198] Its adjacent concept of the 'minimum level of severity', as conceived by the ECtHR, has also been critiqued, as it too has proven 'very difficult to spell out clear-cut standards for appraising'.[199] Given the interpretive uncertainty, an authoritative commentary on the UNCAT proscribes the discussion, proposing instead that the clause 'must simply be ignored'.[200] There is, however, an entry-point here for a critical discussion of the taken-for-granted suffering—often dis/missed by actors.[201]

Avoiding 'lawful sanctions' for almost ten years of operation, the CAT first came to interpret the 'lawful sanctions' clause in rejecting corporal punishment in 1997—long after the ECtHR and UN Human Rights Committee (HRC) had done so. An early commentator found it 'strange that an organ which has been especially set up to combat torture, has been less outspoken in the beginning on the subject than the HRC'.[202] The clause has still not been expansively unpacked by the CAT which to date ruled on it only to accept as inherent and lawful 'imprisonment and the normal conditions of detention [...] as such';[203] fears arising out of deportation;[204] and the use of force by police in affecting arrest.[205] In one particular case, the CAT ruled that the victim's conditions in prolonged detention in a temporary confinement ward (of three and a half months and one month), without bedding, toiletry items, table, toilet, or

[195] Chris Ingelse, *UN Committee Against Torture: An Assessment* (2001) 216.

[196] Chris Ingelse, 'The Committee Against Torture: One Step Forward, One Step Back' (2000) 18 Netherlands Quarterly of Human Rights 307, 311.

[197] The records of the UN working group on the UNCAT offer limited insights on the matter: UN Commission on Human Rights (1980). For the UK: 'to prevent the provisions of the convention from being bypassed, it should not exclude pain and suffering deriving from the use of lawful sanctions' E/CN.4/1984/SR.33 (1984) [25].

[198] Amnesty International, *Torture in the Eighties* (1984) 14.

[199] Antonio Cassese, 'Can the Notion of Inhuman and Degrading Treatment Be Applied to Socio-economic Conditions?' (1991) 2 European Journal of International Law 144.

[200] Nowak and McArthur (n 187) 84.

[201] Two articles to examine the clause do not offer a critical discussion: Celso Eduardo Faria Coracini, 'The Lawful Sanctions Clause in the State Reporting Procedure before the Committee Against Torture' (2006) 24 (2) Netherlands Quarterly of Human Rights 305; Anna Karapetyan, 'A Recurring Phenomenon: The Lawful Sanctions Clause in the Definition of Torture and the Question of Judicial Corporal Punishment under International Human Rights Law' (2016) 36 Polish Yearbook of International Law 137.

[202] CAT Record of Proceedings (1997) CAT/C/SR.294/Add1 [23] in Ingelse (n 195) 319.

[203] CAT-C-19-D-57-1996 [5.4].

[204] CAT-C-35-D-245-204. See also CAT-C-76-D-1049-2021 (conditions of deportation as Article 16 violation) [3.5], not ruled on.

[205] CAT-C-41-D-257-2004 [9.3]; CAT-C-63-D-678-2015 [10.2] citing the ECtHR's formulation that treatment 'must in any event go beyond that inevitable element of suffering or humiliation connected with a given form of legitimate treatment or punishment' [6.1].

sink, without ventilation, hot water, or walks out of the cell, with constant light in the cell and one meal per day, did 'not appear to have caused "severe pain and suffering" '.[206] The reasoning is curt and unconvincing.

What is more, as with IACPPT's Article 6, Article 16 of the UNCAT refers to the prevention of 'other acts of cruel, inhuman or degrading treatment or punishment which do not amount to torture'—recognizing a plurality of categories of harm albeit without further elaboration. Soft law standards have notably aimed to clarify this plurality—but what can be noticed here is that a wide interpretive approach is applied to inhuman and degrading treatment, not torture.[207] Applicants have also faced difficulties in substantiating their arguments that deportation itself would cause suffering in violation of Article 16;[208] that degrading and humiliating treatment at the hands of national judges violated Article 1 or 16;[209] or that being exposed to the living conditions in country of origin would amount to a violation.[210] These practices happen to be more psychological than physical. As at the IACtHR, the caselaw here does not offer more material for further comparative reflection.

A terminological diversity similar to the other institutions, also without due explanation, can be found in CAT's work. In three similar cases issued around the same time, the CAT described the treatment variably as 'anguish and psychological suffering',[211] 'moral and psychological anguish',[212] and 'emotional and psychological suffering'.[213] The CAT has also referred to non-physical pain as 'emotional pain'.[214] Elsewhere it has also resorted to 'mental suffering',[215] 'psychological damage',[216] 'psychological after-effects',[217] and 'anguish and suffering'.[218] It has referred to 'psychological torture', as argued by petitioners, but

[206] CAT-C-52-D-478-2011, 2014, [11.2].

[207] *UN Body of Principles for the Protection of All Persons under Any Form of Detention or Imprisonment*, GA res 43/173, 9 December 1988, General Clause: 'The term "cruel, inhuman or degrading treatment or punishment" should be interpreted so as to extend the widest possible protection against abuses, whether physical or mental, including the holding of a detained or imprisoned person in conditions which deprive him, temporarily or permanently. of the use of any of his natural senses, such as sight or hearing, or of his awareness of place and the passing of time.' Principle 21 (2) reads: 'No detained person while being interrogated shall be subject to violence, threats or methods of interrogation which impair his capacity of decision or his judgement.'

[208] CAT-C-51-D-434-2010 [4.28]; CAT-C-49-D-412-2010.

[209] CAT-C-7-D-9-1991 [1.3].

[210] CAT-C-62-D-721-2015 [7.6] (Bulgaria).

[211] CAT-C-72-D-793-2017 [6.2]; CAT-C-71-D-843-2017 [6.2].

[212] CAT-C-73-D-921-2019 [6.2].

[213] CAT-C-73-D-952-2019 [8.2].

[214] CAT-C-22-D-106-1998 [3.2].

[215] CAT-C-62-D-496-2012 [8.2].

[216] CAT-C-48-D-433-2010 [12.2].

[217] CAT-C-61-D-654-2015 [3.15].

[218] CAT-C-71-D-858-2018 [6.5].

has not used it out of its own initiative.[219] Compared to the other institutions, however, the CAT has done the least to expand on notions of psychological suffering. The CAT has chosen to simply refer to 'provisions of the Istanbul Protocol according to which the methods of torture can be both physical and psychological, and can include deprivation of such basic needs as food, water and medical care, among other things'.[220] In other cases, psychological suffering was assessed to *merely* aggravate the physical or articulate the context (thereby not afforded focus in and of itself).[221]

Conclusions

The three institutions have generally been responsive to psychological suffering since their very first cases. What is less emphasized is a counter-history here of how recognition has been delimited, with arguments made primarily by states against the free recognition of psychological suffering. Much indeed has been excluded, not only from the typical understandings of torture but also as altogether not warranting the protection of the prohibition at all. Reticence (producing variance) points to a contestation inhering in both recognition and categorization, fought on the fronts of exceptionality (that the psychological suffering in question was no more than trivial), necessity (that it was no more than inevitable), and temporality (that it was no more than fleeting).

Recognition of torture and inhuman and degrading treatment therefore cannot be said to have always flowed as freely as assumed—with many moments of exclusion and inclusion, and with exclusions (as delimitations) appearing early and leaving an important legacy. These delimitations can be elaborated as follows: exceptionality is the expectation for torture to require a 'special stigma' more easily satisfied by physically overt practices, deeming psychological suffering as lacking that 'stigma' and thus more fitting of 'lesser' categories (inhuman, degrading, not minimum level of severity). Temporality refers to the determination that short-term psychological suffering is not sufficiently harmful to deserve the protection of the prohibition and incremental long-term psychological suffering was not sufficiently spectacular to amount

219 CAT-C-26-D-147-1999 [2.6]; CAT-C-46-D-399-2009 [3.2]; CAT-C-33-D-223-2002 [4.9]; CAT-C-32-D-202-2002 [2.8].

220 CAT-C-61-D-661-2015 [8.2].

221 CAT-C-55-D-575-201 [5.12]: 'insults aggravate suffering and degradation to torture'; CAT-C-55-D-575-201 [7.6]: aggravated by being forced to 'to remove all his clothes and to sleep handcuffed arms and knees on the very cold cemented ground'.

to torture—as reinforcing the exceptionality criterion. Necessity is the understanding that most practices deemed to be on balance necessary for the state *legitimately* caused psychological suffering.

There are, on these three fronts, strong parallels between inclusion and exclusion at all three institutions. Although the ECmHR–ECtHR and IACtHR seem complex at first glance (especially compared to the CAT), perhaps due to their terminological plurality, there is much lacking in the depth of reasoning relating to how psychological suffering is recognized. As ready as the recognition of psychological suffering reads, there were also immediate delimitations, as sourced from the distinct association psychological suffering has had with degradation and discomfort more than with torture. There is, to put this slightly differently, no consolidated position within the caselaw with respect to 'how' and 'how much' psychological suffering should be included and excluded. The 'how' and 'how much' have been subject to close configuration and contestation since their very inception—leading to vast variation and a lack of precision. The next chapter focuses this examination on categorization.

3

Categorization and its discontents

> Classifications are powerful technologies. Embedded in working infrastructures[,] they become relatively invisible without losing any of that power [and] should be recognised as the significant site of political and ethical work that they are.[1]

How we name, classify, and categorize violence matters. It matters for victim-survivors and states, for academics as much as advocates and adjudicators. Where, this chapter asks, has psychological suffering been categorized in these understandings? As mentioned, no case categorized as torture has included psychological suffering standing on its own: no case of prolonged solitary confinement, irreducible life imprisonment, or threats to life, however serious. What then is typical torture precisely? What practices and experiences have the three institutions associated with the category? What about for related categories of inhuman and degrading treatment? This chapter consists of two sections. In the first ('The "stigma" of torture and categories "lesser"'), I characterize the category of torture as deeply associated with the physical spectacle. I also examine how psychological suffering has found a better 'fit' under the 'lesser' categories. This section also illustrates the interpretive impulses and issues through the example of solitary confinement cases. In the second section ('Contesting categorization'), I start to draw on interviews revealing perspectives not explicit or elaborated on the face of official documents.

[1] Geoffrey C Bowker and Susan Leigh Star, *Sorting Things Out: Classification and Its Consequences* (MIT Press 2000) 319.

Torture and the Recognition of Psychological Suffering in International Law. Ergün Cakal, Oxford University Press.
 DOI: 10.1093/oso/9780198989493.003.0003

The 'stigma' of torture and categories 'lesser'

This section works through the dominant associations the three institutions have made between the nature of suffering and the categories of torture ('Stigma: typical torture') and inhuman and degrading treatment ('"Lesser": inhuman and degrading'). I use solitary confinement ('Solitary as a case study') and the interplay between Articles 3 and 8 ('Other: Article 8 and dissent') to illustrate these dynamics.

Stigma: typical torture

From a sweeping read of the caselaw, the ECtHR's 1978 ruling in *Ireland* is revealed to have had profound repercussions for the politics of categorizing torture and, in the proceeding decades, sustained a deep-seated contestation about what has warranted the label of torture. The ruling consolidated the position that torture required a 'special stigma' and an 'aggravated' intensity of suffering. Despite not ruling out intense psychological suffering, in principle, from being categorized as torture, the conclusion reached in the judgment was that the 'five techniques' did not amount to the required 'intensity', despite the evidence to the contrary, practically foreclosing psychological suffering from the category when singled out.

From 1978 to 1996, until *Aksoy*, as mentioned, the ECtHR did not specifically categorize any of its findings as torture. This shows how the ruling, the bedrock of the field despite its numerous dissents, has cast a long shadow on the present exercise of naming torture, with the device of 'special stigma' rendering an effective hierarchy between torture and inhuman and degrading treatment. Furthermore, it is telling that, across the 3,071 Article 3 cases the ECtHR has ruled on to date (from 1960 to mid-May 2025), a specific finding of torture has only been found in 109 cases (see Annex 4). An exceptionality, or at least a stagnancy, can be observed here. Notably, these cases have been predominantly found in eastern European states, with a few exceptions: Russia (forty-one), Turkey (twenty), Ukraine (eighteen), Italy (six), Moldova (five), Bulgaria (four), Azerbaijan (three), Georgia (two), Macedonia (three), Romania (two), France (one), Moldova and Russia (one), Armenia (one), Albania (one), and Greece (one).

These cases reveal that certain physically overt practices enjoy a closer association with torture. Lengthy police beatings in *Selmouni*, for instance, led to the conclusion that '[w]hatever a person's state of health, it can be presumed that such intensity of blows will cause substantial pain'.[2] The same approach has been taken on electric shocks which the ECtHR has accepted as 'a particularly serious form of ill-treatment capable of provoking severe pain and cruel suffering and therefore falling to be treated as torture, even if it does not result in any long-term health damage'.[3] Despite the well-worn imperative that claims ought to be assessed on a case-by-case basis, such reasoning has created overriding presumptions essentializing the nature of suffering as attached to certain experiences as singular and inarguable.

The ECtHR's 'Guide on Article 3', with its first edition published in August 2022, provides another useful systematic overview. Long used internally as a first point of reference for ECtHR judges and registry, it has recently been published for external use for the first time.[4] For present purposes, it is taken to reflect the logics and considerations present in judicial reasoning—from which I draw some observations. From its outset, the Guide finds that 'Article 3 has been *commonly* applied in contexts in which the proscribed form of treatment has emanated from *intentionally* inflicted acts of State agents or public authorities' (emphasis added). The association between intentional or positive acts and Article 3, despite other authorities explaining that these are not always necessary, is front and centre. Assessments of Article 3, the Guide goes on to find, take into consideration (a) the purpose, (b) the context ('such as an atmosphere of heightened tension and emotions'), and (c) the victim's vulnerability.[5] The need to factor in socio-political standards, as found in *Selmouni*, also features here.[6]

The rest of the Guide lists the types of claims to have been *typically* qualified under which specific violation. Torture, as provided, is exemplified by cases which combined sexual, physical, and psychological ill-treatment, combined physical beatings and psychological coercion, force-feeding, and Palestinian hanging. While the element of psychological suffering is taken into account, the cases cited all involve physical spectacles. There is an implicit indispensability of physicality, according to the Guide, although the Court 'has not ruled out'

[2] *Selmouni v France* [1999] ECtHR 25803/94 [102].
[3] *Polonskiy v Russia* [2009] ECtHR 30033/05 [124].
[4] ECtHR, 'Guide on Article 3 of the European Convention on Human Rights: Prohibition of Torture' (August 2023) [3].
[5] ibid [6].
[6] ibid [11].

> that a threat of torture can also amount to torture, as the nature of torture covers both physical pain and mental suffering. In particular, the fear of physical torture itself may in certain circumstances constitute mental torture. However, it has underlined that the classification of whether a given threat of physical torture amounted to psychological torture or to inhuman or degrading treatment depended upon all the circumstances of a given case, including, notably, the severity of the pressure exerted and the intensity of the mental suffering caused.[7]

This remains in the realm of principle, not having been applied to threat-related cases to have followed (which have instead been associated with inhuman or degrading treatment, if anything).

Beyond the Guide, dissenting judgments have also been revealing as to how categorization is approached. As in *Ireland*, the threshold between torture and inhuman treatment has generated notable dissent in more recent cases.[8] In a rare prescient dissent, Judge Zupancic held that:[9]

> According to medical science, the subjective threshold of pain may vary a great deal from one person to another. Moreover, the physical invasiveness of the procedure is not decisive. Letting water drop for hours on the shaved head of a person, as in a well-known Japanese form of torture during the Second World War, may not seem very invasive, yet it clearly caused severe suffering. […] Nevertheless, except in extreme cases of mistreatment (electroshocks, Palestinian hanging, *falaka*, etc.), it is impossible to generalise. […] In the absence of proof to the contrary and given the principle that everyone is presumed to know the natural consequences of their acts, I am constrained to maintain that the pain and the suffering in this particular case were severe. Thus, we ought to speak of torture.

Differences between what applicants have argued and adjudicators have found in terms of categorization are similarly instructive. For applicants (victim-survivors) themselves, the specific categorization of torture reads to have often held significance. In a case where the victim specifically argued to have 'threats of violence to undress in front of an officer of the opposite sex and perform sit-ups and being threatened with violence or even death' categorized as torture,

[7] ECtHR, 'Guide on Article 3' [11].
[8] *Juanenea and Yarzabal v Spain* [2018] ECtHR 1653/13, dissent of Judge Keller and others.
[9] *Jalloh v Germany* [2006] ECtHR 54810/00, concurring opinion.

the ECtHR disagreed and instead deferred to the domestic finding of 'psychological ill-treatment'.[10] This interest in categorizations was also abundantly clear on the face of the submission in *Volodina* and *Tunikova*[11] which both involved domestic violence. In the latter, two judges separately regretted that the majority did not qualify the experiences of the victim as amounting to torture, with Pinto lamenting: 'I wonder what more is needed to reach a finding of torture under Article 3.' These are revealing moments where discretion and delimitations are brought into stark relief. That the finding should have been 'torture' and not inhuman or degrading treatment also signals the significance placed on the distinction. Inhuman and degrading treatment here are instead taken as offering more conceptual breadth and as more politically amenable than torture, both domestically and for the ECtHR—a point elaborated in the interviews.

As with much else, the IACtHR has long relied on the ECtHR in understanding the prohibition to have 'several gradations'—embracing treatment ranging from 'torture to other types of humiliation or cruel, inhuman or degrading treatment with varying degrees of physical and psychological effects caused by endogenous and exogenous factors which must be proven in each specific situation'.[12] In a recent case, the Court based its torture categorization on needing 'utmost rigor' and the acts in question being 'particularly heinous'.[13] In the same case, it ruled falanka as constituting torture, simply referencing the Istanbul Protocol.[14] Generally, despite the urge for 'rigor', the differences between these categories have not been elaborately explained by the IACtHR. A recent commentary points out that 'not all the norms provided under Article 5 have the same normative content'.[15] In the vast majority of cases, the same commentary argues, the IACtHR 'does not specifically qualify State's abuses as "torture," "cruel," "inhuman," or "degrading" treatment, so that its judgments lack a certain degree of pedagogy'.[16]

A closer reading of the IACtHR caselaw indeed indicates that the practice of categorization remains intuitive and inexplicable. It proves difficult, to put this

[10] *OR and LR v Moldova* [2019] ECtHR 24129/11 [44–60].

[11] *Volodina v Russia* [2019] ECtHR 41261/17; *Tunikova and ors v Russia* [2021] ECtHR 55974/16 [71]: where the applicants argued that 'recognising severe instances of domestic violence as "torture" would emphasise the gravity of the violence in the eyes of the public and the authorities tasked with monitoring and response, empower victims, and discourage or even deter perpetrators'.

[12] *Loayza Tamayo v Peru* [1997] IACtHR [57]. The IACtHR, like the other bodies, has adopted the principle of assessing on a case-by-case basis: *Azul Rojas Marín et al v Perú* [2021] [159].

[13] *Valencia Campos and others v Bolivia* [2023] IACtHR [183].

[14] ibid [183].

[15] Ludovic Hennebel and Hélène Tigroudja, *The American Convention on Human Rights: A Commentary* (OUP 2021) 194.

[16] ibid 195–98.

plainly, to pin down how this content is varied, as reasoning on specific categorization is less forthcoming than the ECtHR. While severe pain is not required by the IACPPT, in numerous cases its presence is noted by the Court in its categorization.[17] When it has, it is telling where psychological suffering has fit into the exercise. In one case involving the life imprisonment of children, the Court found the 'extreme psychological impact' caused by life imprisonment to be inhuman and degrading, whereas the falanka, also established in the case, was found to be torture.[18] The difference in the categorization, though not explicitly justified, can be said to pivot on an implicit hierarchical logic between physical and psychological suffering.

The significance attached to categorization, therefore, has largely remained unclear. In *Cotton Field*, Judge Quiroga wrote that, on the one hand, from 'a practical and juridical perspective, whether or not a conduct is classified as torture does not make much difference' as torture and CIDT are all prohibited but that 'there appears to be no justification for not classifying the treatment applied to the three victims in this case as torture'.[19] Extrajudicially, Quiroga noted that '[i]t is often said that a distinction between different types of conduct must be made in order particularly to highlight torture, as the term torture has a greater stigma associated with it that must be expressed'.[20] Here, she also argued against the IACtHR practice of differentiating between torture and other forms of ill-treatment. There are no other direct insights offered by the caselaw on this point.

As compared to the two others, CAT caselaw has offered no extended articulation on points of categorizing psychological suffering. In an early case the applicants sought to rely on *Ireland* and *Greek* cases to establish a case under Article 1 that torture also covered 'the infliction of mental suffering by creating a state of anguish and stress by means other than bodily assault'.[21] The case in question related to racial intimidation by private individuals to cause Roma residents to flee their homes (namely, a pogrom) without intervention by the police. The CAT determined this to be inhuman and degrading treatment and not torture. In a separate opinion, two CAT members argued that the finding should have been 'torture'—criticizing the majority decision as amounting to

[17] Severity, despite not explicit in the IACPPT definition, has been incorporated into the jurisprudence, despite one commentary finding its use remaining 'relatively indeterminate and fundamentally casuistic': Hennebel and Tigroudja (n 15) 216.

[18] Compare *Mendoza and ors v Argentina* [2013] IACtHR [183] and [211]; *Miguel Castro-Castro Prison v Peru* [2006] IACtHR [326]: 'the Istanbul Protocol establishes that falanga is a form of torture'.

[19] *González et al v Mexico* ('Cotton Field') [2019] IACtHR, separate opinion of Quiroga [2].

[20] Cecilia Medina Quiroga, *The American Convention on Human Rights: Crucial Rights and Their Theory and Practice* (2nd edn, Intersentia 2016) 153.

[21] CAT-C-29-D-161-2000 [8.5].

'a presumption of "severe suffering", certainly "mental" but also inescapably "physical" in nature even if the victims were not subjected to direct physical aggression'.[22] As at the two other institutions, dissent and discrepancy are revealing of the tensions on categorization. Despite its principle against a hierarchy as mentioned at the book's outset, categorization still proved significant at the CAT.

A systematic review of its caselaw shows that the CAT has most frequently categorized torture in cases involving police beatings[23] (or a police shooting).[24] It has also categorized 'the so-called *falaka* and "roast chicken" methods [as being] in essence acts of torture'.[25] It must also be noted that the CAT has also come close, though unconvincingly against the broader backdrop of its categorization practices, to also including detention conditions and solitary confinement as a violation of Article 1. Yet, this is found in a case concerning overt physical practices (e.g. falanka) which allowed the CAT to first find torture before cursorily folding in the psychological practices.[26]

To be clear, the CAT has categorized systematic psychological suffering as torture but only in broader inquiries (namely, Article 20 country inquiries and state reviews). In Peru, the CAT found that 'sensorial deprivation and the almost total prohibition of communication cause persistent and unjustified suffering which amounts to torture',[27] yet categorized as inhuman and degrading other instances in the same inquiry.[28] This categorization was made without coherent reasoning except for pointing to the duration of treatment.[29] In

[22] ibid, individual opinion by Mariño and González Poblete.

[23] CAT-C-59-D-606-2014; CAT-C-63-D-637-2014; CAT-C-47-D-353-2008; CAT-C-62-D-496-2012; CAT-C-51-D-441-2010; CAT-C-72-D-992-2020; CAT-C-60-D-612-2014; CAT-C-55-D-553-2013; CAT-C-35-D-172-2000; CAT-C-56-D-578-2013; CAT-C-59-D-549-2013; CAT-C-52-D-503-2012; CAT-C-71-D-843-2017; CAT-C-51-D-376-2009; CAT-C-60-D-651-2015; CAT-C-52-D-497-201; CAT-C-31-D-187-2001; CAT-C-71-D-759-2016; CAT-C-62-D-493-2012; CAT-C-39-D-269-2005; CAT-C-41-D-257-2004; CAT-C-52-D-402-2009; CAT-C-61-D-654-2015; CAT-C-61-D-661-2015; CAT-C-55-D-575-201; CAT-C-48-D-433-2010; CAT-C-41-D-291-2006; CAT-C-60-D-573-2013; CAT-C-34-D-171-2000.

[24] CAT-C-72-D-793-2017.

[25] CAT-C-74-D-891-2018 [8.2].

[26] CAT-C-74-D-891-2018 [8.3]: 'all the treatment allegedly inflicted on the complainant during his detention also constitutes acts of torture, i.e.: (a) the insanitary conditions in his various cells, (b) the long periods of solitary confinement without the ability to be seen by a doctor of his choice; and (c) the restricted access to counsel and to his family. Accordingly, the Committee does not consider it necessary to examine separately the claims under article 16'. I do not consider the ruling that threats were 'psychological torture' in *Campos and others v Bolivia* [2023] IACtHR [188] to be a singling out of psychological suffering given the backdrop of serious physical and sexual violence in that case.

[27] CAT, Article 20 inquiry on Peru, A/55/44 (2000) [185–86].

[28] ibid [183].

[29] Manfred Nowak and others (eds), *The United Nations Convention Against Torture and Its Optional Protocol: A Commentary* (2nd edn, OUP 2019) 49.

another Article 20 inquiry on Turkey, a similar categorization of torture was made in respect to 'solitary confinement cells known as "coffins"' (described as 'cells measure approximately 60 by 80 centimetres, they have no light and inadequate ventilation, and the inmate can only stand or crouch') as 'in themselves constitut[ing] a kind of torture'.[30] In its state reviews too, the CAT has been more relaxed in condemning sleep deprivation,[31] 'enhanced interrogation techniques',[32] and threats[33] as torture. In a 2006 report on the US following 9/11, it found that 'acts of psychological torture' were

> not limited to 'prolonged mental harm' as set out in the State party's understandings lodged at the time of ratification of the Convention, but constitute a wider category of acts, which cause severe mental suffering, irrespective of their prolongation or its duration [and that the US] rescind any interrogation technique, including methods involving sexual humiliation, waterboarding, short shackling and using dogs to induce fear, that constitutes torture or [inhuman or degrading treatment].[34]

In sum, the distillation of the institutions' precedents typifies torture as *physical* and, in turn, characterizes inhuman and degrading treatment as more accommodating of *psychological* suffering. Given the practices the category has been associated with, there are also indications that torture needs to be a spectacle; an intense event as opposed to an incremental experience.

[30] CAT, Article 20 inquiry on Turkey, A/48/44/Add1 (1993) [52].

[31] CAT, CO Republic of Korea (1996) (A/52/44) [56]: 'The sleep deprivation practiced on suspects, which may in some cases constitute torture and which seems to be routinely used to extract confessions, is unacceptable.'

[32] CAT, 'Sessional/Annual Report of Committee' (1997) A/52/44 [257]: '(1) restraining in very painful conditions, (2) hooding under special conditions, (3) sounding of loud music for prolonged periods, (4) sleep deprivation for prolonged periods, (5) threats, including death threats, (6) violent shaking, and (7) using cold air to chill [...] are in the Committee's view, breaches of article 16 and also constitute torture as defined in article 1 of the Convention.'

[33] CAT, CO New Zealand (1993) A/48/44(Supp) [148]: 'a threat could constitute torture'; CO Germany (1993) A/48/44(Supp) [167]: 'examining gaps in German laws prohibiting certain aspects of torture, such as psychological pressure, threats and intimidation'; CAT-C-55-D-575-201 [5.12]: 'With regard to the mock execution, the Committee against Torture has already been able to highlight that pointing a gun at the temple of individuals constitutes a method of torture. Moreover, both the [CAT and HRC] have repeatedly considered that threats, in particular against the life of a person, associated with other acts constitute torture.'

[34] CAT, CO USA [13, 24].

'Lesser': inhuman and degrading

It is only a close reading therefore that explicates the association between psychological suffering and the categories of inhuman and degrading treatment. Acts and experiences *typical* of inhuman treatment, according to the ECtHR's Article 3 Guide to start, include: threats, destruction of property, disappearance of relatives, witnessing the execution of relatives, and life sentence in poor detention conditions. Degradation, meanwhile, is associated with humiliation and debasement, diminishment of dignity, and arousing 'feelings of fear, anguish or inferiority capable of breaking an individual's moral and physical resistance'.[35]

The CAT too has primarily categorized as Article 16 (cruel, inhuman, and degrading treatment) violations cases involving psychological suffering: restraints in psychiatry (caged bed of a child),[36] solitary confinement (twenty-one days),[37] beating coupled with threats,[38] handcuffing and blindfolding,[39] forced to be naked on a cold floor,[40] denial of healthcare,[41] shackling to bed and confinement in punishment cells,[42] exposure to cold,[43] dry submarine,[44] 'mental anguish' for family of enforced disappeared,[45] overcrowding,[46] and solitary confinement.[47] The distinction between Articles 1 and 16, in sum, has beatings violating Article 1 and poor detention conditions Article 16.[48] It is normal to read, as in the same case, for mental suffering, hooding, restraints, and strip-search while deported, detention conditions to violate Article 16

[35] ECtHR, 'Guide on Article 3' [19].

[36] CAT-C-72-D-890-2018.

[37] CAT-C-62-D-672-2015 [7.3]: 'The Court found that what was known about the complainant's addiction and mental condition should have underlined the potentially harmful effects of an excessive period of cell confinement on his mental well-being. The Committee further notes the complainant's assertion that the sanction caused him mental suffering and affected him physically. [. . .] in view of the complainant's chronic depression, which was known to the authorities, and drug addiction, the solitary confinement that he was subjected to and the length of time for which he was subjected to it were not proportionate to the objective pursued. The Committee therefore finds that the solitary confinement imposed on the complainant amounted to a violation of his rights under article 16.'

[38] CAT-C-75-D-930-2019 [2.2]; CAT-C-72-D-992-2020; CAT-C-60-D-612-2014.

[39] CAT-C-59-D-606-2014.

[40] CAT-C-63-D-637-2014; CAT-C-55-D-494-2012.

[41] CAT-C-61-D-661-2015.

[42] CAT-C-65-D-778-2016.

[43] CAT-C-47-D-353-2008.

[44] CAT-C-48-D-433-2010.

[45] CAT-C-71-D-858-2018 [6.5]; CAT-C-71-D-858-2018 [6.3]; CAT-C-46-D-341-2008; CAT-C-54-D-456-2011 [6.10]: 'the enforced disappearance [. . .] caused anguish and distress for the complainants and that the authorities were indifferent to their efforts to ascertain his whereabouts and fate.'

[46] CAT-C-55-D-575-201 [7.6].

[47] CAT-C-68-D-817-2017; CAT-C-52-D-478-2011; CAT-C-41-D-316-2007; CAT-C-62-D-672-2015; CAT-C-63-D-678-2015; CAT-C-32-D-202-2002.

[48] CAT-C-55-D-575-2013 [7.6]; CAT-C-55-D-553-2013 [7.3–7.4].

when beatings violate Article 1.[49] There have in fact been cases brought which could have developed the jurisprudence if not discontinued, arguing: threats,[50] hooding,[51] heat in detention,[52] six-month detention before deportation,[53] and 'deprivation of personal freedom' to amount to torture.[54] A survey of CAT state reviews also reveals that psychological suffering is strongly associated with Article 16 than Article 1, particularly concerning detention conditions,[55] forced labour,[56] hooding,[57] and intimidation and threats.[58]

There are also inferences readily drawn where the beatings are referred to in the short hand as 'torture', whereas the complaints around solitary confinement are invoked as distinct and separate—arguably not thought as being in the same category of torture.[59] I take cases on solitary confinement, particularly as decided by the ECtHR, as a case study to examine these broader dynamics.

Solitary as a case study

Solitary confinement cases have also been fertile ground for downgrading and dismissal on the basis of differentiation—holding out unduly extreme suffering as the threshold to meet for a violation to be found. To be sure, the ECtHR caselaw is replete with cases on solitary confinement which are found to amount to inhuman and degrading treatment. Yet, in most cases, the ECtHR is at pains to identify with, unduly defer to, and legitimate official actions, in so doing revealing tactics that steer away from deeming solitary confinement a violation. Solitary confinement cases, to follow *Zeidler-Kornmann* and *Ensslin* which were detailed earlier, have exuded a tension between regressive and expansive interpretations, on the part of states and of ECtHR judges themselves, in recognizing the psychological suffering claimed.

49 CAT-C-55-D-553-2013 [7.3–7.4].
50 CAT-C-57-D-531-2012 but argued only Article 22.
51 CAT-C-75-D-1034-2020, which concerned a sheet placed over head (hooding) and too tight handcuffs in detention, was ruled inadmissible due to lack of exhaustion of remedies.
52 CAT-C-62-D-712-2015 [2.1–2.2] (inadmissible).
53 CAT-C-64-D-693-2015 (unsubstantiated and inadmissible).
54 CAT-C-57-D-598-2014 (non-exhaustion and inadmissible).
55 CAT-C-CR-31-4 [6]; CAT-C-CR-31-3 [6]; CAT-C-CR-32-3 [8–9]; CAT-C-CR-29-329 [56]; CAT-C-BIH-CO-1 [14]; CAT-C-TUR-CO-3 [21]; CAT-C-PHL-CO-2 [19].
56 CAT-C-PRY-CO-4-6 [27].
57 CAT-C-CR-34-CHE [4].
58 CAT-C-CR-33-1 [6]; A/54/44 [97, 102 (c)].
59 CAT-C-61-D-654-2015 [7.3]: the CAT 'notes that the complainant was repeatedly tortured, held in solitary confinement and deprived of medical care'.

More contemporary and consistently cited precedents continue to refer to partial contact rights,[60] resilience,[61] dangerousness,[62] relatively 'short' durations,[63] or short breaks in periods of isolation[64] to downgrade or altogether dismiss such cases. The requirement of total isolation (not partial) to amount to a violation, a device of the ECtHR's own invention finding no basis in science, has continued to feature strongly in its caselaw.[65] Although implicit, 'total' and 'partial' isolation operate as proxies for the level of psychological suffering. 'Total' isolation is understood to inflict unacceptable suffering, whereas 'partial' is tolerable. This has attracted both internal and external criticism given that total isolation does not exist and is thus an unattainable threshold.[66] Relatedly, it is also noteworthy that torture has yet to be considered in the Court's reasoning in any such case as the sole question to date has been whether the acts amounted to inhuman treatment.[67]

These cases very much return the discussion to time. To be sure, *indefinite* isolation has been ruled, in principle, to be a violation.[68] Yet, this is a matter of

[60] *Rohde v Denmark* [2005] ECtHR 69332/01.

[61] *Ramirez Sanchez v France* [2006] ECtHR 59450/00 [127–29].

[62] *Öcalan v Turkey (no 1)* [2005] ECtHR 46221/99 [192–96]: 'the Grand Chamber is also mindful of the Government's concerns that the applicant may seek to take advantage of communications with the outside world to renew contact with members of the armed separatist movement of which he was leader. These concerns cannot be said to be unfounded. An added consideration is the Government's fear that it would be difficult to protect the applicant's life in an ordinary prison'.

[63] *Khodorkovskiy and Lebedev v Russia* [2013] ECtHR 11082/06 (a week); *Valasinas v Lithuania* [2001] ECtHR 44558/98 [112] (fifteen days); *Csüllog v Hungary* [2011] ECtHR 30042/08 [33].

[64] In *Savca v Moldova* [2016] ECtHR 17963/08 [27] the applicant argued that his months-long isolation in different centres violated Article 3 but the Court held that 'each period of detention referred to specific events [...] occurred on identifiable dates [and] cannot therefore be construed as a "continuing situation"' in downgrading the harms at play.

[65] *Ulemek v Croatia* [2019] ECtHR 21613/16; *Hansen v Norway* [2018] ECtHR 48852/17; *Fenech v Malta* [2022] ECtHR 19090/20 [34, 74]: Malta argued that thirty-four days was not 'complete sensory deprivation nor total isolation' which the Court accepted in not finding a violation of Article 3. In *Onofriou v Cyprus* [2010] ECtHR 24407/10, Cyprus argued that there 'was no sensory isolation brought about by a substantial reduction in stimulation of the sensory organs' [57] and argued that the applicant did not have medical evidence to show he 'suffered mental or physical deterioration as a result of his confinement or that the physical conditions entailed distress and hardship beyond that which was necessarily incidental to such confinement'.

[66] Antonio Cassese, 'Prohibition of Torture and Inhuman or Degrading Treatment or Punishment' in Paola Gaeta and Salvatore Zappalà (eds), *The Human Dimension of International Law* (OUP 2008) 308.

[67] The CAT's ruling in a case concerning a pre-trial detention detainee of over nine years, with recent years being in solitary confinement conceivably as punishment, provides another prime example here of the problems of categorization. The applicant's lawyers argued for Articles 1 and 16 in the alternative. In its reasoning, the CAT recalled the definition and prohibitions as clear under the UN Nelson Mandela Rules, yet held the treatment to amount not to torture under Article 1 but inhuman and degrading under Article 16: CAT-C-68-D-817-2017 [8.5]. Reading the full breadth of the allegations in the submissions, it is hard to understand how the CAT did not categorize this as torture, and easy to speculate about a connection to the psychological nature of the suffering involved. A similar critique can also be made of the IACtHR in this respect: *Campos and others v Bolivia* [2023] IACtHR [192] involved multiple applicants who 'were kept in solitary confinement for 70 days, incommunicado, and without any sunlight', which the IACtHR categorized as a form of cruel and inhuman treatment.

[68] *AB v Russia* [2016] ECtHR 1439/06.

defining what is indefinite, with Öcalan and Sanchez remaining where they are to this day, decades later, having effectively been indefinitely isolated. While the indefinite is not permitted, the prolonged is problematically permitted. In the *Chamber* ruling in *Ramirez Sanchez*, the Court had noted that the applicant was isolated for eight years and two months.[69] It reviewed durations in other solitary cases in normalizing the eight years. The dissent there foregrounded the duration in arguing against such a comparative normalization and how this could not be considered the use of solitary confinement 'as a last resort' as dictated by the Court's own caselaw. The dissenters thus countered the majority's reasoning both regarding the nature of the act and its impact. In terms of the nature of the act, they held that a 'period of more than eight years cannot stand up to any objective examination'.[70] Delays in visibility of impact are underscored in the following:

> the effects of certain treatment on a person's physical or mental health may not be immediately apparent but become so subsequently. This phenomenon is well known in the sphere of the post-traumatic effects of inhuman or degrading treatment or torture. Similarly, a person in good health may nonetheless suffer from particular forms of ill-treatment. In that connection, it should be recalled that, in one of his objections to a renewal of solitary confinement, the applicant himself described it as 'a form of torture'.[71]

Security reasons, invocations of dangerousness, or adjacent terms such as risk are often argued by state authorities and occasionally agreed to by judges in politically sensitive cases. These justifications have been effective in characterizing applicants as 'hardly [being] considered a genuinely vulnerable type of prisoner',[72] as a 'danger to society',[73] affiliated with the mafia,[74] 'perceived as provocative and threatening',[75] 'violent and dangerous',[76] as a 'potential

[69] *Ramirez Sanchez v France* [2005] ECtHR Chamber 59450/00.

[70] ibid (separate opinion of Judges Rozakis, Loucaides, and Tulkens, 5).

[71] ibid. Other notable remarks include: 'Such a period is not, as the majority note, merely "regrettable", it is also liable to produce harmful effects [and it] substantially exceeds the inevitable level of suffering inherent in detention'; the judges rejected the distinction between 'partial' or 'total' isolation (that the partial 'cannot lead to the conclusion that the regime to which he was subject was not genuine isolation, but akin to an ordinary, even commonplace, measure', 'Prolonging solitary confinement in this way for a period so long as to be virtually permanent [...] bringing the measure into the domain of unacceptable suffering').

[72] *Kardišauskas v Lithuania* [2015] ECtHR 62304/12, concurring opinion [3].

[73] *Enea v Italy* [2009] ECtHR 74912/01 [65]; *Slusarczyk v Poland* [2015] ECtHR 23463/04 [90].

[74] *Messina v Italy (no 2)* [1999] ECtHR 25498/94.

[75] *Ukraine v Kulakov* [2010] ECtHR 12944/02, p 6.

[76] *Wieser v Austria* [2007] ECtHR 2293/03 [37]: 'Authorities had reason to believe that applicant was violent and dangerous.'

threat',[77] with a 'serious lack of moral character',[78] and other indicia of dangerousness.[79] While characterizing itself as 'particularly attentive to restrictions which apply to prisoners who are not dangerous or disorderly' and 'to restrictions which remain in place after the applicant has been assessed as no longer posing a security risk' to avoid arbitrariness,[80] the ECtHR has avoided this promise where there has been a political sensitivity. Deferring to prison authorities, the ECtHR has yielded to such state arguments explaining, for instance, that 'it is not for the Court to specify which security measures may be applied to prisoners'.[81] Over and above drawing in the familiar logics of resilience and partial isolation, the Court rejected that Anders Breivik's isolation violated Article 3. In following the Norwegian courts, the ECtHR did not 'call into question that the applicant's detention posed significant challenges for the domestic authorities and that those authorities considered it necessary to combine his detention with extraordinary security measures'.[82]

Resilience is another device to justify and thus exclude psychological suffering from the prohibition's purview. As with health assessments of individual prisoners, states have made resilience-based arguments in similar cases, pointing to applicants lacking 'normal' resilience because they were a wealthy businessman,[83] or were stronger as they were 'so young that they could not have suffered so badly'.[84] In one case, the ECtHR also pointed to the desirability of having the applicant's 'physical and psychological aptitude for long-term isolation'.[85] Finding the applicant in decent health,[86] for instance, the majority in *Ramirez Sanchez* assessed the measure to not be harmful enough.[87]

In all, these cases mark an exceptionally high threshold of recognition, coming to serve as grounds for states to argue the legitimacy of their restrictive solitary confinement regimes.[88] Non-violations or violations 'less than' torture

[77] *AT (no 2) v Estonia* [2018] ECtHR 23183/15 [83–84].
[78] *Glowacki v Poland* [2013] ECtHR 1608/08 [31–32, 96–97].
[79] *Horych v Poland* [2012] ECtHR 13621/08.
[80] *Babar Ahmad and ors v UK* [2012] ECtHR 24027/07 [211].
[81] ibid.
[82] *Hansen v Norway* [2018] ECtHR 48852/17 [146].
[83] *Casuneanu v Romania* [2013] ECtHR 22018/10 [56].
[84] *Ozdoyev and others v Russia* [2019] ECtHR 9782/08 [313]; *Georgiev v Bulgaria* [2007] ECtHR 61507/00 [61]: no violation despite the overcrowding, 'given that he was twenty-seven years old at the time, did not claim that his physical or mental health was affected in any way and did not complain of any other aspects of the regime'.
[85] *Ramishvili and Kokhreidze v Georgia* [2009] ECtHR 1704/06 [80].
[86] *Ramirez Sanchez v France* [74]: 'the applicant said that his perfect mental and physical health was due to his strength of character, the efforts he had made to keep his mind active and to retain mental stability and his resistance'.
[87] ibid [141].
[88] *Karpenko v Ukraine* [2021] ECtHR 45397/13 [46]; *Geanopol v Romania* [2013] ECtHR 1777/06 [56].

are found, although facts warrant greater recognition. Despite moments of strong recognition, there have been as many missed opportunities—resulting in the dominance of physical suffering.[89] A corollary finding emerges here from how cautiously selective the institutions have been in applying socio-political standards in responding to these practices. This is returned to in the next chapter.

Other: Article 8 and dissent

The association of psychological suffering with categories 'lower' than torture is also evident in the consideration of Article 8 (being the right to privacy and family life) of the ECHR, a provision which also very much focusses on psychological suffering (or rather integrity), particularly where acts 'do not attain a [certain] seriousness'.[90] The strip-search of a twelve-year-old boy with a disability who was left traumatized, for the ECtHR, was an Article 8 not an Article 3 violation.[91] The deportation of an applicant living with schizophrenia, where it was observed that 'mental health must also be regarded as a crucial part of private life associated with the aspect of moral integrity', was ruled in a similar manner.[92] Cases involving online threats,[93] strip-searches,[94] the right to clean drinking water,[95] a child's witnessing their father's handcuffing,[96] where military personnel were investigated and discharged because of their sexual orientation,[97] where a waste-treatment plant close to the applicant's home caused a nuisance,[98] where family members were denied visiting their ten-year-old daughter,[99] where there were insults and threats towards a Muslim

89 Many solitary confinement cases, I would argue, could have amounted to torture and not simply inhuman and degrading treatment. *Renolde v France* [2008] ECtHR 5608/05 (history of mental illness, forty-five days (finding: inhuman and degrading)); *GB v Bulgaria* [2004] ECtHR 42346/98 (regime very restrictive with very little human contact for more than eight years, alone in cell almost twenty-three hours per day (finding: inhuman and degrading)); *AL (XW) v Russia* [2015] ECtHR 44095/14 [75] (solitary confinement in immigration detention for four and a half months with no contact with other inmates, restricted visits from his wife, no access to reading materials, etc. (finding: inhuman)); *X v Turkey* [2012] ECtHR 24626/09 (inhuman and degrading), *AB v Russia* [2010] ECtHR 1439/06 (near-total social isolation for over three years (finding: inhuman or degrading)).

90 *Södermann v Sweden* [2013] ECtHR 5786/08 [84]: for instance, 'malicious misrepresentation' in *KU v Finland* [2008] ECtHR 2872/02.

91 *Wainwright v UK* [2006] ECtHR 12350/04.

92 *Bensaid v UK* [2001] ECtHR 44599/98 [47].

93 *Buturugă v Romania* [2020] ECtHR 56867/15 argued Article 3 but the Court found Article 8.

94 *Dejnek v Poland* [2017] ECtHR 9635/13.

95 *Hudorovic and others v Slovenia* [2020] ECtHR 24816/14, dissent of Judges Pavli and Kūris.

96 *A v Russia* [2022] ECtHR 37735/09.

97 *Smith and Grady v UK* [1999] ECtHR 33985/96 [117–23].

98 *López Ostra v Spain* [1994] ECtHR 16798/90 [58–60].

99 *Deltuva v Lithuania* [2023] ECtHR 38144/20 [45–49].

group,[100] where a woman was forced to abort abroad,[101] and where prison officers showed a lack of courtesy when strip-searching visitors, though there was no verbal abuse or physical contact,[102] were all ruled as Article 8 not 3. Conversely, the Court decided a case under Article 3 even when it was argued under 8.[103] A survey reveals cases where Article 3 violations were found for a Russian conscript on the basis of insults, bullying, and extortion[104] but no violations of Article 8 were found where a young boy was psychologically pressured by police.[105]

How this fit between the two articles is determined lacks clarity. The Court has come to concede that the distinction is not 'clearcut' given that they both require the state to 'safeguard the physical and psychological integrity of a person' and that Articles 3 and 8 along with Article 2 form a 'continuum' to 'provide protection once it has been established that attacks on an individual's integrity were sufficiently serious to necessitate a response'.[106] For one judge, 'in such cases, one cannot speak of one circle but of two circles, where the complaint falls outside the circle of protection of Article 3 but falls within the circle of protection of Article 8'.[107]

The lack of consistency here has attracted internal criticism engendering dissents in important cases.[108] In a case concerning forced sterilization, one judge rejected the majority's finding that the violation was one of Article 8 and not of Article 3.[109] In another case where the majority found children's living

[100] *Georgian Muslim Relations and others v Georgia* [2023] ECtHR 24225/19 [72]. Georgia's response differentiated this case from other cases (though 'serious and offensive by nature') as it did not involve physical violence. It did this successfully in arguing that the minimum for Article 3 was not met.

[101] *ML v Poland* [2023] ECtHR 40119/21.

[102] *Wainwright v UK* [2006] ECtHR [44–49] in *Jalloh* (n 9) [82, 83, and 86]: the applicant, on whom the authorities had forcibly administered medication, 'ha[d] been subjected to inhuman and degrading treatment contrary to Article 3 (and found a violation of that Article), and then held that the applicant's complaint under Article 8, which concerned the same fact, did not give rise to any separate issue'.

[103] *GM and others v The Republic of Moldova* [2023] ECtHR 44394/15; *Akopyan v Ukraine* [2014] ECtHR 12317/06; *VC v Slovakia* [2012] ECtHR 18968/07.

[104] *Filippovy v Russia* [2022] 19355/09 103: the victim 'endured over a protracted period of time despite repeated requests to be transferred and the constant mental anxiety caused by the imminent risk of physical violence by his fellow conscripts'.

[105] *Romanova v Ukraine* [2022] ECtHR 63961/13: 'that Y. was crying during the questioning is in itself [not] sufficient to conclude that the necessary level of severity was reached'.

[106] *Hanovs v Latvia* [2024] ECtHR 40861/22 [45–54].

[107] *Obote v Russia* [2019] ECtHR 58954/09, opinion of Judge Serghides [47]; see also *Melnik v Ukraine* [2006] ECtHR 72286/01 [62]: Article 8 'may extend to situations of deprivation of liberty and may be regarded as affording a protection in relation to the conditions during detention which do not attain the level of severity proscribed by Article 3'.

[108] *Obote* (n 107), opinion of Serghides [48].

[109] *YP v Russia* [2022] ECtHR 43399/13: this is the 'first case involving a woman's forced sterilisation in which the Court has held that, in contrast to earlier similar cases, her ordeal did *not* reach the threshold of inhuman or degrading treatment [...] This latter finding is consistent with the practically unanimous position of [the HRC, CAT, and IACtHR]. [...] Yet, the message sent by today's holding on the applicability of Article 3 is that such treatment was not serious enough to reach the threshold [...]

conditions in a detention centre to violate Article 3, a dissenting judge argued that this lowered the Article 3 threshold and that the question 'should have been dealt with under Article 8'.[110] Moreover, opting for a procedural violation rather than a substantive one led to strong dissent in one case involving slapping, deprivation of food and water, and infliction of psychological pressure on a Roma sixteen-year-old at the hands of the police.[111] Similar dissents have concerned discriminatory insults in a police raid[112] and a trans athlete forced into testosterone-lowering treatment.[113] These cases notably are regularly of a psychological nature, involving intimidation, insults, threats, and related fear and anxiety inducing acts and experiences. If an Article 3 violation is found, it precludes a consideration of Article 8. If a violation is not found under Article 3, the ECtHR assesses the facts under Article 8. This may suggest that the Court first looks for physical violence and presumes it to be evidently serious, whereas non-physical injuries need to be rebutted as not being trivial. It is difficult to understand how this is determined with any certainty.

This close relation between Articles 3 and 8 has also seen Article 8 claims precluded where Article 3 violations are found in the same case. In one case, the Court found a violation of Article 3 but refused to look at the Article 8 allegation of denial of visits in detention 'based on the application of the so-called Câmpeanu formula, a sparing one-sentence consideration that, owing to the fact that the Court "has examined the main legal questions raised in the present application", it is absolved from the "need to give a separate ruling on the admissibility and merits of the [remaining] complaint"'.[114] One judge took issue with this line of reasoning in a partly dissenting opinion, cautioning that, 'if used too often and indiscriminately (even if it may not be not unwholesome in and of itself), [it] may hinder the protection and promotion of various Convention rights on even a broader scale'.[115] In his exploration of the relationship, he ultimately found Articles 3 and 8 were close but not close enough to '*per se* allow treating these two Articles as overlapping', characterizing this

To meet the threshold future victims of forced sterilisation would be required to prove some degree of (undefined) special vulnerability as well as malicious intent on the part of the medical personnel'.

110 *MH and ors v Croatia* [2021] ECtHR 15670/18, dissent of Judge Wojtyczek [1.2].
111 *Adam v Slovakia* [2016] ECtHR 68066/12, dissent of Judge Serghides.
112 *Derrek and others v Russia* [2025] ECtHR 31712/21, separate opinion of Judge Zünd [7]: 'The use of derogatory terms by a police officer during the raid was unacceptable, as was the disclosure of the video footage. I would therefore have concluded that there had been a violation of Article 8, read in conjunction with Article 14 of the Convention, on both procedural and substantive grounds. However, I think the threshold for Article 3 to come into play was not attained.'
113 *Semenya v Switzerland* [2023] ECtHR 10934/21, opinion of Judge Serghides [31–50].
114 *Petukhov v Russia (no 2)* [2019] ECtHR 41216/13.
115 ibid, dissent of Judge Kūris.

judicial device as effectively downgrading and dismissing, or trivializing, claims worth merit.

In sum, Article 8 has offered the ECtHR the option to categorize psychological suffering beyond the categories in Article 3, providing an alternative to simply dismissing a case as falling below the minimum of Article 3. Although the review here does not claim to be exhaustive, the nature of the suffering shifted from the purview of Articles 3 and 8 have been distinctly psychologically oriented. Furthermore, as generally with cases focussing on elaborating on the minimum level of severity pertaining to Article 3, the cases serving to illustrate the interplay between Articles 3 and 8 have engendered strong and apparent dissents as to internal judicial politics, particularly on the severity of suffering and whether it is deserving of categorization under Article 3.[116]

Contesting categorization

My interviews explored the question of categorization and how psychological suffering fit in its contestation. I set out to hear whether categorization was even identified as an issue for psychological suffering ('Identifying the issue'). The explanation, where offered, broached the coupled premises of exceptionality and dilution ('Exceptionality—dilution') and occasionally led to a discussion of comparative (or hierarchical) thinking between cases and forms of suffering ('Comparison (across cases and country contexts)'). Categorization was also very much discussed as an aggregation of views among adjudicators shifting over time ('Composition and deliberation'). I also approached applicant lawyers to hear how victims' (their clients) instructed them (or not) on categorization ('Victims' views').

Identifying the issue

Most interviewees only learned of the absence of any case which categorized psychological suffering as torture during the interview: 'you're telling me that

[116] While this is not a visible issue at the other two institutions, it has occurred at the UN HRC, concerning the isolation of a child: see Brough v Australia [2006] CCPR/C/86/D/1184/2003, where disciplinary solitary confinement of a child for seventy-two and forty-eight hours was found to be a violation of Article 10 (the right to be treated with humanity and with respect for the inherent dignity) not 7 (torture and inhuman and degrading treatment); see also *Taunoa v Attorney-General* (2004) 7 HRNZ 379 Young J [274]. Nor is the slippage between Articles 3 and 5 (right to liberty and security of person) explored: *Rooman v Belgium* [2019] ECtHR 18052/11, dissent of Judge Nussberger [2].

there hasn't been any case where the Court specifically found torture, which stemmed from emotional trauma? I never have really thought about that, that's interesting',[117] 'I'm trying to think if we've had situations of pure sort of mental harm, it's possible, I would have to check';[118] 'I'm not sure that we have caselaw that is clear on this but I would accept the mental torture, it is perfectly possible'.[119] The interviewees often referred to *Gäfgen*,[120] following which I informed them that this was not specifically categorized as torture.

In explaining this away, a host of former lawyers sweepingly affirmed a lack of structured institutional approach to categorization. A former IACtHR lawyer explained that it was 'never really decided where the line was drawn between inhuman and degrading treatment and torture […] maybe that's a good thing, because they don't need to do it; and currently, inhuman treatment is forbidden just as much as torture'.[121] That said, the same lawyer also saw the importance 'for regional courts and international bodies generally, to not to be afraid of calling things by their name but I do realize that sometimes a line drawn is this kind of a grey line, it's not a very bright line […] it's sometimes difficult to decide where the line is drawn'. Another IAmCHR/IACtHR lawyer similarly admitted that

> there has never been too much of a drive to create a methodological approach to judging […] there may be some reasons for this, but that the main one is that the Court actually relies on their perceptions of human understanding […] the Court can actually tap into a notion that you could almost call judicial empathy, which is the ability to not only put a name but also recognize the pain in others. This is what has been relied upon in the notion that understanding the degree of suffering that is brought about by truly inhuman and degrading treatment or punishment […] It's about understanding damage and the notion of damage, and that [at the IACtHR] is a very largely unexplored issue. […] I don't think [non-legal understandings of suffering] have made its way to the doctrine of the Commission or of the Court. We evoke intensity of pain, as a way to provoke traditional empathy, that we do not actually quantify. Quantify is not the right word. We do not have legal language that describes intensity of pain and the consequences.[122]

[117] ECtHR17, senior registry lawyer.
[118] ECtHR8, judge.
[119] ECtHR24, judge.
[120] ECtHR2, senior registry lawyer.
[121] IACtHR7, former senior IACmHR lawyer.
[122] IACtHR4, former senior IACtHR lawyer.

Others at the IACtHR cast the ambiguity in a constructive light. One senior IACtHR lawyer explained, for instance, that 'we maintain the ambiguity because we don't want to give the message that this conduct is not a form of torture, but we don't want to declare it because we don't have proof'.[123] He continued to admit: 'we don't have a consistency in the caselaw' on severity given: 'first of all the composition of the Court, you have some judges [who] have a different opinion about the same conduct than other judges in another moment, and second, the Court doesn't feel very compelled to follow the caselaw in this matter, as they see themselves free to change whenever they want'. The diversity of the Court, for some at the ECtHR, meant a 'diversity of experiences and viewpoints: and the constant need to find common ground'.[124] Discretion was to be preserved to accommodate such diversity. This strongly signified overall (individual and institutional) interests in preserving discretion, not wanting to be bound by what has come before, and not wanting to bind what is to come—placing a premium on discretionary flexibility. I return to the role of composition shortly.

Neither could those interviewed with respect to the CAT recall particular cases where psychological suffering was discussed on its own. Cases generally argued a combination of acts and impacts, particularly if complainants were detained for a long time: 'they've been exposed to all sorts of things'.[125] One UN Office of the High Commissioner for Human Rights (OHCHR) lawyer, centrally involved in processing cases, explained that there were not so many cases that only argue psychological suffering, as often 'it's implicit in the story of the person'.[126] A former CAT member felt that 'there was no problem of having an acceptance of torture, even though it didn't leave bruises' and saw General Comment 2 for having further 'opened the door' for the consideration of psychological suffering particularly by non-state actors.[127] One former member reflected that this could be explained because 'it's much easier to prove physical than the mental'.[128] Yet, there were indeed cases where such deliberation was warranted: *Aarass* and *Coppin* representing two recent occasions where torture could have been underscored as being psychological—which I pick up on in the discussion on state deference in Chapter 5.

123 IACtHR15, senior IACtHR lawyer.
124 ECtHR7, senior registry lawyer; ECtHR5, judge; ECtHR15, judge.
125 CAT3, former member; CAT15, member.
126 CAT20, UN legal officer.
127 CAT3, former member.
128 CAT1, former member.

An applicant lawyer experienced at litigating at the ECtHR did 'not think there [was] any problem',[129] with another lawyer similarly finding that 'there has been a developing awareness, obviously, over the last twenty years or so of what psychological suffering is, with the courts having been more or less forced to acknowledge that'.[130] Other experienced applicant lawyers did, however, relate that 'states put a lot of effort in most cases' to not have a finding of torture against them,[131] that 'words carry a weight and torture is torture', and that 'for the state is very much clear as well, that what they don't want to be called is torturers'.[132] Over-cautiousness as to demoting certain practices, which in principle could have been qualified as torture, only because they were common, was recognized by others.[133] The torture threshold, for the attuned few, was 'very high, unjustly high'.[134] It might matter not personally but politically. Others aimed similar charges at the ECtHR:

> It's quite clear if you go right back to *Ireland v UK* that mental suffering falls within Article 3 as well as physical suffering. But very often mental suffering falls within the scope because it's a consequence of physical suffering. [And ECtHR judges] haven't always taken a straightforward approach. The cross-over between physical and psychological distress is not always clear. One is very frequently a follow on from the other.[135]
>
> [That the ECtHR] would not find torture when it's only psychological suffering means that the Court grades physical suffering as a more severe form of suffering in general than psychological [...] this is a traditional approach to torture. In the Western tradition, torture has to do with severe forms of physical treatment. No one would look at it from the point of view of the psychological suffering.[136]

Giving the IACtHR the benefit of the doubt, an applicant lawyer who had long litigated before the IACtHR didn't identify a premium placed on the torture category, assuming that the Court does not see it to be 'the core of the case', and where applicants run countless arguments, the Court 'focusses its energy on that one [the core] to get it right, and to get the proper standard, and then

[129] ECtHR34, applicant lawyer.
[130] ECtHR38, applicant lawyer.
[131] IACtHR2, applicant lawyer.
[132] IACtHR8, applicant lawyer.
[133] ECtHR29, senior registry lawyer.
[134] ECtHR21, applicant lawyer; ECtHR35, applicant lawyer.
[135] ECtHR32, applicant lawyer.
[136] ECtHR21, applicant lawyer.

sometimes the others kind of fall through the cracks'.[137] A violation of any category was thus sufficient. Characterizing further distinctions as a bit more 'academic', one IACtHR lawyer accepted that 'consensus is enough' explanation on an Article 5 violation, elaborating that although 'mental suffering is very important for us', the focus on physical injuries could be 'because if you have enough elements to show the torture with a physical suffering, that's enough for the Court'.[138]

CAT's categorization, as elsewhere, was also less than methodical and left much room for speculation and association. On the whole, CAT members rejected, in conversation, a clear distinction between Articles 1 and 16 (as they were 'intertwined to avoid having to speak to the difference',[139] 'there is no clear division, you could say that there is a subjective delineation but I don't [differentiate], generally there's not so much discussion on this point; it's all very intolerable',[140] 'it is quite unclear, so you have to be very careful […] you have to recognize the complexity of the threshold […] it can be a complex analysis […] on a case-by-case basis'[141]). The space allowed for articulating the distinction in deliberations was limited ('unfortunately, the Committee does not go very much in depth with these issues'[142]). Another member did not conceptually engage with the question, dryly responding that all 'interpretation must be made in accordance with international law'.[143] Where cases are about methods which the established caselaw have qualified to be torture (like falanka or rape), the CAT 'doesn't need to question too much'.[144] Interviewees attributed CAT's conceptual thinness and variance to a lack of space in official documents,[145] or because it was obvious that 'people being present and beaten up and burned with cigarettes, electric shocks, and all that stuff' fell under Article 1, preventing further discussion (so 'we didn't have much discussion on the scope of Article 1, the definition of torture or mental suffering').[146] Severity was central to the distinction for some ('as long as the pain is intense, because this is in the definition itself, as long as you think it's intense, you just qualify it as torture').[147]

[137] IACtHR1, applicant lawyer.
[138] IACtHR14, senior IACtHR lawyer.
[139] CAT9, member.
[140] CAT8, member.
[141] CAT6, former member.
[142] CAT2, former member.
[143] CAT10, member.
[144] CAT20, UN legal officer.
[145] CAT6, former member.
[146] CAT1, former member.
[147] CAT20, UN legal officer.

Exceptionality—dilution

Reserving 'torture' for the exceptional was a prominent point of discussion more broadly. Judges and registry lawyers admitted to a 'certain disagreement',[148] that it was 'thought differently, that's the logic behind keeping it exceptional'.[149] This exceptionality (of physical spectacle) was a lowest common denominator of sorts, a point on which all could agree. This discussion drew in differences of attitudes but also the history that what was initially envisaged in respective convention frameworks holding torture as exceptional 'started slipping into normal everyday life [and] became applicable to all sorts of different situations […] I personally don't see an issue with this, but I can understand that some people can'.[150]

Interviewees expressed that the ECtHR 'has always been very cautious in qualifying certain treatment as torture',[151] 'to be particularly sure of yourself when you think that there has been a torture',[152] 'unless we are sure 100 per cent […] we just leave it blank […] "Article 3 is violated" and we don't go into the details',[153] 'for a torture finding, the Court needs to be 100 per cent about it'.[154] When asked why psychological suffering when singled out had not been categorized as torture, judges and senior registry lawyers understood this to be the result of evidentiary difficulties with such cases.

Others pointed to their uncertainty as to purpose to have led to categorizations of inhuman treatment and not torture.[155] A lawyer currently working at the IACtHR explained that the distinction between grades 'for the Court would be the severity plus the purpose' and as the purpose was mostly clear in cases, it turned on severity.[156] Reasoning in some cases has indeed pointed to evidentiary uncertainty as to severity[157] and as to intention[158] in justifying not categorizing torture.[159] Interviewees accepted that 'it is difficult to produce

148 ECtHR1, senior registry lawyer.
149 ECtHR2, judge.
150 ECtHR1, senior registry lawyer.
151 ECtHR6, senior registry lawyer.
152 ECtHR25, senior registry lawyer.
153 ECtHR23, senior registry lawyer.
154 ECtHR12, senior registry lawyer.
155 ECtHR4, ECtHR12, ECtHR24.
156 IACtHR16, senior IACtHR lawyer.
157 *Lutsenko and Verbytskyy v Ukraine* [2021] ECtHR 12482/14 [80] didn't 'find it necessary to adopt a position on the particular classification of the ill-treatment […] it being sufficient to note that it was very serious—he had numerous haematomas and contusions on the trunk of his body, limbs, head and face'.
158 *Jevtovic v Serbia* [2020] ECtHR 29896/14 [78].
159 CAT-C-68-D-818-2017 [8.2]: 'established facts of the case constitute, as a minimum [CIDT], within the meaning of article 16 of the Convention, although it is unable to find sufficient evidence to state with certainty that they constitute torture'.

evidence [...] it is much easier to establish inhuman and degrading treatment, and we're happy to find it';[160] that 'it is easier to do so [prove] with physical trauma rather than emotional trauma';[161] and that 'it is just harder to prove, unless there are several very concordant to-the-point psychological reports'.[162] Certainty meant comfort, and its lack meant difficulty in reaching strong conclusions on psychological suffering. The same lawyer wanted to protect the integrity of the jurisprudence from 'frivolous' claims, explaining that thresholds 'need to be kept high'. When asked why:

> And why? Because in many cases, what I also see, I'm not saying like frivolous applications, but sometimes what is transparent from the documents I see is that people were subjected, let's say to some sort of ill-treatment, but maybe it wasn't that bad [...] I mean, of course, it is probably painful at that moment and very regrettable.

Referring to the caselaw on irreducible life imprisonment, one judge explained that 'this can be read as also a sign that the Court is realizing where we should definitely not expand the scope of Article 3 in any context'.[163] Expanding risks 'watering down the protection'; then, this judge predicted, 'we start to introduce Article 3 clause 2', meaning a delimitation clause. The recognition, and its expansion, needed caution and consolidation before any continuation. Caution was also invoked through possible opportunism regarding compensation, with one judge speculating that advocates argued torture to obtain the significant difference ('almost double' that of inhuman and degrading) in just satisfaction,[164] rendering it to have 'a practical impact qualifying torture [...] or not'.[165] Expansionism would only reward such opportunism.

It was widely accepted that 'we record treatment as torture in really exceptional cases' based on the reasoning that 'it will be like losing a sword if diluted',[166] and 'because otherwise you devalue the notion'.[167] The label was taken to have a pedagogical power, as it was 'used to send an educational message to the state concerned [...] they go further domestically'.[168] Another reflected that 'you have to be a bit careful in not being inflationary, we cannot say that

[160] ECtHR15, judge.
[161] ECtHR17, senior registry lawyer.
[162] ECtHR29, senior registry lawyer.
[163] ECtHR14, judge.
[164] ECtHR29, senior registry lawyer.
[165] ECtHR19, former judge; ECtHR22, former senior registry lawyer.
[166] ECtHR6, senior registry lawyer.
[167] ECtHR29, senior registry lawyer.
[168] ECtHR17, senior registry lawyer.

everything is torture […] because you can end up extremely quickly encoding everything torture'.[169] Those inside the IACtHR also struck similar chords as at the ECtHR: 'Not all suffering or ill-treatment is torture; I think it's very important to preserve the key elements of torture';[170] 'you don't call everything torture, because if everything is torture, then nothing really is torture'.[171] One lawyer observed multiple instances when the political significance of torture came to the fore; that there was, for instance, a 'very clear effort to establish that rape was torture […] there was a litigation on the death-row syndrome and whether or not you qualify that as torture'.[172] These created a pressure on the Inter-American system, according to this lawyer, to either 'go beyond legal discussions' and to engage with 'political realities', or at times shy away and 'not rock the boat'. Some practices simply had to be denied entry (conceivably those psychologically oriented). So it was the symbolism, fear of dilution, and opportunism, both as a matter of principle but also as a means to maintaining consensus and controlling caseloads, that emerged for these interviewees as a central imperative.

As at the ECtHR and IACtHR, CAT members also viewed the label of torture as being politically weightier ('torture definitely carries with it a very important statement […] that's why states vehemently oppose it';[173] 'because the treaty treats torture more harshly';[174] that it should be reserved for the hardest and kept as a last resort as 'it is easier to trivialize the word "torture"').[175] Conversely, one former member, though saying, 'I don't mind what enters the concept of torture', saw two risks in broadening the definition: (1) that 'we deviate our attention from the criminal justice system, the detention system, the criminal procedure rules […] the CAT has its strength in poking into the core of the criminal justice system and the rights that are extended to people detained, deprived of their freedom, and accused of crimes' and (2) that we broaden the questions posed in state reviews so that 'with that time allocated, they have no chance even if they wanted to try to answer them all; the more we ask them, the more they cherry pick the questions that they would like to answer',[176] before admitting to having 'always been against the Committee having too many victims'.

169 ECtHR20, judge.
170 IACtHR14, senior IACtHR lawyer.
171 IACtHR7, former senior IACmHR lawyer.
172 IACtHR5, former senior IACmHR lawyer.
173 CAT6, former member.
174 CAT9, member.
175 CAT16, member.
176 CAT2, former member.

These approaches also translated to state deference. A judge implied the desire to have most member states meet minimum protections before lowering them ('if we manage to get at least most of the member states up to the minimum level, you should be very happy, because we are very far from there').[177] The danger the same judge saw in 'fine-tuning' vis-à-vis 'the most stable rule of law member states [...] can be perceived as us not completely understanding the context'. He anticipated state resistance in such instances, putting it as follows:

> we have a crisis in Ukraine, in Turkey, in Poland, Hungary, and you are telling us on these small details you should probably have ... this is a luxury ... we cannot support this. [...] we should not forget of course to 'fine-tune elements' on the top of any visible ones. But we have to realize that most of our cases are quite brutal and there are so many really brutal situations that this Court is not able to deal with.

There was a note of cautious political pragmatism struck in all this. Expansion in categorization could unduly endanger the system. Caution and consolidation were called for. While these accounts were framed and read broadly, they were in response to my specific questions on the recognition of psychological suffering. Accepting that any feeling of outrage or degradation by an applicant should be discussed and considered, one judge nevertheless questioned applicants with a 'very strong imagination, they think that if they are refused access to a bar' who

> feel offended the whole time. They are victims. So what is obvious? Nothing is obvious, but you still have to draw limits, otherwise you do a bad service to the concepts for the real victim. The inflation problem is real. That is a dangerous judgement, insofar as it elevates everything to Article 3. It's a bit like with children. That's a general problem here. If you give a slap to your children ten times a day, they won't even take notice of the eleventh one, but if you do it once a year, then they will notice it and it will have an effect. So if we find violations the whole time, the governments who've coped with it, it won't impress them.[178]

[177] ECtHR14, judge.
[178] ECtHR20, judge.

Bouyid engendered consternation on this front inside the ECtHR with some admitting that 'there are many people who are not convinced by this [. . .] their hesitation comes from somehow downgrading this threshold of severity'[179] and that it 'generated a lot of commentary within the Court'.[180] Another confirmed that 'you still have very conflicting views',[181] and judges elaborated that 'you will notice that it is not as often cited as it would be, why? because we don't like it [. . .] it goes very far',[182] that it is 'not really taken very seriously at the beginning',[183] and that 'it was meant to make our lives easier but it has not'.[184] Severity, at the ECtHR, though 'historically used' as the key differentiator, was observed by some as 'somehow being put aside or at least, ousted gradually [. . .] replaced by necessity' with *Bouyid*.[185] Yet the shift away from severity had created another issue.

Although Article 8 was also recognized as offering breadth,[186] some feared that this too was being diluted.[187] Expansive interpretations required consensus—with consensus relatively easily achieved in categories less than torture. The 'economy' emerged from the pressure to deliver more judgments and engendered institutional politics, 'vicious opposition', from some judges.[188] Seeing 'there to be a dilution', a former senior registry lawyer thought that *Bouyid* was an Article 8 case but 'there were marginally enough factors to put it into Article 3'.[189] Just because the allegation in question was not an Article 3 matter, the Court didn't have to go and fit it under Article 8. Perhaps it was no violation of the ECHR.[190] Similar concerns were raised about 'turning Article 8 into a catchall for unsuccessful Article 3 complaints'[191] and that judges should avoid 'shopping for applicable articles'.[192]

Hard placed to think of discussions such as *Bouyid*, IACtHR interviewees saw the discussion regarding exceptionality and dilution as rare or irrelevant due to the complexion of cases which easily met the threshold ('because the context is very different [. . .] almost all cases that go to the Inter-American

179 ECtHR1, senior registry lawyer.
180 ECtHR8, judge.
181 ECtHR3, senior registry lawyer.
182 ECtHR20, judge.
183 ECtHR19, former judge; ECtHR4, judge.
184 ECtHR25, senior registry lawyer.
185 ECtHR4, judge.
186 ECtHR20, judge.
187 ECtHR10, judge.
188 ECtHR22, former senior registry lawyer.
189 ECtHR16, former senior registry lawyer.
190 ECtHR10, judge.
191 ECtHR23, senior registry lawyer.
192 ECtHR13, judge.

system involve very bad forms of torture, very physical ones';[193] 'I don't know if the Court has had the dilemma […] as the dockets of the Court reflects more flagrant cases';[194] 'because it hasn't been alleged').[195] A former IACtHR lawyer explained that 'if the threshold into Article 5 is not crossed, that's just inconveniences of life'.[196] Referring to *Gäfgen*, a former IACtHR lawyer explained that they didn't see such 'complex, borderline cases', finding it 'very exceptional for an international court to analyse such a particular case'.[197] The nature of psychological suffering was instead said to be more a discussion inside the IACmHR where discussions around prolonged solitary confinement, death penalty methods, and death-row phenomena were said to be more commonplace.[198]

In sounding caution, one CAT member invoked their fear of 'floodgates' that recognition in this case could mean more work for the CAT, explaining that *Coppin* was 'serious, but not professionally speaking'.[199] To the member, it was hard to run institutions for the mentally ill and elderly. So, for them, it became partly a policy consideration: welfare institutions should exist and not made harder to run. In relation to the use of caged beds in Slovakia, the same member could see that the medicine to the applicant was doubled—meaning she had a disorder, that she was dangerous, and that the use of a caged bed in this situation was 'reasonable […] perhaps we could say it was "bad" but not a violation otherwise it is not balanced, to not pay attention to the reality and difficulty of authorities of investigating after decades'. The member had raised the lawful sanctions argument but others had decided according to 'a dynamic of political correctness'. As at the ECtHR, there were those who pushed against caution and conservatism, the rare voice at the CAT who counter-argued the over-caution: 'I am a little bit concerned that under the idea of preserving the stigma, we do not qualify practices that are clearly torture because they are generalized [so] let's [not] leave that to a narrow group of violations'.[200] Some members made a push to shift the established caselaw as 'the composition changed and they want to have their own way and away from the direction of the old jurisprudence'.[201]

193 IACtHR1, applicant lawyer.
194 IACtHR4, former senior IACtHR lawyer.
195 IACtHR16, senior IACtHR lawyer.
196 IACtHR4, former senior IACtHR lawyer.
197 IACtHR12, former senior IACtHR lawyer.
198 IACtHR6, former senior IACmHR lawyer.
199 CAT8, former member.
200 CAT6, former member.
201 CAT11, UN legal officer.

Here, as throughout interviews, much was explained through policy and practical factors. Practically speaking, the disposition of individual petitions did not allow for the resources (time, space, research support) required for an elaborate discussion on the evolving nature of suffering. There were, it is true, not as many cases brought before the CAT calling for such a discussion, given how relatively rare Article 1 and 16 cases were compared to non-refoulement cases. Yet, when cases did present, as in *Coppin*, the resort to policy considerations against invoking evolution, such as the 'floodgates' argument, was more startling.

Comparison (across cases and country contexts)

Comparative thinking served to situate suffering on a spectrum of severity. Registry lawyers reflected on internal discussions where they reasoned 'how could that case be torture if this was not?'.[202] This referred to two different case files on their desk or in their memory. While accepting the psychological suffering evident in *Gäfgen*, a senior registry lawyer argued that this was 'not the worst' in explaining why it was not categorized as torture ('of course he [the victim] was scared' but 'it wasn't awful torture in my opinion'[203])—effectively holding severity as key as well as alluding to a comparison between cases. Although insults and threats were a 'terrible thing', when the adjudicators moved to categorization and asked the question of whether it was torture, it was 'probably not because it's still not comparable to what has happened' in cases involving severe physical suffering.[204] Another lawyer put this as follows:

> in Russia manifestations against the war, people are being shoved into police buses taken to police stations [...] and they claim torture and to me, yes, of course, it is very unpleasant. There are physical traces usually, like bruises, abrasions. But if we find in this case torture had taken place then what about people who went through something like that [...] brain concussion, her nose broken [...] beaten to a pulp literally, with hematomas everywhere. I mean, the medical documents are horrendous. Then what will happen if we in both cases, we say yeah, that amounts to torture [...]?[205]

[202] ECtHR29, senior registry lawyer.
[203] ECtHR29, senior registry lawyer.
[204] ECtHR23, senior registry lawyer.
[205] ECtHR29, senior registry lawyer.

A transcontinental comparison was similarly offered as a prism to assess necessity. If a Nordic member state, explained a judge, 'famous for a rather lenient criminal system […] finds that this is still warranted, then there might be reason for that.'[206] Asked whether there was any political or civilizational reason for why more violations were found against certain states, most interviewees said 'no' and that it was rather simply a representation of the violence on the ground, the lack of safeguards and domestic remedies.[207] That said, the Court was seen to 'appreciate certain national conditions in terms of, let's say, there is a national security issue, or there's a certain atmosphere in the country, say in Turkey it was the PKK' but that 'doesn't ever influence the Court in a real way.'[208]

Comparison was also made between individuals. The problematic figure of resilience and vulnerability pervasive in solitary confinement cases was also invoked here. A senior lawyer, as an example, pointed to a case concerning a house search where both children and adults were present, where the use of a specific vulnerability lens meant violations were found against the children but not the adults, given one adult applicant 'had been a member of the special forces himself, so he would know what these type of operations involve.'[209] Failure to recognize the full range of harm, therefore, amounted to acceptance of some harm.

Comparison took on a conceptual tone at the CAT. Members saw Article 1 as a narrower concept ('a very solid article') than Article 16 which was vast, with one member venturing: 'If we consider emerging issues [intersex rights], Article 16 is our buffer.'[210] Another underscored that inhuman and degrading treatment 'still can cover a lot grotesque and repulsive practices' (giving the example of Nazis making Jewish people scrub floors).[211] Similarly, a former CAT member explained that 'jurisprudence on Article 16 is much weaker in the CAT than Article 1.'[212] A former member explained that the breadth was due to state reviews generally listing practices potentially in violation of Article 16 ('will give you, of course, an idea of what type of practices are usually qualified in principle').[213] When such practices were argued under the individual

206 ECtHR14, judge.

207 ECtHR16, former senior registry lawyer; ECtHR7, senior registry lawyer; ECtHR22, former senior registry lawyer.

208 ECtHR7, senior registry lawyer.

209 ECtHR25, senior registry lawyer.

210 CAT15, member.

211 CAT9, member.

212 CAT4, former member.

213 CAT6, former member.

petitions process, this member explained, the categorization was 'open to change' and qualified as Article 1 violations if substantiated.

Composition and deliberation

Categorization was also contingent on a consensus between adjudicators and their supporting lawyers, resulting in a reserved use of the specific category of torture as also apparent at the ECtHR. As at the ECtHR, an IACtHR judge did not place a premium on how a case was to be categorized under Article 5, but noted that it depended closely on a collective deliberation and an aspiration for consensus.[214] Pragmatism and an openness to the plurality of categories were also underscored by multiple interviewees there. Categorization was essentially dependent on the nature of the case and the desires of judges (if 'they have a project') in developing a specific area of caselaw ('this is a political election of the judges which may collide with what the Court lawyers recommend').[215] The same lawyer also drew attention to the politics within the Secretariat, arguing that it was a mistake to overlook the composition there:

> People outside the Court think that the judges decide everything, but this is wrong. Ninety per cent of the cases are decided by registry lawyers of the Court. The judges wouldn't like me telling you that but this is true [...] in the one hundred Article 5 cases we send to judges seventy-five don't change. [...] in the past, the judges were more conservative and the Registry always was pushing forward. The judges were always trying to stop, to slow down. Now, the opposite is happening; the Registry is more conservative.

Categorization was thus rendered contingent on a consensus between judges and the Secretariat, resulting in a reserved use of torture as also apparent at the ECtHR.

Categorization between substantive and procedural violations also emerged in this line of discussion, as an expression of the difficulties adjudicators faced in accommodating diverse demands. Avoiding strict categorization was also achieved, interviewees admitted, through 'procedural' or 'judicial economy' (where having dealt with the 'main thrust of the case', the Court moves to dispose of the case),[216] through the breadth offered by 'global', 'unspecified', or

[214] IACtHR10, judge; IACtHR5, former senior IACmHR lawyer.
[215] IACtHR15, senior IACtHR lawyer.
[216] ECtHR15, judge; ECtHR6, senior registry lawyer.

'procedural' violations. A trend towards global violations was explained as being a 'personality' and a compromise-based solution, especially where the composition consisted of 'a majority of those who have a stricter view'.[217] This was also a means of avoiding criticism, as a senior lawyer explained that the Court

> does this to avoid criticism [or] they want to avoid delays […] Some applicants don't know the categories. If the Court needs to move on with a judgment, they don't feel that specifying a violation as either torture or inhuman or degrading is needed. Otherwise the victim is delayed. […] If someone thinks some violation is torture and others inhuman or degrading, why wait for a year for a specific violation?[218]

This too was a device of convenience, 'more useful for the Court to say there has been a violation of Article 3, without saying that it was the violation of the procedure, or the so-called global violation is in some cases advisable'.[219] The judge continued to explain that 'for the Court it is much easier to say that there has been a violation of the procedural obligation here; and not to go into detail'. Admitting that this was a 'problematic solution', the judge thought that this was what 'the government wants to receive', to explain to its public that 'okay, there have been some irregularities in the investigation at the domestic level but there has been no violation on substantive aspects'.

Doctrine had become coded into process by other institutional mechanisms of coherence-maintenance. One senior registry lawyer explained that some cases falling clearly below the minimum-level threshold, or being called 'trivial', was a matter of studying the Court's filtering mechanism, explaining that 'we have all sorts of crazy applicants making all sorts of allegations like saying, "I don't want to live in such a regime and that amounts to torture for us", complaining about governance in a particular country'.[220] Exploration of the filtering mechanism, which is an unpublished process, met a dead end, with others explaining that there was nothing to see. This nevertheless preserved precedent related to recognition—summarily excluding cases conceivably on procedural grounds (insufficient substantiation) and on substantive grounds ('crazy … allegations'). How psychological suffering might fit here remained unexplored. The question of composition is returned to in the next chapter.

217 ECtHR13, judge.
218 ECtHR12, senior registry lawyer.
219 ECtHR4, judge.
220 ECtHR6, senior registry lawyer.

Victims' views

Where did advocates and their clients feature in this contestation? Despite indications identified earlier to the contrary, applicant lawyers characterized victims as demonstrating a lack of awareness of psychological suffering and categorization. Applicants 'express suffering', explained one lawyer, but did not 'recall actually having had that type of [legal] language owned by victims'.[221] Applicants, that is to say, did not 'understand that they were subjected to any treatment that can be contrary to international standards',[222] or 'focussed on the physical effects of the treatment which they had received',[223] explained one lawyer, recalling that applicants had an issue

> establishing in their own mind that they had been tortured, because of their expectations as to how they were going to be treated. I remember one particular conversation with an applicant who had been held in a cell, with no bed, no clothes, no toilet facilities, freezing temperatures, without a coat, or shoes, or socks or anything. But as far as they were concerned, that wasn't ill-treatment, ill-treatment didn't arise until you got beaten up by the gendarmerie. We had to educate the applicants into identifying themselves as having been ill-treated.

This reflection accorded with the limited scholarship on how psychological suffering is overlooked by some victim-survivors, who fail to 'authorize' their words and to overcome the 'insurmountable barrier between victims and those with whom they wish to communicate' and simply because 'it is hard to ascertain clear, visible marks of torture, citizens can be uncertain whether pain was in fact experienced'.[224]

In one ECtHR case, an applicant 'pointed out that he was not complaining about the use of handcuffs and chains during his transfer to hospital—that being a routine if abnormal and degrading practice—since he had simply suffered embarrassment and only mental rather than actual torture'.[225] Further to the point of applicants' express instructions, it was important to hear, as

[221] IACtHR4, former senior IACtHR lawyer; ECtHR32, applicant lawyer.
[222] ECtHR40, applicant lawyer.
[223] ECtHR38, applicant lawyer.
[224] Darius Rejali, 'Modern Torture as a Civic Marker: Solving a Global Anxiety with a New Political Technology' (2003) 2 (2) Journal of Human Rights 153, 157; see also Darius Rejali, *Torture and Democracy* (Princeton University Press 2007) 30.
[225] *Henaf v Turkey* [2004] ECtHR 65436/01 [43]; *Alhowais v Hungary* [2023] ECtHR 59435/17 [149]: the applicant 'did not complain about the adverse psychological effects of the police operation'.

in earlier discussions, that the specific categorization of torture was not always expressed by applicants or sought by their advocates. Applicant lawyers I spoke to explained that, on the whole, it was generally up to themselves to *legally* categorize the case in their submissions as victims seldom expressed such an instruction, primarily based on a lack of knowledge on the part of applicants as to the different categories.[226] Applicants who explicitly instructed their lawyers to argue for the torture categorization were seen as rare and rather 'sophisticated'.[227]

Conclusions

While there has been expansion when viewed broadly, a specific focus on categorization reveals that torture requires physically overt suffering while psychological suffering has come to be associated with the inhuman and degrading. The concept of 'special stigma' crafted in *Ireland* has endured to conceivably underpin this position. As a result, solitary confinement, like other psychologically oriented practices, has had an easier configuration with inhuman and degrading treatment compared to the category of torture, but contestation in categorization has persisted. Although the category of torture was, in principle, not foreclosed to predominantly psychologically oriented practices and experiences, in practice the conclusions of the entirety of the caselaw exude such a position.

To be clear, the point here is not that such practices should not be understood as torture (as, in most cases, it is not difficult to accept that they inflict severe suffering). The point, rather, is that in typifying torture, associating it with such practices, it privileges them in the hierarchical legal imaginary, rendering them potentially easier access than other practices. In all, the material presented exhibits an ambivalence simultaneously concealing and revealing: that categorization does not matter but then again it does, and then dependent on various factors. While reasoning as to how psychological suffering is categorized is limited on the face of its judgments, the IACtHR and CAT have occasionally revealed positions similar to that of the ECtHR: that the threshold for torture should be fixed high and that certain practices are to be associated with inhuman and degrading treatment, not torture. State practice of denying the

226 ECtHR38, applicant lawyer; ECtHR21, applicant lawyer; ECtHR35, applicant lawyer; ECtHR35, applicant lawyer; IACtHR1, applicant lawyer; IACtHR2, applicant lawyer.

227 IACtHR3, applicant lawyer; IACtHR8, applicant lawyer; IACtHR7, former senior IACmHR lawyer; IACtHR6, former senior IACmHR lawyer.

label of 'torture', over and above other categories, has also helped imbue it with a political symbolism. Expansive positions as to interpreting the prohibition were established early, rejecting the primacy of the physical at least in principle, against state interests.

These were confirmed and crystallized in my interviews with advocates and adjudicators. Almost all did not know that psychological suffering when standing on its own had not been categorized as torture; nor did a vast number register the issues given their pragmatism in securing a violation. This led me to examine interpretive practice more broadly than planned. Doing so, I heard that considerations of exception, caution, and comparison resulted in preserving high thresholds. These were grounded in reservations around being receptive to too many claims (resembling the 'floodgates' fear) and needing evidentiary certainty before invoking the category of torture, as well as striving towards institutional consensus. These were presented as strategies to deal with certain difficult cases or considerations. Some, however, were more convincing than others—internally among adjudicators and institutional lawyers and externally among users and observers of the three institutions. That adjudicators did not see the need to expand their interpretation also problematized the figure of dynamic interpretation—indicating that pragmatic and potentially conservative considerations were being prioritized over the progressive. I explore this more specifically in the next chapter.

4

Recognition and the socio-political

> Is it sufficient for an adjudicator to say that his or her interpretation is evolutionary? Or are there more objective criteria? Is it possible to presume a situation of evolutionary interpretation where no mention is made of it?[1]

> And how does one know that a certain standard can be considered representative for contemporary feelings? When it comes to the international legal norm of torture, this difficulty must not be exaggerated. [...] are we to look at what legislators say, what judges say or what people say? This begs the question to what extent public opinion should be decisive. Is it not the task of the legislator and judiciary apparatus to mould the public opinion, and to set the beacons of the tolerable and intolerable?[2]

The dominant narrative of the prohibition's interpretation has been characterized by expansive and responsive, not resistant or evasive, recognition. While applicable to the entirety of the ECtHR, IACtHR, and UN treaty body frameworks, it is noteworthy that the inception of the 'living instrument' doctrine is found in *Tyrer v UK*, a case involving the prohibition. In *Selmouni*, to repeat, recognizing the 'living instrument' doctrine, the ECtHR promised to broaden the protection under the prohibition in accordance with evolving socio-political values and expectations for stronger protection.[3] Conceivably, this articulation allows for a closer insight into the prevailing logics here—primarily one of historical progression, as contingent on purposive, progressive, and not merely pervasive values.

[1] Gabrielle Marceau and Clément Marquet, 'About the Book' in Georges Abi-Saab and others (eds), *Evolutionary Interpretation and International Law* (Hart 2019) 5.

[2] Steven Dewulf, *The Signature of Evil: (Re)defining Torture in International Law* (Intersentia 2011) 142.

[3] *Selmouni v France* [1999] ECtHR 25803/94 [101].

Torture and the Recognition of Psychological Suffering in International Law. Ergün Cakal, Oxford University Press.
 DOI: 10.1093/oso/9780198989493.003.0004

Although *Tyrer's* formulation of 'present-day conditions' and *Selmouni's* 'fundamental values of democratic societies' are accepted, how they are applied is far from clear from a caselaw review. As asked by others more broadly, 'how can judges identify and reflect the changing views of society when interpreting rights provisions?'[4] More pointedly, despite precedents and prescriptions, it is far from clear how 'dynamic interpretation' has served the recognition of psychological suffering. I therefore proceeded to ask: how (and how consistently) has the doctrine of dynamic interpretation been invoked in the prohibition-related caselaw? What impact have these considerations had on the recognition of psychological suffering? The following discussion scrutinizes this terrain that has often, although not entirely, been uncritically accepted and repeated. As I do not have *direct* evidence (namely, of direct observations of adjudicatory reasoning), I instead examine how advocates and adjudicators *talk* about socio-political standards. I trace the contours of how actors have negotiated regressive (narrow) and progressive (expansive) socio-political considerations under dynamic interpretation of the prohibition at the three institutions.

The material is presented in three sections. The first ('Establishing evolution') identifies the general conceptual bounds of the doctrine, broadly and in its relationship with the prohibition. The second ('Invoking evolution') examines how the doctrine has been used (or not) at the institutions towards engaging emerging understandings around suffering—drawing both on my systematic review and interviews. The final section ('Selecting standards') draws attention to the selective uses of external standards. This is a more expansive chapter than earlier chapters, examining the broader institutional conditions which determine the weighing up of socio-political standards pertaining to psychological suffering. While a broad examination of how dynamic interpretation features and functions in the caselaw could read as remote, it remains a potentially critical condition for the expansive recognition of psychological suffering warranting further examination.

[4] Kanstantsin Dzehtsiarou and Conor O'Mahony, 'Evolutive Interpretation of Rights Provisions: A Comparison of the European Court of Human Rights and the U.S. Supreme Court' (2013) 44 Columbia Human Rights Law Review 309.

Establishing evolution

The principled expectation is for the prohibition's interpretation to evolve and extend to emerging understandings associated with suffering on the grounds of the 'living instrument' doctrine and dynamic interpretation. There is also a close relationship, accepting the logic in *Selmouni*, between evolution and categorization: that evolving understandings not only shape recognition broadly but could potentially see what was considered degrading, over time, as more severe, as torture. Yet, as the foregoing has shown, this promise has been left unfulfilled especially with categorizations still requiring high thresholds, remaining fixed on the physical. In what follows, I start with a caselaw and literature review on how and how much the institutions have invoked evolution before drawing on interviews.

Early history

Preceding the *Tyrer* decision by a couple of years, the coupling of 'social change' and the ECHR as being a 'living legal instrument' appears prominently in Max Sørensen's presentation 'Do the rights set forth in the European Convention on Human Rights in 1950 have the same significance in 1975?', delivered in November 1975 at the fourth international colloquy on the ECHR held in Rome before judges and state representatives. There, Sørensen, then a judge of the European Court of Justice and soon to be a judge of the ECtHR, argued in favour of using 'living instrument' to introduce an element of dynamism and progress to keep pace with general social change'.[5] Viewing ECHR's Article 3 as a 'classic example of vague phraseology', he took it as duly open to a 'liberal' interpretation 'according to current attitudes in society', 'evolution of ideas and values generally accepted in society', and 'in such a way as to keep pace with social change'.[6] The ensuing oral interventions by state representatives, to have been recorded, read as receptive to notions of living, evolving, and dynamic interpretation, and as accepting that the prohibition of torture 'has rightly become the evolutive article par excellence', but also anticipate the

[5] Max Sørensen, 'Do the Rights and Freedoms Set Forth in the European Convention on Human Rights in 1950 Have the Same Significance in 1975?' (1975) 89; Humphrey Waldock, 'The Evolution of Human Rights Concepts and the Application of the European Convention on Human Rights' in Paul Reuter (ed), *Mélanges offerts à Paul Reuter: Le droit international—Unité et diversité* (Padone 1981) 547, a former ECtHR judge, held that the ECHR was drafted to 'evolve in response to changes in legal or social concepts'.

[6] Sørensen (n 5) 89.

difficulties in determining the limits of such an approach.[7] The complexity as foretold is borne out in the discursive developments that followed.

Outside of the drafting debates of the ECHR, discussion around social and historical groundings which culminated in the doctrine can be found even earlier than *Tyrer*. Although *Tyrer* is the first appearance of the term 'living instrument' in its jurisprudence, the ECmHR and ECtHR had been implicitly adopting an evolutive approach in earlier cases.[8] The *Greek Case* could be identified as the first instance where torture's sociality was considered at any of the three institutions. It is also instructive, as mentioned, that it represents the first relevant case to grapple with the phenomenon of psychological suffering. Rejecting that the 'slaps and blows during, or shortly after, their arrest' violated Article 3 rights of the prisoners, the ECmHR remarked that society had 'tolerated […] and even taken for granted […] a certain roughness of treatment'.[9] The ECmHR further reasoned that the degree to which 'the public may accept physical violence as being neither cruel nor excessive, varies between different societies and even between different sections of them'.[10]

An early study to problematize dynamic interpretation in the *Greek Case* argued that legal interpretation should not be made 'subject to societal preference in so straightforward a manner as implied', particularly as citizens are usually disinclined to comprehend or care about the treatment of prisoners.[11] While the obscurity of the public knowing (or indifference to) what happens in prisons may well hold, this critique has arguably been rendered obsolete by the ECtHR's current explicit requirement that social attitudes be harnessed progressively and not regressively. The ECtHR has presumed a very particular and linear model through *Selmouni*—seemingly impervious to breaks in form of revolutions, regime change, or state backlash. Then again, with a view to the ECtHR's state deference such as to 'dangerous' prisoner justifications in solitary confinement cases, already detailed, this argument, that dynamic interpretation lets in regressive elements, could conceivably still ring true at a technical level.

Keeping to early cases, in *Tyrer* too, conservative public opinion on the Isle of Man was similarly and unsuccessfully put forward by the UK government

[7] Sørensen (n 5) 116.

[8] Ed Bates, *The Evolution of the European Convention on Human Rights: From Its Inception to the Creation of a Permanent Court of Human Rights* (OUP 2010) 328.

[9] *Denmark, Norway, Sweden and Netherlands v Greece* [*The Greek Case*] [1969] ECmHR 3321/67, 3322/67, 3323/67, 3344/67, p 501.

[10] ibid.

[11] John Vorhaus, 'On Degradation Part Two: Degrading Treatment and Punishment' (2003) 31 Common Law World Review 65, 85.

as supportive of corporal punishment—as local attitudes were overridden by the national. The UK argued that corporal punishment 'did not outrage public opinion in the Isle of Man'. The passage in question from the *Greek Case* was also directly relied on by the UK.[12] The adjudicators instead preferred to look afield and found that the 'great majority of the member States of the Council of Europe, judicial corporal punishment is not, it appears, used and, indeed, in some of them, has never existed in modern times'.[13] The ECmHR ultimately ruled that 'simply because the measure [corporal punishment] has been in use for a long time or even meets with general approval', it can still be degrading and 'that, should one go by public opinion, it would be very difficult indeed to make progress in criminology'.[14] Commissioner Kellberg underscored the importance of progressive values, explaining that the ECmHR 'could well have reached a different conclusion in such a case twenty-five years ago. But much has changed since then and the meaning must be given to notions of fundamental rights in present-day circumstances'.[15]

There has been no shortage since of adjudicators evoking socio-political standards or social change in one way or another. Social change has occasionally been debated in and outside of judgments at the ECtHR. During a judicial seminar organized by the ECtHR on dynamic interpretation, for instance, the then ECtHR President Costa spoke of how the ECHR needed to be 'interpreted, and applied, by adapting it to the changes that have taken place over time—to changes in society, in morals, in mentalities, in laws, but also to technological innovations and scientific progress'.[16] On this footing, the ECtHR has broadly understood its interpretation of 'the concepts of inhuman and degrading treatment and punishment [to] have evolved considerably since the Convention came into force in 1953'.[17]

Proxies of expansion

In her review of the ECtHR caselaw, Ezgi Yildiz concludes that Article 3 has indeed *evolved considerably* to now cover 'violations arising from omissions and

[12] *Tyrer v UK* [1976] ECmHR 5856/72 [23].
[13] ibid [38] per Commissioner Kellberg.
[14] ibid [84].
[15] Report of the public hearings held on 17 January 1978, 57–58.
[16] ECtHR, 'Dialogue between Judges: What Are the Limits to the Evolutive Interpretation of the Convention?' (2011) 5.
[17] *Khamtokhu and Aksenchik v Russia* [2017] ECtHR 60367/08 [73].

emphasizing procedural obligations'[18] and that accordingly the 'threshold to define acts as torture and inhuman or degrading treatment has been lowered', progressively so.[19] She also finds that the 'developments within the Convention system mirrored what had been in progress outside of it'.[20] Building on early analysis,[21] she identifies that the range of issues covered under Article 3 has expanded, noting how with Dougoz v Greece[22] the ECtHR accepted detention conditions to be violations when it previously did not.[23]

While protection has indeed been expanded, this discussion suggests that evidence of progress depends on the markers (or proxies) chosen. Despite promises of progress, for instance, there was no *specific* finding of torture from *Ireland* (1976) until *Aksoy* (1996).[24] There was also no finding of any Article 3 violation (namely, inhuman or degrading treatment) from *Tyrer* to *Tomasi* (1992).[25] Again, while the grounds have expanded, in cases dated 1967–2006, Yildiz herself finds them to be met with high numbers of dismissals.[26] In her review of the Article 3 caselaw, Natasa Mavronicola concludes that the ECtHR 'has only made findings of torture in cases of infliction—and not of instigation, consent or acquiescence—by State officials'.[27] On these proxies, the *Selmouni* promise could read as unfulfilled.

Evolution in recognition has thus been far from a product of linearly expansive interpretive preferences; not 'a moral or legal matter but one of political expediency as well'.[28] Strongly corroborative here are numerous occasions where the ECtHR cautiously refrained from invoking 'progress' or 'improvement' in controversial cases (at the time) such as: the right to die;[29] the right to abortion;[30] prohibition of the death penalty;[31] conviction and sentencing

[18] Ezgi Yildiz, 'Interpretative Evolution of the Norm Prohibiting Torture and Inhuman or Degrading Treatment under the European Convention' in Anne-Lise Kjær and Joanna Lam (eds), *Language and Legal Interpretation in International Law* (OUP 2022) 312.

[19] Ezgi Yildiz, 'A Norm in Flux: The Development of the Norm Against Torture under the European Convention from a Macro Perspective' (2016) iCourts Working Paper No 45.

[20] Ezgi Yildiz, 'A Court with Many Faces: Institutional Identities and Interpretive Preferences: The Case of the European Court of Human Rights and the Norm against Torture', PhD thesis, IHEID Geneva (2016) 235, 201.

[21] Antonio Cassese, 'Prohibition of Torture and Inhuman or Degrading Treatment or Punishment' in Paola Gaeta and Salvatore Zappalà (eds), *The Human Dimension of International Law* (OUP 2008) 296–331.

[22] *Dougoz v Greece* [2001] ECtHR 40907/98.

[23] Citing *Dougoz v Greece* [2001] ECtHR 40907/98 in Yildiz (n 20) 199.

[24] *Aksoy v Turkey* [1996] ECtHR 100/1995/606/694.

[25] *Tomasi v France* [1992] ECtHR 12850/87.

[26] Yildiz (n 20) 187–89.

[27] Natasa Mavronicola, *Torture, Inhumanity, and Degradation under Article 3 of the ECHR: Absolute Rights and Absolute Wrongs* (Hart 2021) 89.

[28] Yildiz (n 20) 311–13.

[29] *Pretty v UK* [2002] ECtHR 2346/02.

[30] *A, B and C v Ireland* [2010] ECtHR 25579/05.

[31] *Öcalan v Turkey (no 1)* [2005] ECtHR 46221/99.

age of criminal responsibility;[32] and the right to marry.[33] In rejecting the available progressive interpretations, judges have reified regressive interpretations. Progressive promises have thus been tempered in some areas and by some judges as needing to be reactive and reflective and not proactive, innovative, or anticipatory.[34]

Irreducible life imprisonment cases illustrate such oscillations—between regressive and expansive impulses. These cases, particularly through several separate opinions, offer expanded reasoning on the nature (and limits) of evolutive interpretation. Predating the variable flurry of cases involving life imprisonment to follow, in *Leger v France*, it was a dissenting judge who intuitively advanced that the 'time was ripe to make a step forward' in moving against the practice.[35] *Vinter v UK*, characterized as a highwater mark, held that irreducible life imprisonment, given it defeated 'hope',[36] was inhuman. Two years later, in the rulings in *Hutchinson v UK*, however, the *Vinter* was effectively reversed in finding no violation of irreducible life sentences.[37] Subsequent chamber decisions in *Matiošaitis v Lithuania*[38] and *Petukhov v Ukraine (no 2)*[39] saw *Vinter* resurface and followed, pointing to an exceptional treatment of the UK, to say the least, based on political considerations in *Hutchinson*—arguably an attempt to appease an important member state. Following *Vinter*, ECtHR's Grand Chamber, in *Khamtokhu and Aksenchik*, also failed to find an international trend to abolish life imprisonment, despite accepting that exempting some groups from the practice could be identified.[40] Hungarian use of the practice has been recently summarily found to be a violation.[41]

[32] *T v UK* [1999] ECtHR 24724/94; *V v UK* [1999] ECtHR 24888/94.

[33] *Johnston and others v Ireland* [1986] ECtHR 9697/82.

[34] *Helsinki Bizottsag v Hungary* [2016] ECtHR 18030/11, concurring opinion [3]; *X and others v Austria* [2013] ECtHR [GC] 19010/07, p 139, dissenting opinion [23]; Rudolph Bernhardt, 'Evolutive Treaty Interpretation, Especially of the European Convention on Human' (2000) 1999 German Yearbook of International Law 22: broadly reflecting on evolutive interpretation, former ECtHR president Rudolf Bernhardt admitted that he felt obliged, as an international judge, to be more conservative than progressive.

[35] *Leger v France* [2009] ECtHR 19324/02 [16], dissent of Judge Fura-Sandstrom. Running the 'these things take time' argument, for instance, the Bulgarian government explained in *Iorgov v Bulgaria* that 'the delay between the moratorium on executions in 1990 and the final abolition of the death penalty in 1998 had been inevitable as the public debate and the evolution of societal attitudes had required time'.

[36] *Vinter and ors v UK* [2013] ECtHR [GC] 66069/09, opinion of Power-Forde.

[37] *Hutchinson v UK* [2015] ECtHR 57592/08 [2017] [GC].

[38] *Matiošaitis and ors v Lithuania* [2017] ECtHR 22662/13 [135].

[39] *Petukhov v Russia (no 2)* [2019] ECtHR 41216/13 [187].

[40] *Khamtokhu and Aksenchik v Russia* [2017] ECtHR 60367/08 [86]. Judge Pinto de Alberquerque's separate opinion [25–38] is well worth reading here, in which he held that categorizing 'whole life' sentences as amounting to inhuman treatment 'undeniably constitute[d] progress', highlighted 'the international trend in favour of abolishing this type of punishment and the requirement of an evolutive and pro persona interpretation', and argued against a 'State-centred conception of consensus'.

[41] See *Bancsók and László Magyar v Hungary (no 2)* [2021] ECtHR 52374/15 and cases referring to it such as *Keszthelyi and others v Hungary* [2024] ECtHR 44977/20.

What these series of cases reveal is an oscillating expansion susceptible to socio-political considerations both progressively as regressively. The variance is not self-explanatory or amenable to doctrinal analysis. This informed my choice to discuss with relevant actors when 'evolution' in socio-political standards was invoked in their practice—particularly in their work on cases involving psychological suffering.

Thin reasoning

My survey of the caselaw revealed that, since *Tyrer*, the ECtHR explicitly invoked 'living instrument' only *once* more in Article 3 caselaw,[42] opting instead for analogous concepts to be listed shortly. Similarly, *Selmouni* has been cited more than 600 times since it was delivered but only a handful of cases cite and use its evolutionary principle. In a vast majority of cases, what is drawn upon is its reasoning around (i) the absolute nature of the prohibition, (ii) that good health before detention and bad health when released gives rise to a presumption, (iii) to spell out the prohibition is 'a value of civilisation', and (iv) that it requires a 'special stigma'—indicating a negligence of its progressive promise as it is used to make responsivity to emergent understandings of suffering more difficult.

That said, legal creativity since the two cases has been extensive, with the notion of 'evolution' found throughout ECtHR caselaw and often attributed to *Tyrer*—manifest in a kaleidoscope of phrases gesturing at change and contemporaneity in values: 'present-day conditions and changing circumstances in society'; 'the most modern experience and thinking'; 'the standards of civilised behaviour that are the hallmark of a democratic society'; 'required in present-day democratic societies in Europe'; 'changing conditions'; 'modern-day conditions'; 'contemporary social attitudes'; 'a rapid evolution of social attitudes'; 'societal changes and evolving views'; 'social progress'; 'conscience of Europe'; and '*perspective humanitaire*'.

How these values have been determined and situated has predominantly been through assessing the regulatory 'consensus' on a matter, or 'common ground' as found 'amongst modern societies';[43] considering 'the notions currently prevailing in democratic states;[44] in 'national and international law';[45]

[42] The exception was *Soering*. See also Ezgi Yildiz, *Between Forbearance and Audacity: The European Court of Human Rights and the Norm against Torture* (CUP 2023) 122.
[43] *Marckx v Belgium* [1979] ECtHR 6833/74.
[44] *Guzzardi v Italy* [1980] ECtHR 7367/76.
[45] *Damir and Baykara v Turkey* [2008] ECtHR 34503/97.

'developments and commonly accepted standards in the penal policy';[46] 'in harmony with other rules of international law of which it forms a part';[47] 'evolving convergence as to the standards to be achieved'; and a 'clear and uncontested evidence of a continuing international trend'.[48] While this plurality seems solid at first, it favours sources of international law over a more social scientific or otherwise empirical grounding. National and international law, to put this differently, are taken by and large as proxies for socio-political standards.

Based on the variance of stances, devices, and sources normally relied on by actors to substantiate socio-political standards, the doctrine of dynamic interpretation is charged with being imprecise, counter-majoritarian, activist, and a reformist 'fig-leaf', as lacking predictability and foreseeability[49] and engendering legal uncertainty.[50] It was indeed difficult in my own search to find *empirical* support for how the doctrine has been precisely applied—with a 'sparseness' of justifications and evidence for the doctrine as it is applied 'with virtually no explanation of its origins, benefits and limitations'.[51] This has opened the ECtHR, in particular, up to critiques of 'policy-making' and 'subjective ad-hockery' without judicial elaboration and empirical grounding.[52] Calls to 'objectivize' dynamic interpretation and to 'scientifically analyse social trends and changes of mentalities' have been made here.[53] These critiques have been occasionally accepted by adjudicators, conceding that this exercise has not been 'an exact science and it is hardly surprising that views will differ even among the judges themselves as to whether it has been sufficiently established and, if so, as to the weight to be given to it'.[54] The terrain remains, therefore, far from settled.

The 'living instrument' doctrine has thus been criticized as thinly reasoned. Although *Tyrer* conceptually linked history, values, and legal reasoning, scholars have pointed out that it 'did not give any reasons for its

[46] *Tyrer v UK* [1978] ECtHR 5856/72 [31].
[47] *Mamatkulov and Askarov v Turkey* [2005] ECtHR [GC] 46827/99.
[48] *Goodwin v UK* [2002] ECtHR 28957/95 [84–85].
[49] Jens Vedsted-Hansen, and Ida Koch, 'International Human Rights and National Legislatures: Conflict or Balance?' (2006) 75 Nordic Journal of International Law 3, 11.
[50] *Golder v UK* [1975] ECtHR 4451/70, separate opinion of Judge Verdross.
[51] Alistair Mowbray, 'The Creativity of the European Court of Human Rights' (2005) 5 Human Rights Law Review 57, 71.
[52] ibid.
[53] Gloria Gaggioli, 'The Strength of Evolutionary Interpretation in International Human Rights Law' in Georges Abi-Saab and others (eds), *Evolutionary Interpretation and International Law* (Hart 2019) 114.
[54] Nicholas Bratza, 'Living Instrument or Dead Letter: The Future of the European Convention on Human Rights' (2014) 2 European Human Rights Law Review 120, 123; ECtHR (n 16) 9–10.

characterisation' or how 'commonly accepted standards' should be weighed.[55] Torture's supposed 'special stigma', sitting at the heart of its conceptualization, is another direct reference to law's socio-political context. This too has been without much elaboration—a consequential differentiator between torture despite 'virtually no jurisprudential development of what is meant by stigma or what exactly it is that the Court seeks to stigmatize'.[56] The conceptual depth of similar devices is unmistakably rare—with exceptions drawing on the social significance of the face,[57] evolving understandings of sexual autonomy,[58] or 'civil' or 'social death'.[59] In his dissent in *Jalloh v Germany*, a case concerning the suffering inflicted by a forced emetic, Judge Zupancic urged that the Court needed to tend to what he termed 'the zeitgeist':

> Most worrisome of all in all of this, however, is the already apparent change in the zeitgeist and the consequent degradation of minimal standards. What in 1952 was patently 'conduct that shocked the conscience' has in 2006 become an issue that must be extensively—and not just in this case—pondered, argued and debated. Despite their apparent evolution, this transmutation has little to do with the scholarly differentiation of juristic standards as, for example, between 'inhuman and degrading treatment' on the one hand and 'torture' on the other. Particular conduct on the part of the police will or will not shock the conscience of those appointed to consider it and to assess it. If it does they will condemn it as torture. If it does not they will deem it tolerable. [...] This assessment derives from a certain hierarchy of values—assimilated by everyone from the policeman holding down the person in whom a tube is to be inserted through which an emetic will be administered, to the medical doctor administering the tube and the emetic, to the judge admitting evidence so cruelly obtained. These hierarchies of values are the real origin of all

55 Bratza (n 54) 144.

56 Kathleen Cavanaugh, 'On Torture: The Case of the "Hooded Men"' (2020) 42 Human Rights Quarterly 519, 532; see also Michelle Farrell, 'The Marks of Civilisation: The Special Stigma of Torture' (2022) 22 (1) Human Rights Law Review 1.

57 *Bouyid v Belgium* [2015] ECtHR [GC] 23380/09 [104]: 'A slap has a considerable impact on the person receiving it. A slap to the face affects the part of the person's body which expresses his individuality, manifests his social identity and constitutes the centre of his senses—sight, speech and hearing—which are used for communication with others.'

58 *X v Cyprus* [2025] ECtHR 40733/22 [109]: 'The Court has previously observed that the evolving understanding of the way rape is experienced by the victim has shown that victims of sexual abuse often put up no physical resistance because of a variety of psychological factors or because they fear violence from the perpetrator. Moreover, the development of law and practice in that area reflects the evolution of societies towards effective equality and respect for individuals' sexual autonomy' (references omitted).

59 *Matiošaitis* (n 38): irreducible life 'described as a social death sentence'; *Ülke v Turkey* [2006] ECtHR 39437/98 [59] 'civil death'.

the secondary ratiocination and, more worrisome, often the apparent lack of sensibility and interest.

Such depth of reasoning as Zupancic offers here does not often appear in the caselaw. What he identifies is a link between the socio-political with the sense-centric, that recognition is shaped socially, informing visceral and legal reprehension and response. Similar logics, despite not always explicit in decisions, were readily provided in the interviews: that 'good judges are good at making the correlation between the law and the world'[60] or 'judges, lawyers come and go, and their perception, reflection, education varies in time; we are also living in modern societies, so we are not disconnected from developments, we do take them into account'.[61] I'll come to these shortly.

Like the ECtHR, the IACtHR has also occasionally, though less often, invoked the doctrine of dynamic interpretation, holding that, as *Tyrer*, 'human rights treaties are living instruments whose interpretation must consider the changes over time and present-day conditions'.[62] The *Selmouni* principle has also been cited by the IACtHR[63] as well as the IACmHR[64] in torture-related cases. Like the ECtHR, the IACtHR's approach to assessing evolution has also been left open-ended, with assessments looking to regional and global normative frameworks and, to a lesser extent, notions of consensus. The scholarship is thin on this front. It has importantly asked, however, why the IACtHR has 'appeared to give insufficient consideration to the consent of the regional community of states as a factor in the evolutive interpretation of a human rights treaty'—finding one 'evident reason for the less frequent reliance on "regional consensus" in the Americas is the comparative prevalence of systematic human rights abuses directed against the core of the protected rights'.[65] Unlike the ECtHR, regional consensus has been too low to be accepted by the IACtHR.

My own review of the IACtHR torture-related caselaw revealed that the doctrine's invocation there was rare to be sure. Notably, it was Judge Trindade

[60] ECtHR10, judge.

[61] ECtHR6, senior registry lawyer.

[62] *Right to Information on Consular Assistance* [1999] [114]; *Gómez Paquiyauri Brothers v Peru* [2004] IACtHR [165]; see also IACtHR, Advisory Opinion OC-10/89, *Interpretation of the American Declaration of the Rights and Duties of Man*, of 14.07.1989, Series A, n 10, p 45, [37]: it is 'necessary to point out that to determine the legal status of the American Declaration it is appropriate to look to the inter-American system of today in the light of the evolution it has undergone since the adoption of the Declaration, rather than to examine the normative value and significance which that instrument was believed to have had in 1948'.

[63] *Cantoral-Benavides v Peru* [2000] IACtHR [99].

[64] IACmHR, 'Towards the closure of Guantanamo', OAS/Ser.L/V/II.Doc 20/15 (2015) [111].

[65] Gerald Neuman, 'Import, Export, and Regional Consent in the Inter-American Court of Human Rights' (2008) 19 European Journal of International Law 101, 107.

who almost exclusively invoked the doctrine of dynamic interpretation in the history of the IACtHR: as being compatible with the Vienna Convention on the Law of Treaties, solely progressive and responding to changing realities,[66] and as bound with social and civilizational factors.[67] The *Selmouni* principle also appeared in the IACtHR jurisprudence mainly through the writing of Trindade who variably underscored evolution and the civilizational aspects of the prohibition of torture,[68] on one occasion insightfully reflecting that 'progress in this area has not been linear but rather—as often happens—pendulous'.[69] Writing extrajudicially, as an exception to Trindade, Judge Quiroga too held that the ACHR 'calls for an elaboration of aspects of rights to adapt them to the evolution of society. In short, interpretation must be a dynamic process'.[70] There have been others who have weighed in on these points (but exceptionally so).[71]

The use (and influence) of socio-political standards at the CAT were essentially explicitly absent from official documents but those interviewed referred to numerous examples of interpretive expansion based on an increased social recognition of psychological suffering. While never having explicitly cited *Tyrer* or *Selmouni*, the CAT on a few occasions has used similar language around evolution in needing to respond 'to evolving threats, issues, and practices'[72] and expressing that its 'understanding of and recommendations in respect of effective measures are in a process of continual evolution, as, unfortunately, are the methods of torture and ill-treatment'.[73] The CAT has otherwise not elaborately historicized or explicitly linked torture's evolution to socio-political factors in a similar manner.[74]

[66] *Bámaca-Velásquez v Guatemala* [2000] IACtHR, separate opinion [34, 114]; *Pueblo Bello Massacre v Colombia* [2006] IACtHR, separate opinion [50]; *Mapiripán Massacre v Colombia* [2005] IACtHR, separate opinion [5]; *Ximenes-Lopes v Brazil* [2005] IACtHR, separate opinion [46]; *Blake v Guatemala* [1998] IACtHR, separate opinion [12]; *The Ituango Massacres v Colombia* [2006] IACtHR, separate opinion [50].

[67] *Servellón-García et al v Honduras* [2006] IACtHR, separate opinion [24]; *'Street Children' (Villagran-Morales et al) v Guatemala* [1999] IACtHR, separate opinion with Abreu [11]; *Blanco-Romero et al v Venezuela* [2005] IACtHR, separate opinion; *Barrios Altos* [2001] IACtHR, separate opinion referring to 'dictates of public conscience' [25] and 'affront to the juridical conscience of humanity' [26].

[68] *Baldeón-García v Perú* [2006] IACtHR, separate opinion of Trindade [5]; *Cantoral-Benavides* (n 63), separate opinion of Trindade [99]; *Tibi v Ecuador* [2004] IACtHR, separate opinion of Trindade [29]; *Bámaca-Velásquez* (n 66), separate opinion of Trindade [35].

[69] *Myrna Mack Chang v Guatemala* [2003] IACtHR, separate opinion of Trindade [8].

[70] Cecilia Quiroga, 'The Inter-American Court of Human Rights 35 Years' (2015) 33 (2) Netherlands Quarterly of Human Rights 118–22.

[71] Exceptions to Trindade: *Fermin Ramirez v Guatemala* [2005] IACtHR, separate opinion of Garcia Ramirez cited civilization, evolution, and 'social consciousness'.

[72] CAT, 'General Comment No 2' (2008) [1].

[73] CAT-C-65-D-758-2016, dissent [4–6].

[74] Except noting the evolution as a peremptory norm: CAT-C-67-D-854-2017 [2.13].

Invoking evolution

I now turn squarely to the perspectives and positions interviewees expressed on these points. As already alluded to, the recognition of psychological suffering was readily put in a historical trajectory by interviewees, of changes in 'society and state', which were described now 'as less aggressive physically' than in the nineteenth century, whereas now 'the state is more and more aggressive but non physically'.[75] One senior registry lawyer also confirmed that judges indeed regularly discussed 'social morals', understanding them as the shared ideas around 'what is normal and what is not normal, what is civil, and what is not civil'.[76] Keeping with how early precedents shifted boundaries and exuded a receptivity to including psychological suffering, all interviewees at the ECtHR, judges and senior registry lawyers, accepted that intense suffering meeting the prohibition's threshold could well be psychological in nature, dismissing any charge of a 'general bias in favour of states for judges not accepting psychological ill-treatment'.[77]

Foreshadowing the next section on external standards as well as the connection between socio-political standards and scientific expertise to follow in the next chapter, one senior registry lawyer demanded that any invocation of socio-political standards be corroborated by evidence:

> society and judges need proof—they would not go into something unless they are on solid ground […] lawyers need to inform them […] judges need to be helped to imagine how a victim felt. Lawyers need to rely on more studies, academic studies. If we at the Court need to follow the evolution of society, you as a lawyer need to bring your argument. We do look at what's going on. If none of the parties bring it to the case, we sigh. We don't follow the continental system where the judge has a more active role.[78]

This position also mirrored multiple accounts which attributed the Court's expansionist interpretation to its users, placing the responsibility on this front on the users' competence to convince the Court to make a move. A former senior registry lawyer explained that for a long time

[75] ECtHR12, senior registry lawyer.
[76] ECtHR28, senior registry lawyer.
[77] ECtHR15, judge.
[78] ECtHR12, senior registry lawyer.

> there was no knowledge of the Convention system, no expertise in the legal community to bring these cases. And it was only when people like Kevin Boyle, Francoise Hampson, and Philip Leach [...] the involvement of NGOs and lawyers aware of the UN materials, aware of the emerging international standards on torture [...] the Court can only react when cases are filed by it, and certainly [this was the case] for the Commission.[79]

On this premise, others pointed to the rarity of such cases being argued ('it does not happen often',[80] 'what accounts for that is the rarity of acts of mental suffering which could be qualified as torture'[81]). Again, this was akin to the explanation that the Court could only decide on cases that were submitted. Cases involving serious threats, irreducible life imprisonment, or prolonged solitary confinement as identified in previous chapters seemed not to count.

Implicit invocation

ECtHR judges and senior registry lawyers I interviewed were ready to accept the doctrine but questioned the extent of its use. When asked why *Tyrer* or *Selmouni* was not regularly cited to expand protection, one senior registry lawyer explained that 'it could nowadays have become more or less a self-understanding [...] if nobody raises it as a particular issue, I have a feeling it is kind of a thing that goes without saying'.[82] While *Selmouni* was still being employed, claimed another registry lawyer, the change in cases being brought to the Court (from 'rough treatment' to now involving detention conditions) was not the ideal ground for distinct application of dynamic interpretation.[83] Another offered a similar explanation, of the lack of explicit invocation of the 'living instrument' doctrine, in finding that it was 'not always necessary to reason with it'.[84] A senior registry lawyer underscored that the conception and use of 'living instrument' was a product of necessity (that 'it comes gradually, it comes necessarily, by the way work is conducted') and as an exercise in explicating the implicit ('we have not actually invented anything; we've just put words into already existing concepts'[85]).

[79] ECtHR22, former senior registry lawyer.
[80] ECtHR24, judge.
[81] ECtHR23, senior registry lawyer.
[82] ECtHR1, senior registry lawyer.
[83] ECtHR6, senior registry lawyer.
[84] ECtHR7, senior registry lawyer.
[85] ECtHR3, senior registry lawyer.

Although not explicitly or extensively invoked, interviewees argued that the doctrine of dynamic interpretation had also featured in the work of the IACtHR. When asked for examples of evolution from interviewees at the IACtHR, the examples of gender-based violence (and the recognition of the inhering psychological suffering)[86] and enforced disappearance (and the associated 'right to truth')[87] were regularly advanced as where the Court had evolved. The role of an evidence-sensitive civil society in litigating cases was taken as instrumental but here too, as at the ECtHR, 'dynamic interpretation' was normally left intuitive and implicit. Applicant lawyers explained that evolutive interpretation was used in 'asking the Court to interpret a specific article in a way that it has not done before' as in a case of forced labour against Brazil and sexual slavery against Venezuela.[88] These in the lawyer's view were 'quite innovative' but, given that the IACtHR had been 'quite progressive' on its own initiative on mental suffering from early on, the expectation was that the IACtHR would not need to be pushed to accept 'new concepts'. The applicant's demand, explained this lawyer, remained 'implicit' where it was 'just a question of developing the standard a little bit more or for the Court to make a certain interpretation'. Another applicant lawyer similarly explained that the importance the IACtHR placed on scientific understandings meant that evolutive interpretation didn't have to be explicitly argued before it.[89]

CAT interviewees, as at the ECtHR and IACtHR, also listed progressive developments as including 'explicit reference to the European Court and its practices',[90] following UN, European, and Inter-American jurisprudence,[91] the introduction of feminist approaches,[92] enforced disappearances and suffering of families,[93] invalidating amnesty laws and *N v Switzerland* (refoulement regarding rehabilitation),[94] and 'responding to many types of cases which we had not considered or had been reluctant to consider in the past [...] considering this psychiatric issue'.[95] Linking progressive interpretation to psychological suffering, members claimed that 'psychological suffering is getting more attention, particularly the notion of "meaningful human contact", solitary

[86] IACtHR14, IACtHR lawyer; IACtHR7, former IACmHR lawyer; IACtHR6, former IACmHR lawyer; IACtHR4, former IACtHR lawyer; IACtHR10, judge.
[87] IACtHR14, senior IACtHR lawyer.
[88] IACtHR1, applicant lawyer.
[89] IACtHR2, applicant lawyer.
[90] CAT2, former member.
[91] CAT4, former member.
[92] CAT16, member.
[93] CAT3, former member.
[94] CAT6, former member.
[95] CAT13, member.

confinement and irreducible life imprisonment',[96] and that 'there is a general sense that these things change over time; perhaps this applies to psychological suffering more than physical pain'—with the latter mostly remaining the same.[97] Individual decisions were supportive of how some former CAT members had a hard time remembering having discussed dynamic interpretation—who instead saw 'more the clearcut situations' and not so much cases 'breaking jurisprudential ground [where] that is something that could be discussed'[98] or, similarly put, 'cases that are very severe cases where it's very tough physical injury treatment, not like solitary confinement and other mental suffering issues'.[99]

As at the ECtHR and IACtHR, applicant lawyers at the CAT did not generally rely on evolving interpretation, finding their claims to be obvious.[100] One experienced lawyer, although inclined to invoke dynamic interpretation, found word limits on the CAT application to be 'a hindrance to making innovative arguments' ('how can you actually pretend to advance jurisprudence to make the point for social implications, root causes, give them the background?'[101]). When I relayed this account in subsequent interviews, a UN lawyer admitted that the 'system itself is not legal 100 per cent', and not conducive to extensive conceptualization or elaboration of such doctrines.[102] The disadvantage of offering more detail, this UN lawyer continued, was narrowing jurisprudence in that 'if you are starting to explain everything, then you might become maybe too narrow in the standards that we are imposing to each complainant, it is a way of leaving the door open to a large category of people coming in to complain'. This account returned the discussion to the point of caution and dilution. In adding to the pattern emerging of keeping evolution implicit and reserved, it pointed to the practical reasons for why reasoning remained implicit.

In all, that the interpretation of the prohibition was evolving was generally accepted by interviewees. The central doctrine through which this evolution could be realized, namely dynamic interpretation, was, however, rarely explicitly used and the possibility of such use raised consternation especially among judges. Advocates, as adjudicators, took the position that it was best applied implicitly and sparingly. Interviewees also argued that some cases did not allow its use given how well the precedent was established—without acknowledging

96 CAT16, member.
97 CAT9, member.
98 CAT6, former member.
99 CAT1, former member.
100 CAT7, applicant lawyer.
101 IACtHR8, applicant lawyer.
102 CAT20, UN legal officer.

the potential for this approach to pre-empt reflection on why certain instances were being excluded. This articulated a caution in invoking evolution, a caution amplified when the category of torture entered the equation.

Common sense as conduit

Interviewees invoked notions of common sense or personal experience instead as standing in for dynamic interpretation. Reinforcing implicit invocations, the notion of 'common sense' was viewed as a conduit to bringing shared understandings to bear in deliberations: 'to the community';[103] 'to order the messiness of life';[104] to ensure that 'we are not isolated from outside, we follow the developments, we are human beings'.[105] For one registry lawyer, it was only a matter of time before the Court recognized that certain values are coalesced into common sense—which was what happened with cases around domestic violence, though the Court was 'awfully late to look at this'.[106] Another senior registry lawyer preferred 'legal sense', compared to 'common sense' in gesturing to shared values regarding what was right and wrong, as a notion which 'guides us subconsciously' and is used to 'make assumptions'.[107] Common sense was invoked 'quite often' as a starting point towards a more rigorous 'objective' assessment in using 'common sense or the normal experience that we would have as humans' to ask: 'how would this normally be perceived?' The judge preferred to use the term 'socially validated'.[108]

While common sense was seen to have its proper time and place, it was not seen to be apt for the Court which ought instead to thoroughly operate on the basis of evidence, or apt 'for questions that require consensus'.[109] Another judge dismissed the notion of 'common sense' as 'not a good reference' as for them it was 'not the spirit of the international protection of human rights'.[110] Instead, this judge saw their job to 'have to apply the rules, for which we have so many tools, and have to see also the comparative law'. Another judge called it a 'dangerous concept' but admitted that there were occasions where common sense led to 'straightforward' and 'quick' rulings on experiences which were

103 ECtHR14, judge.
104 ECtHR13, judge.
105 ECtHR6, senior registry lawyer; ECtHR21, applicant lawyer.
106 ECtHR28, senior registry lawyer.
107 ECtHR24, judge.
108 ECtHR14, judge.
109 ECtHR3, senior registry lawyer.
110 ECtHR10, judge.

'obviously torture'.[111] Against this approach, one judge viewed it as 'purely caustic' and 'very unprofessional'.[112]

Drawing on personal and professional experience as others did 'common sense', one judge related that 'at the time it was quite standard' to accept physically disciplining boys, seeing and hearing it through family members and clients, and identifying a time around the 1970s where social responses shifted, 'an evolution of thinking' occurred.[113] Another judge also responded with a similar reference to experience

> First of all, [judges] live here and now. They live in present society; they're not living in an ivory tower. They're not excluded by the rest of the world. So they sense by their own being what's going on around them, and they are themselves sensitive to developments. We may also ask for our research report. What is, let's say the perception of school punishment, the first source of understanding? It's a judge him or herself. They're not isolated in contact with the outside world. The judge of 2023 is not the same judge like the judge in 1959. […] When I grew up, it was perfectly normal that I get slapped by my teacher if I was making trouble class in the class. Now it's a capital crime. So of course, when the case arises a judge will take the floor and say, 'Yes, back in my time, that was okay but now it's no longer acceptable'. Many of the judges, for instance, have kids themselves. So everybody brings in their own experience, their own perceptions, and their own understanding of how things should be. They don't say, if that's what you ask, 'Oh, yeah, we're a living instrument, we should look into the twenty-first century', it comes naturally. [114]

So for this judge too, 'living instrument' was supplanted in deliberations by individual experiences of suffering. Experience and common sense were, pithily put, conduits channelling shared standards. Continuing this explanation, the same judge offered that:

> What people require from judges is that they live on the moon, but are aware of everything that happens. […] Every judge is also a human being who participates in society. […] You don't need to have lost somebody yourself to imagine how the suffering is […] it's not because you have studied law books,

[111] ECtHR20, judge.
[112] ECtHR19, former judge.
[113] ECtHR26, judge.
[114] ECtHR20, judge.

> it's because you participate in life that you can assess what it is. No law book provides for any standard of how much you give. […] The problem is that these are basically abstract legal concepts […] But if you come to what a human being feels in his own flesh […] you try to be the average, reasonable person.

In reflecting such sentiment and using the same 'moon' metaphor, another judge identified a similar inevitability of experience in applying abstract legal concepts: 'we don't come from the moon. […] Thirty or forty years ago, we thought that corporal punishment of children by teachers was okay, now we don't have separate legal regimes for illegitimate children. Now, we find the term offensive and harmful. That's been an evolution for entire societies'.[115] This discussion on common sense more broadly will be returned to in Chapter 6.

Evolution as revolution

What if evolution would mean a deviation from doctrine, from precedent? Where there was established caselaw, explained one judge, on a particular issue or an adjacent issue that can be imported, 'living instrument' was not invoked ('normally that's it') unless 'compelling reasons' existed to not follow it.[116] For this judge, this meant that the 'living instrument' doctrine was used where judges want to either 'deviate' from or 'develop' jurisprudence. Invoking the 'living instrument' doctrine, for one senior registry lawyer with whom this resonated, mostly depended 'on the courage and on the willingness of the judges […] if they are visionaries, if they want to introduce some new standards, not necessarily reflecting our current caselaw' as well as 'personality and background'.[117] In their own work, this lawyer expressed a preference for 'restraint', holding strong to precedent, explaining: 'I wouldn't be proposing anything revolutionary; I don't think that's my role'. A sitting judge explained that some fellow judges would offer 'the new visions, the new lines, and then some will be more conservative, more prudent, more trying to guard what we already have'.[118] So the doctrine was understood to announce a strong stance, so strong it could mark one out as a visionary or revolutionary.

[115] ECtHR8, judge.
[116] ECtHR14, judge.
[117] ECtHR23, senior registry lawyer.
[118] ECtHR14, judge.

Standing against its overuse, one judge characterized the 'living instrument' doctrine as 'complicated and disputed', which he saw as not necessarily to expand but 'to keep the Convention alive', reflecting that the Court 'already went very far, according to some too far, in broadening the scope of Article 3 [...] wanting to see to virtually anything that is bad'.[119] Sounding such a note of caution, the same judge explained that there was a 'need to take a step back' in the expansion of Article 3 given that it was an absolute right (and as such 'considered to be the most serious provision in the Convention') and because of the need to remain legitimate and persuasive vis-à-vis member states. Whether the protection of the prohibition according to this view was to be extended was a matter of political persuasion—that the broader integrity of the prohibition was to be protected.

These accounts continued to confirm previous research on the application of the 'living instrument' which has found it to be 'rather unproblematic in cases where there have been obvious changes in state practice or relevant rules of international law and it is inevitable to interpret a given treaty in light of these changes'.[120] Interviewees generally admitted to the caution with which institutions have acted—with clear implications for expanded recognition of psychological suffering.

Dynamic interpretation was perceived as progressive and, as such, potentially expanding state obligations. It was best, some thought, to argue that what was being asked for from the IACtHR was *merely* to explicate established standards, not expand them. This indicated a pragmatic sense of caution around how much psychological suffering could be recognized explicitly. In sum, while invoking evolution was accepted as uncontroversial in principle, and as manifest in the recognition of emergent forms of suffering, interviewees from both inside and outside the IACtHR focussed on the contingency on the composition of the judges and the Secretariat and opted for a cautious and constrained use. Invoking evolution around changing socio-political standards on psychological suffering, as this broader avoidance of stoking contestation conceivably meant, required careful consideration and could not always be freely foregrounded.

In speaking caution against dynamic interpretation, one sitting CAT member preferred to rule on the socio-political standards in 'historical' cases

[119] ECtHR14, judge.

[120] Daniel Moeckli and Nigel White, 'Treaties as "Living Instruments"' in Dino Kritsiotis and Michael Bowman (eds), *Conceptual and Contextual Perspectives on the Modern Law of Treaties* (CUP 2018) 156.

such as *Coppin* and *Zentveld v New Zealand*[121] which were prevalent at the time of the experiences complained about, telling me:[122]

> we asked ourselves what was normal at that time in society […] we had to prove to ourselves that the matters in question were illegal [under customary international law] at that time. We knew it was bad from today's standards but can't hold states to account like that, otherwise we would have a lot of historical cases. The NZ case involved use of electro shock therapy. We asked ourselves whether the CAT can even assess historical cases by today's standards. It was a technical discussion. It was difficult to say: was UNCAT even applicable then?[123]

The reluctance to invoke 'living instrument' was confirmed by applicant lawyers at all institutions. One take was: 'we used to do that all the time, because we were trying to get the Court to look at the facts in a different way; where there were violations which didn't appear on first sight to be violations [which needed] progressive interpretation.'[124] The point had been accepted by the Court, and the argument packed away by this advocate. Another found it to have worked within limits: 'what a judge might say fifty years ago, "it is just aches and pains when forced to stand up for X hours", now all realized, no, that's a deliberate thing to break someone's spirit […] but there is a limit to where the Court will go, because it is ultimately an international tribunal, they're not a small claims court.'[125] Others paid no attention as they found their cases to be flagrant and obvious.[126] Another was straight-up pessimistic: 'all courts are by their nature conservative. […] if you're lucky, you will get a dissent, or a separate opinion, which will push the boat forwards.'[127]

Other applicant lawyers had no qualms about invoking 'living instrument' as it assisted in opening up the consideration of societal therefore structural issues[128] or could imagine that there could be an occasion when 'you have some past jurisprudence against you, then you have no other option, you have to say, you Court, you need to change the way you're interpreting this treaty, so

121 CAT-C-68-D-852-2017.
122 CAT8, member.
123 This was effectively a denial of dynamic interpretation in historical cases. What is more, Elizabeth Coppin not only argued historical suffering but also one that was continuing, especially given the lack of redress and recognition.
124 ECtHR38, applicant lawyer.
125 ECtHR31, applicant lawyer.
126 ECtHR21, applicant lawyer; ECtHR34, applicant lawyer.
127 ECtHR30, applicant lawyer.
128 IACtHR8, applicant lawyer.

as to stay with the times'.[129] To spell this out, however, could amount to an admission that 'you're on unproven ground so it's better to avoid it and just say, "look, under the standards that we've all agreed to, and they've already established these"'. Arguing that the IACtHR should recognize sexual violations as being more than just rape, the applicant lawyer admitted, was wanting 'slightly dynamic interpretation, but we didn't say it that way' but that 'it's important to explicitly recognize these forms of torture which already fit your standards but just haven't been explicitly analysed this way before'. Much more than evolutive interpretation, this lawyer characterized this as 'original' interpretation because 'we're still at a preliminary stage of that analysis, it wouldn't even be dynamic, as those words have been on the books for years'. Progressive interpretation followed only 'once they have established certain standards, then they want the jurisprudence to be evolving'.[130]

Composition and consensus

That evolution operated implicitly or 'naturally' occasionally led to the expression of the view that assessment and disposition of cases was a collective exercise ('we do consult each other because it's a collective effort to prepare a sound judgment'[131]). Relatedly, weekly meetings between all the section registrars and the Jurisconsult to 'discuss where the caselaw is going' was another means of ensuring the coherence of caselaw took place.[132] Some Grand Chamber cases were deliberately composed, one judge cynically claimed, to achieve a certain disposition.[133] Deliberations, including around categorization detailed in the previous chapter, were influenced by the interest to preserve collegiality and to achieve consensus ('a collegial majority, not necessarily unanimity')—seen as more difficult the bigger the composition in a given case.[134]

Despite lengthy deliberations, one judge explained that judges were 'very often in agreement' as the judge rapporteur's draft was often followed and unquestioned.[135] The Guide and its 'knowledge-sharing platform' were seen to shut down contestation, with many interviewees at the Court asking me whether I had consulted it. Some judges and senior registry lawyers pointed to

129 IACtHR9, applicant lawyer.
130 IACtHR1, applicant lawyer.
131 ECtHR6, senior registry lawyer.
132 ECtHR3, senior registry lawyer.
133 ECtHR19, former judge.
134 ECtHR26, judge.
135 ECtHR20, judge.

the platform for improving jurisprudential coherence and consistency.[136] For some, it meant that Article 3 'is not as complicated as you might think',[137] with precedent and the guidance of the Jurisconsult being straightforward on the distinction.[138]

Composition also played a part at the IACtHR—with progressive judges being the lynchpins in evolution. Evolution, for a senior IACtHR lawyer, was contingent on a composition of judges with a 'tendency to find more violations',[139] which the lawyer attributed to a tendency or a 'general mood' and change in the Latin American context to debate new forms of rights such as social, environmental, or indigenous rights ('to victimize some conduct that ten years ago we didn't'). This translated to the Court being 'softer than in the past' in terms of finding torture violations, requiring less evidence. Compositions also disabled. A previous all-male older composition did not want to move on certain issues like rape.[140] When cases moved from rape to include other forms of sexual violence, there happened to be two very proactive women on the bench.[141] As one applicant lawyer explained: 'there are cases in which you don't expect the Court to say something, and they come up with a very innovative or very progressive standard (because you have one judge who has an agenda)'—with Judge Medina seen as an example concerning cases on sexual violence who had a 'very good ear' and who was 'very willing to dedicate part of the case to that analysis'.[142]

As at the IACtHR, the potential for progressive interpretation was also subject to the CAT's composition.[143] Situating the discussion in a historical context as at the ECtHR, a CAT member explained that states shift their practices ('physical torture was also the norm before centuries ago'); with each shift there is a 'need for someone to identify this as a human rights violation; you also need to watch out for the aim of prison; if people walk out worse, then something is happening'. Compared to the ECtHR, where normative consensus was more readily identified, this was not as easy 'at the universal level' because 'whereas Europeans have an easier time to reach consensus on common values, when you add Russia and China, it becomes different'.[144] Another member explained

[136] ECtHR1, senior registry lawyer; ECtHR4, judge; ECtHR24, judge.
[137] ECtHR20, judge.
[138] ECtHR13, judge.
[139] IACtHR15, senior IACtHR lawyer.
[140] IACtHR5, former senior IACmHR lawyer; IACtHR10, judge.
[141] IACtHR5, former senior IACmHR lawyer.
[142] IACtHR3, applicant lawyer.
[143] CAT2, former member; CAT10, member; CAT15, member; CAT4, former member.
[144] CAT10, member.

that this meant that there was an 'individual approach, not a collective sense at the CAT'.[145]

Experience was implicit yet instrumental: 'this is inherent in the decision-making process unless we get to using electrodes',[146] 'it is difficult to forget this aspect when we have to discuss, when we come into the room with our background',[147] 'work experience obviously counts but personal qualities count too',[148] 'consciously we operate professionally, unconsciously experiences are also at play',[149] 'we all come with our own traditions; I can see that me and the Chinese member have both brought with us the contexts in which we were conditioned'.[150] The influence of composition was returned to time and again, indicating a growing tension between regressive and progressive approaches. These exchanges pointed to questions of competence returned to in the next chapter.

In rejecting the premise that evolution did not really feature in the jurisprudence of the CAT, one former member retorted, 'in fact, it does', going on to explain that this was often the terrain on which conservative members (the 'legal positivists') restrained the progressive members from expansive interpretation, arguing that 'this is not what the states signed up to'.[151] The 'legal positivists', or as another member characterized them, those wanting 'a strict interpretation of international law', were viewed as a barrier to expansionist recognition. Counting himself in the expansionist camp, he countered that 'when states ratify a convention, they also ratify perhaps implicitly the right of the Committee to interpret the Convention in a more protective beneficial direction for victims over time'. He continued

> But in much of my time as a member of CAT this was strongly blocked by a combination of people that were representing conservative states that did not want CAT to develop. [...] So there were victories where we, I can safely say, moved forward the boundaries. So it wasn't that it didn't happen but it happened to a very limited degree, I admit, which was also quite demotivating for me, personally, that fighting and fighting was with very limited results.

[145] CAT16, member.
[146] CAT9, member.
[147] CAT10, member.
[148] CAT14, member.
[149] CAT8, member.
[150] CAT9, member.
[151] CAT2, former member.

So it was a conservative composition as promoted by states that encouraged narrow interpretations. It must be remembered that members sit in their own right, independently of their country of origin.

In all, it was difficult to gauge how such considerations sensitized the interviewees, here as elsewhere, to psychological suffering with precision beyond general prescription. There had been growing tension between narrow and expansionist positions. There were indeed expansive or evolutive advances made over the years, but the current composition slowed this momentum.

Selecting standards

All three institutions opened up for socio-political standards through importing external standards pertaining to how suffering was more broadly understood as un/acceptable. While actors readily accepted the role of these sources, there remained questions of their utility, of *when* and *to what extent* they were used. How were these to be reconciled against the broad caution just expressed? What became clear is how the wide discretion to resort to these sources has produced a variability and unpredictably in this practice. Previous research has raised a similar question in quantifying the parallel phenomenon of 'subsequent practice', identifying two distinct sets of issues, presuppositions of which are rarely unpacked: '(i) *whose* practice is relevant; and (ii) *what* kind of practice one should take into account'.[152] This, as previous research has argued, involves preferences and is not a neutral process. Looking at formal documents such as judgments, for instance, is advanced as such a *selection*. Finding a similar selection in my caselaw review, I sought to unpack it through the interviews. I found that while there is a broad recognition that external standards existed including on psychologically oriented practices such as solitary confinement, caution bred a selectivity in how these standards were applied.

Consensus—time—caution

When asked what judges looked at in gauging socio-political standards, sources mostly included international material and consensus among states' domestic

[152] Andrea Bianchi, 'Law, Time, and Change: The Self-Regulatory Function of Subsequent Practice' in Georg Nolte, (ed), *Treaties and Subsequent Practice* (OUP 2013) 134.

law.[153] Most interviewees at the ECtHR, to start, explained that external standards were a central means of gauging socio-political considerations, especially from the CPT.[154] The principled stance here was one of receptivity that the Court 'is always attentive to positions held by other international institutions such as the CPT and the United Nation's Committee Against Torture'—although this did not come without an assessment of and differentiation between sources, having done so in surveying the international law on restraints in psychiatry.[155] Suffering, that which met the minimum severity threshold, was to be assessed by reference to such standards.[156]

Receptivity to broader standards was readily accepted in principle at the IACtHR—for which it is widely recognized.[157] Standards were viewed as key to moving the IACtHR in 'changing the narrative' and in 'convincing judges that something has changed',[158] as a means of 'building its defence against the accusation of judicial overreach, to sort of build a convincing judgment'.[159] As with the ECtHR, this required most work to be done outside the IACtHR including through the use of the Istanbul Protocol, UN, and IACmHR reports.[160] Yet, the IACtHR has selected standards with little explanation—'consider[ing] itself absolutely free to determine when and how the ACHR evolves'.[161] Moreover, the IACtHR's treatment of consensus has been criticized within[162] and its lack of justification for how it uses external sources (as 'cherry-picking') and how these have 'influenced the dynamic interpretation of the ACHR' has received criticism from outside the Court.[163] Beyond identifying the lack of systematic approach to IACtHR's selection of standards, neither my caselaw review nor

[153] ECtHR14, judge.

[154] ECtHR10, judge; ECtHR26, judge; ECtHR16, former senior registry lawyer; ECtHR6, senior registry lawyer; ECtHR3, senior registry lawyer; ECtHR25, senior registry lawyer. CPT reports, in short, document the conditions and practice in places of deprivation through periodic visits to CoE member states. While the CPT is not an adjudicatory body and does not strictly juridically determine conditions and practices as falling afoul of the prohibition, its findings are taken as indicative and instructive to that end.

[155] *Aggerholm v Denmark* [2020] ECtHR 45439/18 [100].

[156] ECtHR12, senior registry lawyer; ECtHR29, senior registry lawyer.

[157] IACtHR10, judge; IACtHR2, applicant lawyer. The IACtHR can use external international standards under Article 29 of the ACHR (that it can incorporate international jurisprudence) to make it easier to invoke new understandings.

[158] IACtHR3, applicant lawyer.

[159] IACtHR4, former senior IACtHR lawyer.

[160] IACtHR10, judge.

[161] Alvaro Paul, 'Decision-Making Process of the Inter-American Court: An Analysis Prompted by the "In Vitro Fertilization" Case' (2014) 21 (1) ILSA Journal of International & Comparative Law 87, 114.

[162] *Atala-Riffo and Daughters v Chile* [2012] IACtHR per Judge Perez-Perez [20–21].

[163] Taína Garcia Maia, 'External Sources and Inter-American Court of Human Rights' (2023) 72 International and Comparative Law Quarterly 977, 1011.

the interviews yielded much more information at the IACtHR—particularly as relating to psychological suffering.

Everything was fine where there was regional normative consensus, but what about when there wasn't? Normative consensus was invoked by a senior registry lawyer as especially enabling the ECtHR to advance its jurisprudence (to take a stronger stance vis-à-vis outlier states) but in the absence of consensus among adjudicators, the lawyer explained, 'the Court will wait, it will not push'.[164] This was also characterized as a means of denying recognition through engendering a caution within the Court, with rape as torture discussed in these frames ('If you look at rape, these is no consensus across Europe; some say all rape is torture and others say no, nonsense. You hear these discussions').[165]

External standards, reported a former judge expressing a more critical view, were treated with scepticism inside the ECtHR because they were either soft law ('in spite of all the consensus, the Court simply wants to ignore them and say that there should be leeway to not consider') or because there was not always consistency between external authorities ('you can find very interesting cases where the Court is a bit divided between different standards provided by medical science; the Court should have gone further, should have had a serious medical debate').[166] A senior registry lawyer pinned this on a reluctance to be proactive and receptive to broader social change:[167]

> We are not a Court that is always ready to make a breakthrough. More and more we look at the notion of consensus. I wish we would give this up. Consensus is easily evoked if it is a case involving a practice in the last government of Europe. No consensus equals no violation. The Court does not now or in the past say 'this is a new society—let's change things'.

Waiting for any normative consensus, including psychological suffering, meant the wait for recognition would be longer. Others agreed that things took time but instead naturalized it.[168] Taking time was a procedural issue that standards also had to be adopted or domestic remedies exhausted at a national level, meaning that developments came to the Court later. An inevitability

[164] ECtHR3, senior registry lawyer.
[165] ECtHR12, senior registry lawyer.
[166] ECtHR19, former judge.
[167] ECtHR12, senior registry lawyer.
[168] ECtHR6, senior registry lawyer; ECtHR22, senior registry lawyer; ECtHR28, senior registry lawyer.

was sounded on having to wait for external developments—with one senior registry lawyer explaining that 'we see those changes in the society through the applications […] for example, this issue of domestic violence'.[169] A senior registry lawyer referred to the fact that the Court first judged on domestic violence 'awfully late', despite being mindful that 'there is a time […] public discussion and debate needs to take place in order to get there' which made the Court 'more of a reactionary mechanism'.[170] It took time, in a senior registry lawyer's reckoning, for standards to be developed internationally (referring to the Minnesota Protocol, NMR, and relevant UN and CPT standards) which the Court becomes aware of through pleadings by applicants and third parties.[171] Continuing, the same lawyer offered: 'there's a certain inevitability about it, I don't really want to use the language of "living instrument", the Court would say that there now seems to be movement […] a consensus at the international level'. Consensus was repeated time and again.

CAT practice was, in contrast, largely internally referencing. It referenced its state reviews where it could but otherwise did not explore international legal standards outside of certain well-established precedents as emanating from the European and Inter-American systems. That the CAT had effectively its own source of fact-finding through its state review process demonstrated a reliance on its OHCHR personnel to bring UN standards to bear on individual decisions, and rarely referred to standards outside of the UN system, at least in cases on Articles 1 and 16. Caution at the CAT, as elsewhere, was explained away in understanding that changes take time. When discussing why Article 1 violations were so focussed on the physical, a former member explained: 'frankly, it has to do with evidence' but also that these 'treaties have been in place a few decades only, you only have hundreds of cases in many of these systems, except with the European system which is much more developed in this regard—and the issue of mental suffering or illness has been a taboo in many developing countries, and not so developing countries'.[172] While European caselaw had come far, the same could not be expected of other regions of the world. Perhaps it was that victims outside of Europe were not arguing mental suffering given lack of awareness and access to expertise. Further to the invocation of time, an OHCHR lawyer working with individual communications explained that 'there hasn't been a sudden change, as all is incremental and gradual, with general comments making jurisprudence much more complex'.[173] Cases took time

[169] ECtHR29, senior registry lawyer.
[170] ECtHR28, senior registry lawyer.
[171] ECtHR22, former senior registry lawyer.
[172] CAT6, former member.
[173] CAT11, UN legal officer.

to exhaust domestic remedies before getting to Geneva—this meant for one sitting member that they could not really be at the forefront of developing jurisprudence as it will happen at a domestic level first.[174]

Selectivity and solitary

In examining selection, I asked how and when adjudicators referred to external standards on solitary confinement as promoted by the CPT and the UN NMR, which have had a negligible impact on the caselaw to date. While not all potentially torturous practices which might not leave physical marks (e.g. life, threats and restraints) come with explicit bright-lines (i.e. clear rules on when it becomes harmful and prohibited), solitary confinement is one of the rare few which now does. In 2015, informed by legal and health experts,[175] the UN revised its framework on the use of solitary confinement in the UN NMR[176] which have been followed to some degree by the CPT[177] and CoE.[178] The ECtHR, until very recently, had not cited the NMR.[179] The ECtHR's extensive caselaw on solitary confinement thus remains undisturbed—despite such shifts.[180] I asked why.

One judge explained that they were 'generally not viewed seriously by states […] many countries have always been very far from implementing the 1955 edition of the Standard Minimum Rules […] they never adhere to lower standards, and they accepted higher standards, because they didn't think it was serious'.[181] Another senior registry lawyer explained even if it was not as strict as the NMR, 'we'll stick to the European'—meaning the European Prison Rules.[182] This was 'obviously political', this lawyer said, who saw the Court 'let

[174] CAT15, member.

[175] Jennifer Peirce, 'Making the Mandela Rules: Evidence, Expertise, and Politics in the Development of Soft Law International Prison Standards' (2018) 43 (2) Queen's Law Journal 263; see also UN SRT, Report (2016) A/66/268.

[176] UN NMR rules 43 and 45.

[177] CoE, CPT 'Solitary Confinement of Prisoners', CPT/Inf(2011)28-part2.

[178] EPR 60.6.a: 'the confinement of a prisoner for more than 22 hours a day without meaningful human contact, shall never be imposed on children, pregnant women, breastfeeding mothers or parents with infants in prison'.

[179] *Schmidt and Smigol v Estonia* [2023] ECtHR 3501/20 [134].

[180] The ECtHR has (fleetingly and vaguely) referred to the UN SMR/NMR only on a handful of occasions in relation to the removal of prisoners, contact with the outside world, separation of prisoner categories, cell conditions, and restraints. A forceful exception to this is in a dissent lamenting the majority's failure to consider the UN SMR/NMR and the CoE's own soft-law standards in the EPR and associated commentary (*Muršić v Croatia*, separate opinion [37, 62]). That regional regulatory harmony is resisted in the name of flexibility is telling here.

[181] ECtHR4, judge.

[182] ECtHR12, senior registry lawyer.

the other European authorities go first as we need more cohesion between them but if a judge has a particular interest and is willing to accept the consequences, they can go ahead and make their case'. Another lawyer agreed with as much: 'we always felt that we have our own European set of standards, our own legal instrument, which was for us sufficient and good'; that nobody had yet brought a well-argued case focussing on solitary without 'slipping into other issues'.[183] The 'slipping' was picked up by another registry lawyer who elaborated that 'solitary confinement doesn't come on its own before the Court; it's always combined with its harsh sentence or inadequate material conditions'.[184] This repeated the earlier argument that it was visionaries or revolutionaries that shifted the standards. In fact, no judge or senior registry lawyer saw an issue with the ECtHR caselaw on solitary confinement ('I don't think the Court very much lags behind';[185] *Öcalan* and *Ramirez Sanchez* relied on CPT and EPR standards, finding 'certain treatments are inherent in the detention itself'[186]).

One interviewee, an independent expert on solitary confinement, was more critical in observing that 'both decisions [*Öcalan* and *Ramirez Sanchez*] are wrongly decided, quite frankly. It's just unbelievable that the Court would find that solitary confinement, more specifically, that lasted several years in both cases, did not arise to the level of torture'.[187] The expert thought that the ECtHR 'yielded to the pressures of state not to call torture only because the victims were, in both cases, well known people accused of terrorism'. To my question of why no case of prolonged solitary confinement had so far been categorized as torture, the same interviewee held that 'it's a matter of time before a case with all the characteristics that we're talking about comes before a court and then we'll have a little more clarity', though the current trend in litigation focussed on overcrowding. Again, the 'these things take time' line was invoked to sustain hope and trust in the process. So it was not only actors within institutions whose interpretive frames are controlled but also those without.

For the IACtHR, international standards 'like the Nelson Mandela Rules played a role in assessing objectivity' in solitary confinement cases. According to one senior lawyer having made their own study here, weight attributed to the Rules could not be generalized because they were

183 ECtHR1, senior registry lawyer.
184 ECtHR25, senior registry lawyer.
185 ECtHR4, judge.
186 ECtHR6, senior registry lawyer.
187 IACtHR7, former senior IACmHR lawyer.

> not decisive, because it really depends on what other evidence there is in the case, but it's important because in this area of solitary confinement, and even of the expansive interpretation of torture, we are in the middle of the development of international standards, and there's still a lot to explore. The former Special Rapporteur can say this or that, but if what you argue is based on a non-binding but authoritative standard, like the Nelson Mandela Rules, that's very helpful, because they have been around since the 1950s. […] And they determine whether the prison conditions are such that they violate the prohibition. […] Same goes for, for example, the Istanbul Protocol and the Minnesota Protocol.[188]

As with the IACtHR, the interviews failed to yield much on the CAT, particularly as it related to standards of psychological suffering. The selectivity apparent at the CAT, despite the established nature of standards such as the NMR and IP, not only indicated institutional limitations to deliberate and decide cases (arising out of personnel and time restrictions) but was also suggestive of a lack of expertise at a level that is expected from *the* international torture expert body.

In sum, interviewees rarely identified selectivity in standards as problematic, which was comfortably explained away by procedural and institutional factors. Time was again invoked for international standards to be developed and adopted by states before a normative consensus could be identified. External standards did exist and could be helpful but required an incentive or some inclination to be considered. So despite the position that time was required for consensus, even where sources were established, they were conveniently overlooked in realizing conservative findings—with no omission starker than the UN NMR in solitary confinement cases. A close use of standards resulted in the deferral of discretion, the preservation of which was viewed with a premium.

Conclusions

It is striking how rarely explicitly and deeply the doctrine of dynamic (or evolutive) interpretation features in the caselaw—accepted by and large as operating implicitly and intuitively. While receptivity to social and scientific understandings was accepted in principle in how actors recognized psychological

[188] IACtHR7, former senior IACmHR lawyer.

suffering, how these impacted individual cases could not be readily elaborated. In all, the social world, though influential, was never determinative of legal dispositions. There emerged from all this two dominant, though not mutually exclusive, strands of explanation: informational (and environmental) and political (and policy-oriented).

Informational explanations stressed that actors depended on colleagues and conditions, near and far, in shaping decisions. The institutions could not, interviewees repeated time and again, develop an understanding out of their own initiative or in the absence of incontrovertible information—cases and their corroboration had to be brought to them. The institutions had to be *compelled* by their users. The institution needed to be *made* to understand the gravity of the suffering experienced by applicants, given its complexity and subjectivity. That social changes took place gradually 'over time', that the time was not right, and restricted expansive protection were similarly explained as being beyond the control of the three institutions. Caution and consensus also influenced the selection of standards. Evolution, operating implicitly and intuitively, to accept interviewees' accounts has been contingent on composition and, in turn, the ability to reach consensus. Consensus, as many interviewees claimed, took time.

The more political (or policy-oriented) arguments held that caution had to be exercised to preserve authority vis-à-vis a certain state or that the composition of judges or members was not conducive to moving in a direction towards recognition. These were also guised in the guarded and confused sorting, often justified on procedural pragmatism, consensus, and collaboration. When, where, and how actors looked for socio-political standards had implications for how cases were reasoned and substantiated. Looking at consensus among states engendered a conservatism as grounded in a lowest-common-denominator logic. The politically oriented preferences evident here, between constraint and expansive interpretation, confirm previous research which has looked at the changing political contexts in which the institutions have operated since their inception.[189] The positions of the interviewees proved too varied to reliably plot them along any kind of pragmatism–idealism scale.

Choices were, nevertheless, made between pragmatism on the one hand and idealism on the other. The selectivity and lack of transparency as identified here also confirm the broader scholarship critiquing uncritical repetition, intangibility, slipperiness, and oversimplification, finding that their meaning is taken to be obvious, neat, and tidy when nothing could be further from

[189] Yildiz (n 20); Yildiz (n 42).

being the case.[190] To be sure, interviews helped explain some decisions but also raised other questions, particularly in connecting recognition to questions of experience and common sense (which carried quite some weight for adjudicators). How well placed were institutional actors in even processing expertise? How much weight was even placed on the expertise? The grounds of evolution evinced, instead, the interpretive struggle between different interests, not simply technical or legal—tensions which continue to flow through the next chapter.

[190] Kanstantsin Dzehtsiarou, 'European Consensus and the Evolutive Interpretation of the European Convention on Human Rights' (2011) 12 German Law Journal 1730; Kanstantsin Dzehtsiarou, *Can the European Court of Human Rights Shape European Public Order?* (CUP 2022) argues that these are similarly left 'conveniently' vague, intuitive, unclear, and unusable.

5
Scientific expertise

> When it comes to the Convention as a 'living instrument' as a developing concept, the Court will take account of novel scientific understandings which were not prevalent in the 60s, 70s, and 80s.[1]

> The difficulty with stealth tortures is precisely the difficulty of finding a home in the body, a place that authorizes the process of asking for acknowledgement and recognition.[2]

Experience has established distinct evidentiary difficulties in torture-related cases—arising out of the availability (due to state denial) and assessment (due to the need to establish gravity and causality) of evidence. Scientific expertise has been developed and deployed, in this light, to improve documentation practices and, in turn, improve legal decision-making. There is an ostensible significance ascribed to scientific expertise in substantiating psychological suffering, for which questions of evidence are amplified given its invisibility and complex causality. In contrast to physical suffering, for instance, psychologically oriented practices might produce damage that appears months or even years after an experience at the hands of the state, if at all. This has invited doubt on the part of states and adjudicators as compared to physically overt suffering.

As noted from the book's outset, for these and other reasons, the ECtHR itself has even 'concede[d] that there are certain difficulties involved in assessing claims relating to alleged mental suffering or humiliation in the absence of actual bodily injury'.[3] The recognition of psychological suffering has thus necessitated a more rigorous assessment than with physical suffering—closely

[1] President Judge Robert Spano, Talk, 'What role for human duties, obligations and responsibilities in our European human rights discourse?', 2 December 2021, University of Copenhagen, responding to my question on how well placed the ECtHR was in gauging invisible phenomena such as mental suffering.

[2] Darius Rejali, 'Modern Torture as a Civic Marker: Solving a Global Anxiety with a New Political Technology' (2003) 2 (2) Journal of Human Rights 161.

[3] *Dzerkorashvili and others v Georgia* [2023] ECtHR 70572/16 [68].

Torture and the Recognition of Psychological Suffering in International Law. Ergün Cakal, Oxford University Press.
 DOI: 10.1093/oso/9780198989493.003.0005

binding shifting socio-political standards on suffering to the building of a scientific evidence-base on which advocates and adjudicators regularly purport to base their assessments.[4] The then president of the ECtHR, Robert Spano, said as much in the epigraph to this chapter, holding up the coupling of the 'social' and 'scientific' as facilitating a more complete and correct adjudication. Scientific expertise, by which I primarily mean evidence produced based on recognized biomedical and psychological methodologies, has indeed ascended to an authoritative role in the anti-torture field—particularly with the skills of doctors and psychologists routinely sought to reliably investigate and document allegations.[5]

Since the 1970s, on such a premise, scientific experts (namely, medical doctors and psychologists primarily associated with civil society organizations) have worked to reach a consensus on how psychological suffering figures in documentation: that torture 'can be life-threatening even though no physical marks can be found at the objective examination—even shortly after torture';[6] that 'the absence of such physical evidence should not be construed to suggest that torture did not occur, since such acts of violence against persons frequently leave no marks or permanent scars';[7] that documenting psychological, as compared to physical, suffering remains limited;[8] that direct (first-hand) evidence is 'highly elusive',[9] particularly if it does not leave physical marks;[10] and that a clear causality between act and impact should not be expected.[11] Such understandings underpin contemporary practices of medico-legal documentation. What is foregrounded in this complex calculus has been relevant

[4] Disciplines such as psychology or psychiatry did not always enjoy the same level of authority as today. These significations change over time—with legal, medical, and psychological actors needing to recognize this and respond accordingly.

[5] Darius Rejali, *Torture and Democracy* (Princeton University Press 2007) 16; Basak Can, 'Human Rights, Humanitarianism, and State Violence: Medical Documentation of Torture in Turkey' (2016) 30 (3) Medical Anthropology Quarterly 342–58.

[6] Hans Draminsky Petersen and Peter Jacobsen, 'Life-Threatening Torture without Visible Marks' (1985) 13 Scandinavian Journal of Social Medicine 87, 88.

[7] Istanbul Protocol I (1999) [161].

[8] Pau Pérez-Sales, *Psychological Torture: Definition, Evaluation and Measurement* (Routledge 2016) 126; UN HRC, CCPR-C-107-D-1945-2010 (2013): given the difficulty of proving psychological methods, 'investigation of such acts should be exhaustive'.

[9] Gabriella Echeverria and others, 'Panel IV: Challenges to Proving Cases of Torture before the Committee against Torture' (2013) 20 (4) Human Rights Brief 33, 36.

[10] Claudio Grossman, 'The Normative Value of the Istanbul Protocol' in IRCT, *Shedding Light on a Dark Practice: Using the Istanbul Protocol to Document Torture* (IRCT 2009) 11.

[11] For Pérez-Sales (n 8) 274–75, it is a fallacy to expect 'an unequivocal *causal* relationship between certain practices and their consequences in order to determine the limits of torture' and 'When medicine in general and specifically psychiatry face the issue of defining torture, they can establish practices with a *high risk ratio* [relative risk] of causing damage, and [...] this damage is of sufficient magnitude to be banned internationally. [...] They can also establish operational (reviewable) criteria that allow a combined group of techniques to qualify as "torture" based on the relative likelihood that these combined practices will cause physical or psychological harm.'

actors' ability to precisely and persuasively argue and apprehend suffering in the face of invisibility and deniability—as compared to physically damaging, hence 'visible', suffering.[12]

This chapter presents how actors have used (or not) scientific evidence based on such understandings in substantiating psychological suffering before them. The discussion is presented in three sections. The first section ('Absence') establishes the institutional recognition formulated around the evidentiary absence (availability, flexibility, and difficulties), broadly but also as pertaining to psychological suffering. The second section ('Competence') explores the factors problematizing evidentiary practice in terms of the advocates' and adjudicators' ability to understand, argue, and/or assess the scientific expertise submitted to corroborate cases involving psychological suffering. The third section ('Deference') then examines how advocates and adjudicators defer to, or are respectful of or receptive to, scientific expertise—how much weight it is afforded and why.

Absence

The absence, or availability, of evidence in the following discussion consists of two aspects. The first (in 'Difficulty—flexibility—plurality') relates to how the particular difficulty of readily appreciating psychological suffering, and torture more broadly, has been accepted at the three institutions in principle. It also looks at how the institutions have flexed given the absence of direct evidence, but also coming to prefer medical expertise, somewhat problematically particularly when it is not available. The second ('Subjectivity—objectivity—visibility') relates to how much testimony standing on its own, in the absence of other evidence, counts.

Difficulty—flexibility—plurality

The question of what standard of proof should apply in torture-related cases, given that much evidence is suppressed by states, appeared as a point of contention in the first international case. The *Greek Case* fixed the standard at 'beyond reasonable doubt' which it understood as 'not a doubt based on a merely

[12] Psychological suffering can be visible in a multitude of ways, for instance through a victim's behaviour, but this, again, may not readily be captured as a scar in a photo.

theoretical possibility or raised in order to avoid a disagreeable conclusion'.[13] The reasoning there helpfully went on to recognize 'certain inherent difficulties' in substantiating torture-related cases because:

> First, a victim or a witness able to corroborate his story might hesitate to describe or reveal all that has happened to him for fear of reprisals upon himself or his family. Secondly, acts of torture or ill-treatment by agents of the police or armed services would be carried out as far as possible without witnesses and perhaps without the knowledge of higher authority. Thirdly, where allegations of torture or ill-treatment are made, the authorities, whether the police or armed forces or the Ministries concerned, must inevitably feel that they have a collective reputation to defend, a feeling which would be all the stronger in those authorities that had no knowledge of the activities of the agents against whom the allegations are made. In consequence there may be reluctance of higher authority to admit, or allow inquiries to be made into, facts which might show that the allegations are true.

Finally, the ECmHR drew attention to the notion that 'physical traces of torture or ill-treatment may with lapse of time become unrecognisable, even by medical experts, particularly where the form of torture itself leaves little external marks'.[14] One of the more prescient rearticulations of evidentiary difficulty since has characterized torture as 'practiced in secret, often by experienced interrogators who are skilled at ensuring that it leaves no visible signs on the victim [with] those who are charged with ensuring that torture does not occur—courts, prosecutors and medical personnel—are complicit in its concealment'.[15]

In countering such evidentiary difficulty (due to absence, complexity, asymmetry, or evasiveness), one primary discussion has centred on evidentiary flexibility, namely adjusting (shifting or sharing) standards and burdens of proof.[16] To this end, all three institutions have ascribed to a free and flexible

[13] *Denmark, Norway, Sweden and Netherlands v Greece* [*The Greek Case*] [1969] ECmHR 3321/67, 3322/67, 3323/67, 3344/67, p 196 [30].

[14] ibid, p 197 [31].

[15] *Othman (Abu Qatada) v UK* [2012] ECtHR 8139/09 [276].

[16] ECtHR, Procedural rule 44C (1) relies on presumptions of onus in addressing evidentiary asymmetry; *Selmouni v France* [1999] ECtHR 25803/94 [87] states that 'where an individual is taken into police custody in good health but is found to be injured at the time of release, it is incumbent on the State to provide a plausible explanation of how those injuries were caused'; see *Salman v Turkey* [2000] 21986/93 [100]; *Iskandarov v Russia* [2010] ECtHR 17185/05 [108]; *Ribitsch v Austria* [1995] ECtHR 18896/91 [34]; *Timurtas v Turkey* [2000] ECtHR 23531/94 [66]; CAT, General Comment 1 (1997) A/53/44 [5].

evaluation of evidence in torture-related cases—holding themselves out as the 'master' of their own procedures. The IACtHR, for instance, has claimed for itself an 'ample flexibility to assess the evidence tendered before [it] in accordance with the rules of logic and based on experience'[17] and firmly rejected 'a rigid rule regarding the amount of proof necessary to support the judgment'.[18] Difficulty has also underpinned the CAT's evidentiary regime to not, in principle, expect a high standard of proof[19] especially in order to allow for inconsistencies where immaterial or not raising questions about the general reliability of the case.[20] This flexibility, or unfettered discretion to view and weigh evidence, is closely guarded across all institutions.

This is all important commentary indeed, one which navigates a need for certainty while accommodating the flexibility needed given evidentiary difficulty. That said, how these standards have been applied more broadly has not been entirely consistent or transparent, as they have been variably applied more on a case-by-case basis, lowered in some and heightened in others. Even the apparent adoption of this standard in *Ireland* (1978), which added that the standard could be satisfied by 'the coexistence of sufficiently strong, clear, and concordant inferences, or of similar unrebutted presumptions of fact', has been critiqued as having operated entirely differently in that case—rendering it a 'gift to *raison d'état*' through fixing the *prima facie* burden unduly high.[21]

This discretion, however, has often obscured how the institutions precisely deal with evidentiary difficulties concerning psychological suffering. The clearest instance at the CAT, for example, was where the respondent state referred to a lack of obvious traces of violence which the CAT rejected, explaining that torture 'may leave non-obvious but real traces of violence' and noting that the certificate produced by the complainant reported a neuropsychiatric disorder.[22] In a case involving a handcuffing and blindfolding for eight days, the

[17] *Tibi v Ecuador* [2004] IACtHR [67].

[18] *Velásquez-Rodríguez v Honduras* [1988] IACtHR [127–28].

[19] CAT-C-60-D-653-2015 [9.7]: 'complete accuracy is seldom to be expected by victims'. Fanny De Weck, *Non-Refoulement under the European Convention on Human Rights and the UN Convention Against Torture: The Assessment of Individual Complaints by the European Court of Human Rights under Article 3 ECHR and the United Nations Committee Against Torture under Article 3 CAT* (Brill 2016) 369, 465: the CAT is 'particularly generous in accepting inconsistencies or omissions in cases in which it is established by medical evidence that the complainant has been a victim of torture and is still suffering as a result'.

[20] CAT, General Comment 4 (2017) [49 h–i]: 'Bearing in mind the status of physical and psychological fragility encountered by the majority of complainants such as asylum seekers, former detainees, victims of torture or sexual violence etc., which is conducive to some inconsistencies and/or lapses of memory in their submissions.'

[21] See Marie-Bénédicte Dembour, 'Beyond Reasonable Doubt at Its Worst—But Also at Its Potential Best: Dissecting *Ireland v the United Kingdom*'s No-Torture Finding' (2023) 4 European Convention on Human Rights Law Review 36.

[22] CAT-C-31-D-189-2001 [10.5].

CAT remarked in passing the applicant's reference 'to an article in TORTURE, volume 11, where it is criticized that psychological symptoms do not receive the same recognition by authorities as physical symptoms'.[23] In another case, it noted that the ill-treatment applicant changed after a meeting with a prosecutor, as 'the methods of torture used became more sophisticated, as the police officers were aiming to leave fewer marks on the complainant's body'.[24] The CAT has missed many such opportunities, however, to elaborate how it dealt with the evidentiary difficulties as arising beyond just identifying them.

Acknowledgements of difficulty, and the ensuing self-ascribed flexibility, have also generally informed the wide admissibility of forms of indirect (or circumstantial) evidence: medico-legal reports; similar medical records; testimonies of witnesses and family; administrative information from records and other documents in the place of detention; photos or videos, including from social media; and weapons and other physical evidence, as well as NGO reports.[25] Corroborative circumstantial and contextual evidence has also become significant in certain cases,[26] including through a reliance (though selective) on international standards.[27]

However, the highest chance of success, it has been said, is where victims seek medical attention and documentation promptly following their ill-treatment and bring it to the authorities' attention for fuller investigation.[28] Medico-legal reports, a more sophisticated sub-set of such evidence as prepared by medical doctors and psychologists, have occasionally proven probative in substantiating claims of severe pain, both physical and psychological.[29] Medico-legal

[23] CAT-C-28-D-180-2001 [5.2].

[24] CAT-C-51-D-441-2010 [2.4].

[25] Michael O'Boyle, 'Proof: European Court of Human Rights (ECtHR)' (2018) Max Planck Encyclopedia of International Procedural Law 7; Álvaro Paúl, 'Evidence: Inter-American Court of Human Rights (IACtHR)' (2018) Max Planck Encyclopedia of International Law 24. The CAT too does not appear to be strict in what form of proof it will consider, but often cross-references its findings in state reviews in individual communications.

[26] *Godínez-Cruz* [1989] IACtHR [155]; *González et al v Mexico* ('Cotton Field') [2019] IACtHR [114–64]; *Velásquez-Rodríguez* (n 18) [131–32]; *La Cantuta v Perú* [2006] IACtHR [17–20].

[27] See force-feeding in *Nevmerzhitsky v Ukraine* [2005] ECtHR 54825/00.

[28] Two senior ECtHR registry lawyers having stated as much. See OMCT (Hasan Bakirci and Ugur Erdal), *Article 3 of the European Convention on Human Rights: A Practitioner's Handbook* (OMCT 2006) 136: 'If the applicant is suffering from psychological disturbances as a result of the ill-treatment, it is particularly important that these effects be documented since the finding of such effects requires the Court to make an assessment of a number of subjective elements. A psychological assessment, carried out by a trained specialist, preferably a psychiatrist, "linking" the applicant's psychological problems to his or her allegations will assist the Court in its examination and is strongly recommended.' In terms of medical evidence, the IACtHR expected that it 'should be undertaken regardless of the length of time since the torture'. *Cabrera García and Montiel Flores v Mexico* [2010] IACtHR [122]; *Bueno-Alvez v Argentina* [2007] IACtHR [111–12].

[29] *Savin v Ukraine* [2012] ECtHR 34725/08 [61]: 'the Court attaches weight to the forensic medical experts' findings according to which the applicant's disability was a direct result of the ill-treatment in question'; *Lyapin v Russia* [2014] ECtHR 46956/09 [116]: 'There is medical evidence of the applicant's

documentation, though an umbrella term covering a broad methodology, has come to be represented by a particular civil society movement centred around a particular instrument, the UN Istanbul Protocol (IP), which has championed evidence-based documentation of psychological suffering. Although a *cursory* reading of the caselaw indicates that the IP has garnered general institutional recognition, a more complicated relationship becomes apparent upon a *closer* reading, particularly in cases such as *Coppin* where the IP-compliant evidence is footnoted and forgotten. This will be discussed below on the question of 'deference'.

Subjectivity—objectivity—visibility

In aligning themselves broadly with evidence-based understandings, all three institutions have duly established that suffering is subjective[30] and relative to each victim,[31] and that its visibility does not equate to its gravity.[32] That torture is especially difficult to prove as it may leave no visible signs has also underwritten an acknowledgement that victims should not be subject to unattainable or rigid evidentiary burdens. The ECtHR has gone as far as to hold that 'it may well suffice that the victim is humiliated in his own eyes, even if not in the eyes of others'.[33] Yet, testimony has not normally been afforded such unscrutinized

injuries following his release from police custody including reports by forensic medical experts, which corroborates his account'; *Daşlik v Turkey* [2017] ECtHR 38305/07 [44]; *Mamasakhlisi and others v Georgia and Russia* [2023] ECtHR 29999/04 [389]. See also *Mendoza and ors v Argentina* [2013] IACtHR [183]; *Fernández Ortega and others v Mexico* [2010] IACtHR.

[30] *Cabrera García and Montiel Flores* (n 28) [2010] IACtHR [129].

[31] *Ireland v UK* [1978] ECtHR 5310/71 [162] assessments to consider 'duration of the treatment, its physical or mental effects and, in some cases, the sex, age and state of health of the victim'; *Fleury et al v Haiti* [2011] IACtHR [73]; *Gómez-Paquiyauri Brothers v Peru* [2004] IACtHR [113].

[32] *Tomasi v France* [1992] ECtHR (Chamber) 12850/87 [113] citing and following the ECmHR reasoning that '[a]lthough the injuries observed might appear to be relatively slight, they nevertheless constituted outward signs of the use of physical force on an individual deprived of his liberty and therefore in a state of inferiority'. *Jalloh v Germany* [2006] ECtHR 54810/00 citing US case of *Cooper v Casey*, 97 F3d 914, 917 (1996): 'to require a threshold showing an "objective" injury, the sort of thing that might reveal itself on an X-ray, or in missing teeth, or in a bruised and battered physical appearance, would confer immunity from claims of deliberate indifference on sadistic guards, since it is possible to inflict substantial and prolonged pain without leaving any "objective" traces on the body'. *Labita v Italy* [2000] ECtHR 26772/95, dissent of Judge Ridruejo and others [2]: 'not all of the types of treatment complained of by the applicant before the Court would have left physical or mental scars detectable on medical examination. There would not necessarily have been any signs left by insults, threats or acts of humiliation, by being kept handcuffed during medical examinations, or being required to run along a slippery corridor leading to the exercise yard while warders hurled insults'.

[33] *Bouyid v Belgium* [2015] ECtHR [GC] 23380/09 [89].

weight in practice. Cases involving threats,[34] insults,[35] and pepper-spray[36] have been dismissed in the absence of evidence beyond the testimonial. Against principle and in the absence of additional evidence, assessments of testimony-centric cases have effectively been anchored to an 'objective' measure, or a presumption that 'must have' or 'would have' been harmful enough for 'anybody'.[37] States have also strategically used these ambiguities, pointing to how suffering was 'beyond the evaluation of the law enforcement authorities and could not be objectively measured, as it related to psychological aspects, such as the emotions and personalities of the individuals concerned'.[38] An acknowledgement of subjectivity (or relativity), to put this bluntly, has buckled under demands for greater evidentiary certainty,[39] resulting in an impulse to objectify (or verify) suffering despite knowledge of the difficulty here.

The interviewees also started out on a tone of deferring to testimonial evidence before shifting to their preference to have this verified somehow. In the absence of evidence of psychological suffering, a registry lawyer explained, 'it would be helpful to have a very detailed explanation by the person to get back to this victim's perspective'.[40] A similar emphasis was also placed on detailed description as follows:

> When you speak about physical injuries, the applicant can always attach a medical certificate, which proves the claims. [...] Mental suffering is all about description, personal subjective perception of the applicant. There can be maybe psychologists' reports speaking about the stress or something anxiety, and you will never know what is the direct cause of such a condition [...] How do we tackle this? By paying very careful attention to what the applicant alleges, what is the story behind how he or she describes it, whether

[34] *Süleyha Aydin v Turkey* [2005] ECtHR 25660/94 [94]: 'other than her own allegations, there is no evidence to support her complaint. The Court is unable, therefore, to reach to a conclusion in this respect'.

[35] *Sladkova v Czech Republic* [2023] ECtHR 15741/15 [81].

[36] *Oya Ataman v Turkey* [2000] ECtHR [GC] 26772/95 [25]: the Court rejected a case involving pepper-spray, finding 'no shred of evidence to substantiate her allegations'.

[37] See *Campbell and Cosans v UK* [1980] ECmHR [1982] ECtHR 7511/76 [30]: 'threat directed to an exceptionally insensitive person may have no significant effect on him but nevertheless be incontrovertibly degrading; and conversely, an exceptionally sensitive person might be deeply affected by a threat that could be described as degrading only by a distortion of the ordinary and usual meaning of the word'.

[38] *Akhiyadova v Russia* [2008] ECtHR 32059/02 [82].

[39] *Jevtovic v Serbia* [2020] ECtHR 29896/14 [78]: 'the Court cannot but note that this conclusion was again essentially based on the applicant's own accounts of what had happened and the severity of the injuries sustained by him on that occasion'.

[40] ECtHR7, senior registry lawyer.

> it is consistent with the versions which the applicant brought both before the domestic authorities and before us.[41]

Applicants were 'free to send whatever they wanted' but it would not necessarily 'be decisive',[42] and that the Court was ready to 'understand that an applicant would not have any evidence to prove their case' if only they 'explain why they only have that'.[43] Others emphasized the need for detailed testimony but needed it to be 'backed up':

> A statement by somebody who has suffered is good, because absent such a statement, it's difficult to persuade the Court that the person has indeed suffered. But the statement by the applicant is not worth a lot, if you haven't got a psychologist's report, backing it up. So the suffering, which they have gone and are undergoing is clinically diagnosed or factually presented in some way.[44]

Against this backdrop, one judge referred to a case concerning a student who was verbally abused by a teacher who later went to see a doctor who diagnosed him with PTSD.[45] The judge reflected that 'if the boy didn't have this, I don't know how the Court could have only relied on his words that he felt distressed'. Alternatively, when you had no evidence beyond the testimonial, according to a former CAT member, it was down to making convincing arguments or hoping the state didn't respond ('just have a look at cases against Burundi […] you will see the CAT actually finds the violation based on what the victim says, without going too much into discussing or examining really thoroughly the facts because the state party has not rejected them'[46]).

The need to 'back up' testimony was also the norm at the CAT: 'you really have to rely on professionals who are capable of delivering this information to you in the form which gets more convincing for you';[47] 'if there are no reports, saying that the mental suffering is a very high level, then it's difficult';[48] 'I can't think of a case where I wouldn't want corroborative evidence from some mental health specialist, a psychologist, psychiatrist, somebody of that

[41] ECtHR23, senior registry lawyer.
[42] ECtHR17, senior registry lawyer.
[43] ECtHR16, former senior registry lawyer.
[44] ECtHR32, applicant lawyer.
[45] ECtHR1, senior registry lawyer.
[46] CAT20, UN legal officer.
[47] CAT4, former member; CAT12, member; ECtHR36, applicant lawyer.
[48] CAT7, applicant lawyer.

nature'.[49] These sentiments also resonated at the IACtHR: 'if you have an expert who is persuasive, and appears in person, [it] has a tremendous impact'.[50]

Testimonial evidence was not enough because it rarely stood unscrutinized—apparently being 'not worth a lot' in practice. Another judge explained that applicants often 'did not substantiate where, when, how, who of their allegations [...] just saying I was psychologically abused'—attracting rejections through the single-judge formation.[51] Others were even firmer on this front: 'if you come to the Court and say listen, I am suffering or it is likely I am in imminent danger or real risk of harm, you have to produce some sort of proof [which] could be a medical certificate'.[52] This was mirrored in other accounts:

> The applicant cannot come to the Court and say, I was taken into custody and I was tortured over a period of three days. The Court will say, manifestly unfounded, the applicant has not produced a shred of proof. [...] you need medical evidence [...] to show that the physical injuries are consistent with your allegations.[53]

One applicant lawyer crystallized generally accepted issues with relying on testimonial evidence as follows:

> Physical is much easier to document [...] saying how much the individual has suffered, psychologically, as a consequence of what happened, that's very often subjective. It's not so easy to document objectively. Even if you've got a psychologist's or psychiatrist's or a trauma expert's report. If my right hand has been cut off, you can see it's not there. I've been beaten, you can see that I've got injuries to my body. But if I just explained that I haven't been able to sleep for five years because of this that's much, much harder to document. [...] it's an explanation for why the court also is quite reluctant to find that there has been a substantive violation of Article 3, but much more prone to find a procedural violation.[54]

Ultimately, no evidence likely meant failure ('there is nothing you can do about it';[55] 'beyond reasonable doubt means we have a suspicion and that you must

[49] CAT21, applicant lawyer.
[50] IACtHR3, applicant lawyer.
[51] ECtHR15, judge.
[52] ECtHR26, judge.
[53] ECtHR22, former senior registry lawyer.
[54] ECtHR32, applicant lawyer.
[55] ECtHR29, senior registry lawyer.

convince us; [whereas] you might easily believe a victim outside in another role than in here';[56] 'there have been cases in my experience as well when no violation was found even though you have this gut feeling that something was wrong').[57] Registry lawyers were also firm in that they could not look beyond the materials the parties presented: that the Court could 'not solely rely on applicant testimony or go to the mass media and look for it. [...] it's not our business'[58] or that the Court 'must be reluctant in basing its finding on information or standards which never form part of the case file'.[59] This last lawyer explained like others that, as powerful as a testimony could be, it stood to be checked against 'objective factors':

> Everybody is afraid when they are arrested, everyone is afraid that the police will beat them up, everyone is afraid that their friends or their parents will find out that they have been taken into custody. [...] being taken into custody is of itself a matter which gives rise to stress, anxiety and for certain people. [...] For some people, they will never get over it. It was shameful. They were wrongly suspected, they may be on tablets for the rest of their life, they may lose confidence, their marriage may break up, they may hit the bottle, they may start taking drugs because they are suffering mentally because they were arrested and detained. But that does not mean that there was a breach of Article 3. [...] The subjective of long-term impact going through the police cell and police processes could be grave, but that needs to be checked against the objective factors of necessity or proportionality and another basis of legitimacy.

In dealings with doubts around psychological suffering, interviewees looked for medical evidence that applicants 'consulted doctors, or the psychologist, or been prescribed some kind of medication',[60] or provided some sort of 'expert evidence',[61] 'an expert forensic psychiatrist [...] the way they answer, how their personality has suffered, has been almost ruined',[62] 'the assessment of psychiatric experts or psychologists who can say that this person is suffering from post-traumatic stress',[63] 'expert reports, sometimes prison records—of solitary confinement'.[64]

[56] ECtHR2, judge.
[57] ECtHR23, senior registry lawyer.
[58] ECtHR23, senior registry lawyer.
[59] ECtHR22, former senior registry lawyer.
[60] ECtHR25, senior registry lawyer.
[61] ECtHR12, senior registry lawyer.
[62] ECtHR4, judge.
[63] ECtHR6, senior registry lawyer.
[64] ECtHR15, judge.

Otherwise objective impulses directed actors to work primarily with physical or visible suffering. Certain cases concerning a combination of physical and psychological indeed indicate that, where having found a violation on the physical allegations, adjudicators explicitly chose to overlook the non-physical, to 'not consider it necessary to go on to assess whether the other allegations of physical or psychological abuses are true, particularly in view of the difficulty of proving such treatment'.[65] Psychological suffering, albeit present, is backgrounded, indicating a lack of attention to the full spectrum of suffering born out of practical considerations, with the complexity pertaining to the nature of psychological not physical suffering.

Despite the principled flexibility and receptivity as espoused, previous research too has found that 'from an evidentiary perspective it is much easier to give legal significance to physical injuries than to psychological experiences'[66] and that 'actual bodily injury' still seems to hold the most valuable evidentiary currency.[67] The expressions used in judgments exemplify these preferences in the analysis: '"numerous acts of violence", "large number of blows", "numerous injuries", and "numerous and widespread" injuries'.[68] While there is no necessary medical or otherwise empirical hierarchy established in the scientific expertise between visibility, physicality, and gravity of suffering,[69] the need for convenience devices such as visible marks remains present. These accounts confirm to some extent previous research that visibility can be worth more than words—with purportedly objectifiable evidence given more weight.[70] Such preponderance on visible acts and impacts has worked 'to facilitate

[65] *Bati and others v Turkey* [2004] ECtHR 33097/96 [115]; *Dikme v Turkey* [2000] ECtHR 20869/92 [83]; *Yavuz v Turkey* [2006] ECtHR 67137/01 [39].

[66] Liana Morica Muntean, 'Determining Torture in Interrogation Cases: Comparative Analysis of the Case Law of the European Court of Human Rights, the UN Bodies and the US Courts', Doctor of Juridical Science thesis, Central European University, Budapest (2017) 147–48: that there is a 'habit of inferring certain aspects without adequately strengthening its arguments or placing psychological ill-treatments on a secondary position (sometimes ignoring them altogether) when other treatments causing visible injuries have been proven'.

[67] Natasa Mavronicola, *Torture, Inhumanity, and Degradation under Article 3 of the ECHR: Absolute Rights and Absolute Wrongs* (Hart 2021).

[68] Muntean (n 66) 90.

[69] Metin Başoğlu, Maria Livanou, and Cvetana Crnobarić, 'Torture vs Other Cruel, Inhuman, and Degrading Treatment: Is the Distinction Real or Apparent?' (2007) 64 Archives of General Psychiatry 277.

[70] Tobias Kelly, 'The Causes of Torture: Law, Medicine and the Assessment of Suffering in British Asylum Claims' in Ian Harper and others (eds), *The Clinic and the Court: Law, Medicine and Anthropology* (CUP 2015) 88; Hedi Viterbo, 'Seeing Torture Anew: A Transnational Reconceptualization of State Torture and Visual Evidence' (2014) Stanford Journal of International Law 50 (2) 281–317, 316; Stanley Cohen, *States of Denial: Knowing about Atrocities and Suffering* (Polity 2001) 168–95; Nimisha Patel, 'The Psychologization of Torture' in Mark Rapley and others (eds), *De-medicalizing Misery* (Palgrave 2011) 428; Mary-Jo DelVecchio Good (ed), *Pain as Human Experience: An Anthropological Perspective* (UC Press 1994) 8–10.

further silencing of bodily pains, since it becomes difficult to "prove" torture on the body', frustrating the pursuit of accountability.[71]

Putting all this together depicted a tension between the *principle* of appreciating difficulties as arising from the absence of direct evidence and the *practice* of legal assessment, which saw difficulties defeat specific cases. This tension is returned to in the question of evidentiary certainty discussed in 'Deference'.

Competence

There emerged from the caselaw review as well as the foregoing discussion a distinct difficulty of following, with any degree of precision, how the three institutions have weighed evidence in assessing the gravity and veracity of alleged instances of psychological suffering. Beyond identifying this issue, previous research has not empirically engaged with how adjudicators have drawn on scientific expertise in substantiating psychological suffering.[72] So I set out to explore this question through the lens of competence, particularly on the technical capacity required to assess evidence of psychological suffering ('Psychological suffering, squarely'), affording extended space to one particularly critical expert take on the question ('A critical take'). I conclude with a brief exposition of broader factors invoked by interviewees ('Training—translation—time').

Psychological suffering, squarely

As mentioned, expertise on torture evidence is not one shared widely, and not readily granted to advocates and adjudicators by virtue of working on torture-related cases. It is rather generally seen to be the realm of medical doctors and psychologists. A vast number of those interviewed with legal training accepted this premise. Others with experience in anti-torture work provided rather sophisticated reflections. One judge without much prompt offered:

> There can be physical suffering that can leave mental suffering—it often goes hand in hand. Usually if mental suffering goes with physical suffering, the applicant can more readily prove their case. We are quick to accept that

[71] Victoria Canning, *Torture and Torturous Violence* (Bristol University Press 2022) 33.

[72] The ECtHR, for instance, is found to 'not regularly engage in its own technical evaluation of the physical or mental pain or suffering': Mavronicola (n 67) 95.

> physical suffering led to mental suffering. There are also cases where there is physical ill-treatment with no traces—this is harder for applicants to shift the burden.[73]

Another judge with a similar professional background distinguished between the 'input' (psychologically oriented practices) and 'output' (psychological consequences).[74] These interviewees also firmly rejected a strict distinction between the physical and psychological, finding these 'so mixed up […] because anything physical may have psychological consequences'.[75] Applicant lawyers similarly did not place much emphasis on the distinction between physical and psychological suffering.[76] Despite their initial objection, these interviewees appreciated the premise of my research.

That certain individuals or cultures could be sensitive to psychological suffering more than others also entered the conversation.[77] A judge, for instance, wanted to draw attention to his observation that 'people can suffer from being insulted verbally, such as from being beaten with a truncheon', as some applicants from Turkey had argued before the Court that the worst thing for them was not the physical part but the threats to their relatives. The judge continued:

> That's actually one of the difficulties and that's also linked to the whole notion of moral suffering. […] So much depends on the individual concerned. […] everyone who is experienced will tell you that like most people with a southern temperament cannot bear like other people can. It's always dangerous to start some racist discourse, but it's just objectively how it is.[78]

Although believing that victims could be differentiated, this judge stopped to avoid essentializing cultural traits. Exceptionally few interviewees, it must be said, however, demonstrated such a sophisticated conceptual understanding of psychological suffering. A vast majority of the interviewees had not been trained in scientific expertise whatsoever and pointed this out quite freely: 'this is a Court, this is not a university, we're not researchers. […] we're not scientists; we're not equipped; we're not educated to deal with complex scientific evidence';[79] 'because we're not that expert on the subject [of psychological

[73] ECtHR15, judge.
[74] ECtHR2, judge.
[75] ECtHR2, judge; ECtHR25, senior registry lawyer.
[76] CAT7, applicant lawyer.
[77] ECtHR12, senior registry lawyer.
[78] ECtHR4, judge.
[79] ECtHR14, judge.

suffering]; we're not a specialized body';[80] 'we don't have the expertise, there's no psychological or psychiatric background in the Registry that could eventually provide the scientific knowledge, none whatsoever';[81] or that 'judges don't feel legitimate to make these kind of assessments, don't feel specialized. […] We're lawyers, not doctors to make a medical assessment […] it's just uncomfortable taking a position on something which [judges] don't feel knowledgeable enough to have an opinion'.[82]

Interviewees affirmed that psychological suffering was 'very difficult to prove',[83] 'a little bit trickier to assess',[84] 'intrinsically difficult to prove',[85] 'would require some skills' (whereas physical wouldn't necessarily even need a lawyer),[86] entailed 'an unknowability […] when compared to physical harm as much in the nature of the harm remains hidden and, as such, is difficult to prove',[87] 'verbal aggression; how do you prove that? asking for a medical certificate that you've been insulted?';[88] 'not obvious because there's no marks, you don't see, it's inferred'.[89] Such accounts underscored evidentiary doubt, the demand for more certainty, and the limited institutional competencies to assess psychological suffering without expertise.

I engaged interviewees on what explained terminological variation as noted earlier in the book. Some put it down to 'a matter of style, not just talent; some people prefer to be more […] poetic'.[90] Some guesswork was involved: 'to me suffering is more general and trauma requires some substance, some sensation, that means that there was something so traumatic that it left an imprint'. When asked if the 'psychological' and 'emotional' could be differentiated, a senior lawyer speculated that the emotional is 'something more temporary in a way, and it's because emotions change easily but something mental is a long-lasting, persistent idea, but then again, I'm not a shrink'.[91] The use of more 'medical-ish sounding' terminology in petitions, however, created an expectation for the same senior registry lawyer to see corroboration, animatedly adding:

80 ECtHR6, senior registry lawyer.
81 ECtHR19, former judge.
82 ECtHR28, senior registry lawyer.
83 ECtHR6, senior registry lawyer.
84 ECtHR25, senior registry lawyer.
85 ECtHR27, senior registry lawyer.
86 ECtHR24, judge.
87 ECtHR9, judge.
88 ECtHR4, judge.
89 ECtHR20, judge.
90 ECtHR28, senior registry lawyer.
91 ECtHR29, senior registry lawyer.

show me a document! [...] as soon as it's more medical-ish sounding, I need substantiation. [If] it's a kind of this [general] kind of anguish you have, you worry, and you have no idea what's happening. And you sort of imagine all sorts of worst scenarios in your head. It's a very human, a more general condition. But if someone says, 'I have this mental trauma etc.', then I'll be, 'how do they substantiate', trauma is a very serious word [which] implies a medical process. There should be substantiation to that. That's just me.

While the Court freely and creatively determined terminology, it could hold advocates to account when doing the same.

As at the ECtHR, there was no formal induction for new IACtHR judges as they were expected to learn the ways of the Court 'on the job' and that partly meant learning from the Secretariat.[92] A sitting IACtHR judge explained that it was more difficult for new members joining the composition to immediately understand torture-related caselaw.[93] Judges' previous experience had a real impact on what they readily understood, with 'a judge from Argentina usually knowing what the concept of a disappearance means, but a judge from Costa Rica doesn't have suffering in their history'.[94] A senior IACtHR lawyer supported this position in finding that the Court was not prepared to analyse psychological suffering in depth because they did 'not have a formation in psychological matters, this is case by case, it depends on the judges, some judges have more information concerning the psychological aspects, but in general, we don't know about psychology. This is a fact'.[95]

At this point, I again inquired as to terminological variance at the IACtHR. The difference between 'psychological' and 'moral' was vague for some, with one former IACmHR lawyer associating 'mental' with the psyche and 'moral integrity' with notions of dignity and humanity.[96] Terminological shifts such as the introduction of the term 'ambiguous loss or frozen grief', for one applicant lawyer, made it easier for judges and lawyers to understand psychological suffering.[97] Experts also decried the reductive use of concepts such as trauma and PTSD[98]—'a broad conceptual view is needed to help understand the consequences' of suffering over time (medium- to longer-term impacts) on the

[92] IACtHR14, senior IACtHR lawyer.
[93] IACtHR10, judge.
[94] IACtHR14, senior IACtHR lawyer.
[95] IACtHR15, IACtHR lawyer.
[96] IACtHR5, former senior IACmHR lawyer.
[97] IACtHR8, applicant lawyer.
[98] IACtHR13, expert; IACtHR17, expert.

family and community.[99] These concerns were conveyed with full appreciation that, as experts, their influence was limited.

As an institution, the CAT conceivably had more grounds to exude confidence on the question of competence. The presence of prominent anti-torture doctors and psychologists sitting on the CAT over the years has meant that it appeared well equipped to evaluate the evidence of health impacts presented by petitioners. Former CAT members have included renowned medical anti-torture doctor and former chair Jens Modvig, who coordinated the revision of the Istanbul Protocol; another Danish doctor, Bent Sørensen, who co-founded one of the first civil society organizations working on the documentation of torture; and psychologist professor Nora Sveaass, another prevention and documentation specialist. This has also shored up authority for the CAT's observers. Those with a complex understanding of psychological suffering existed but exceptionally. For a former member:

> You will always have scars in the mind, sometimes those will be accompanied by bruises, sometimes not. The torture that is difficult to identify for lack of physical bruises […] The psychological impact is the one that lives because having spoken to people, they can, for instance, say the cuts and bruises they are healed, but the fact that somebody did it to me, and the fear that I felt and the anxiety and the pain and all those things do not leave me.[100]

Invoking a discussion about the immediate invisibility of some psychological suffering, the same former member, remembering a child's rape-related abortion, underscored the temporality of psychological suffering in its recognition as follows:

> it may be sometimes some of these acts are defined as a simple act happening once and then it's over. They don't see that act in itself may have disturbed and changed that twelve-year-old girl for the rest of her life. At least what I often found myself doing was talking about the psychological and social consequences of torture […] because it's often seen as strictly defined physical acts with a beginning and an end, which I believe torture does not have. It has a beginning, but it doesn't have an end.

[99] IACtHR17, expert.
[100] CAT3, former member.

Another member pointed to their previous experience working as a prison monitor, and their 'specialized trainings on identifying, documenting and reporting traces of torture, including on Istanbul Protocol'.[101] Yet, their expertise could not be attributed to all CAT members. Another former member, a contemporary of Modvig and Sveaass, explained that the presence of experts did not necessarily solve all issues:

> It's not that easy, even for the members who are quite experienced, especially when it's a borderline case [...] where it's not that easy to establish where it really reached the level of severity to establish the violation. So when Jens Modvig will tell you about particular medical evidence provided the rest would listen.[102]

Yet, committee work remained a collective and confidential enterprise—with members lamenting that: 'whatever I say, this is inherent in the decision-making process, and unless we get to using electrodes and we're never gonna get there, these are always gonna be approximations, some coming from a "shared sense"';[103] or that 'members have different approaches, backgrounds. Some of them are judges, either acting or former prosecutors, some of them are doctors, some of them are human rights lawyers and academicians from universities'.[104] Without such support, others found it to be 'a real challenge'.[105] When asked about how to assess psychological suffering, a member said: 'I thought about this until it made my head hurt'.[106] Having been offered no initiation, this member was left clueless, left alone to work out a complex concept.

Psychological suffering, applicant lawyers across all institutions accepted, was open for them to argue. Yet, advocates also spoke of themselves as lacking competence to argue psychological suffering: 'not a skill they pick up',[107] or 'wouldn't even know what question to ask [...] professionals like clinical therapists do'.[108] One expert noted how a lack of basic competence on the part of litigating lawyers could significantly impact on cases as 'lawyers at times don't know the extent of the psychological report they were asking for'[109] and had to be instructed as to the questions to ask. Applicant lawyers, therefore, saw

[101] CAT14, member.
[102] CAT4, former member.
[103] CAT9, member.
[104] CAT4, former member.
[105] CAT15, member; CAT4, former member; CAT14, member.
[106] CAT9, member.
[107] ECtHR31, applicant lawyer.
[108] ECtHR39, applicant lawyer.
[109] IACtHR13, expert.

the need for expertise as essential: to bolster evidence, 'we recently started working with a [psychology] organization';[110] 'for material injuries you can normally take the photos [but for anything non-material] if you don't have a medical report, I should admit that it is very difficult to argue'.[111] So evidentiary difficulties coupled with limits to competence closely impacted on how cases were argued by advocates—leading to the prioritization of more physical aspects, chosen 'tactically' or for 'practical reasons', as it took 'a bit of work and creativity' to argue psychological suffering.[112]

A critical take

An expert, with extensive experience writing IP-compliant reports in both CAT and IACtHR cases, was adamant that 'dominant discourses' needed to be challenged through awareness-raising training and a sustained dialogue between members and health professionals, particularly for all new CAT members. It was unthinkable, reflected the expert, for members to 'join a committee and make decisions on such huge matters with no training whatsoever. What is torture? What does it do? How does it impact on the individual, the family, the community? All of that'. The dialogue would provide them the opportunity for 'unpacking their reasoning: how did you make sense of that? And if at the very least, to ensure that they are held accountable for their decision, that they're transparent as possible around the assumptions that they're making there'. The counterfactual was 'like putting a team of health professionals in the CAT with one or two lawyers, maybe, and making a decision about the law without really understanding the law', which would never happen but it does where lawyers enjoy positions to assess and determine non-legal questions.

This expert went on to identify the primacy of the body or physical evidence over psychological evidence:

> There is no parity between how medical evidence and psychological evidence is considered despite the Istanbul Protocol, despite all the years of health professionals like myself and others talking about this, there is no parity. That is not the fault of the Committee or the courts. This is a bigger problem, globally, in terms of how our understanding of psychological difficulties and

110 ECtHR35, applicant lawyer.
111 ECtHR36, applicant lawyer.
112 ECtHR31, applicant lawyer; ECtHR40, applicant lawyer; ECtHR38, applicant lawyer; ECtHR34, applicant lawyer.

> harms is not as old as medical sciences, and therefore, less understood, less accepted, but there's also stigma in all communities, including members from communities from which Committee members or court are. These kinds of stigma and shame in our own communities and families also makes us more ignorant of psychological harm, and what it looks like, because if you really understood it, you'd see it in your family members, you'd see it in your friends, you'd see it in your everyday work you do. There's a sort of fearful avoidance response to anything to do with psychological. […]
>
> In our professional lives, lawyers and psychologists and other health professionals are complicit and engaging in psychological harm towards people that we think we're trying to help. […] my experience is that often it's addressed, it's read, it's acknowledged, and it's not disputed. But then it will go back to technicalities or other issues. So, it's almost like saying, we're not able to contest the evidence but we don't see this as touching the core of the legal arguments we're making […] A typical way of disguising gendered bias in these decisions or these opinions is to simply not engage. It's not just in law, you see this everywhere, you just don't engage with women's experiences, bodies, autonomy.[113]

The premium lawyers placed on a stricter formulaic biomedical practice of diagnosis (of PTSD and depression) reinforced these issues, which some psychologists reject as 'unreliable, not valid, and not universally and culturally valid' and as 'invalidat[ing] anybody that doesn't meet that threshold for a diagnosis, but nonetheless has been psychologically harmed'. Instead, the expert advanced a more nuanced 'psychological formulation which actually goes much deeper to look at the sort of psyche, the social, the interpersonal, then pieced all of that together to create an opinion'. Much was missed and reduced by a biomedical diagnosis, particularly those with political or religious meaning-making systems that helped them manage their suffering away from a PTSD diagnosis, with the expert explaining that:

> appreciation for the complexity of human beings and the complexity of psychological suffering is beyond decision-makers, because they're not experts. I don't expect them to be experts, but at least respect that psychological evidence to have parity with medical evidence, and that psychological opinions as formulations are not speculations. They're born from experience, research and deep knowledge. […] With medicine […] you observe the signs and

[113] IACtHR13, expert.

symptoms, you try and establish a pattern, you're trying to then establish and infer a causal relationship, you then try and establish whether there are parallel or other possible explanations or other possible, diagnosis or medical problems that could account for the symptoms and patterns. […] Psychology is really different because the signs and symptoms are not always observable because they're behavioural, the emotions are also expressed, physically and they are also expressed verbally. […] However, this knowledge isn't held by medical doctors, or by lawyers. With medicine, you're just looking at the body, the physical, nothing else. It requires more thinking to try and understand it. It's easier to dismiss psychological evidence and look for shortcuts, where medical doctors will say 'yes' or 'no'.

That the UN's expert body had failed on such fundamental points of competence irritated this expert to no end. CAT's recent performance on appreciating scientific expertise placed before it, and the avoidance of ready solutions to institutional issues, fuelled this irritation (bordering on anger).

Training—translation—time

Not all saw this general lack of competence as critical. Although there was no institutional training on 'how to assess medical evidence', any judge in need could seek clarifications from parties[114] or that a report be 'written in a way aimed at the outside world'.[115] Numerous interviewees mentioned registry lawyers with a medical[116] and psychological[117] background, 'a special eye with a medical vocabulary through the roof',[118] who were often sought out impromptu to aid in assessing medically technical cases. Others rejected that evidence was complex, that it was 'usually very concrete things that people complain of, for instance, prison conditions […] which we could assess or we can check' (through CPT or NGO reports, national jurisprudence, or affidavits by other inmates who have been in the same conditions).[119] An applicant

[114] ECtHR3, senior registry lawyer.
[115] ECtHR7, senior registry lawyer.
[116] ECtHR28, senior registry lawyer.
[117] ECtHR19, former judge; ECtHR6, senior registry lawyer; ECtHR1, senior registry lawyer; ECtHR28, senior registry lawyer.
[118] ECtHR29, senior registry lawyer.
[119] ECtHR25, senior registry lawyer. CPT's influence on the ECtHR, perhaps with the exception of solitary confinement cases as discussed, has been confirmed by research: see Tom Daems and Luc Robert (eds), *Europe in Prisons Assessing the Impact of European Institutions on National Prison Systems* (Springer 2017).

lawyer agreed, explaining that 'judges are there to evaluate the information that is put before them; and if that information is technical, expert information, be it from a physical doctor or a psychologist or an engineer, or some other kind of discipline expert, it's important that the lawyer is able to translate. [...] That's what lawyers and judges do all the time'.[120] No longer having a fact-finding function was seen to make things difficult for the ECtHR in coming to such conclusions faster and fuelled reliance on the CPT[121] ('a real limitation',[122] 'we rely on the submissions made by the applicants and respond to them so they have to be consistent'[123]). This was also seen to be the basis of 'free evaluation of evidence'.[124] Relatedly, processual limitations also directly impacted evidentiary assessments.

Despite indications of 'nothing to see here', there were indeed issues around competence at all three institutions. The ECtHR has explicitly admitted to challenges in assessing scientific evidence, for instance, in regularly noting that the '"adequacy" of medical assistance remains the most difficult element to determine'.[125] A high number of rejections in such cases is likely the culmination of the recognized difficulty, the desire for evidentiary certainty, and a lack of receptivity of non-legal understandings.[126]

There was no scientific expertise within the OHCHR assisting the CAT.[127] Despite no formal requirement, there was a premium placed on being legally trained at the CAT.[128] Those who had such a background prided themselves on being competent: 'because I am an international human rights lawyer, I already knew [but] when I got here I was disappointed because others don't know anything about international law, they do not differentiate between national and international law'.[129] One CAT member, a doctrinal international lawyer by

[120] ECtHR32, applicant lawyer.
[121] ECtHR2, judge.
[122] ECtHR14, judge.
[123] ECtHR17, senior registry lawyer.
[124] ECtHR17, senior registry lawyer; ECtHR23, senior registry lawyer.
[125] *Kolesnikovich v Russia* [2016] ECtHR 44694/13 [70]; *Klimov v Russia* [2017] ECtHR 54436/14 [60].
[126] Ezgi Yildiz, 'A Norm in Flux: The Development of the Norm against Torture under the European Convention from a Macro Perspective' (2016) iCourts Working Paper No 45, 22, found that 'the Strasbourg institutions decided that the suffering caused by treatment was below the threshold in 46% of cases concerning failure to provide sufficient (medical) care'.
[127] CAT16, member.
[128] Composition at the CAT is geographically and culturally diverse but with many members operating without anti-torture expertise. At the time of the interviews, the CAT was composed of two anti-torture specialists (Racu and Puce), a former international criminal law judge (Tuzmukhamedov), a human rights generalist (Rouwane), four international law professors (Maeda, Liu, Buchwald, and Touzé), and two retired career diplomats (Heller and Iscan). It is difficult to predict how certain allegations are corroborated by evidence (or not) in collective deliberation.
[129] CAT8, member.

training, dryly said that dealing with scientific expertise was simply 'not difficult'.[130] Despite such accounts, questions of competence were also pressing at the CAT as I heard: 'just because one is legally trained it doesn't mean that they can do anti-torture work'.[131] As one publicized interaction between an IP expert and CAT members revealed, basic questions about how the IP could be used in adjudication remained:[132]

> a Committee member said there tended to be problems in differentiating between torture and other inhuman or degrading treatment. However, the Committee did make that difference and thus wished to know whether the Istanbul Protocol was useful regarding this differentiation. What was the experts' view on this? Also, could the experts speak about the degree of reliability of the Istanbul Protocol in terms of assessing post-traumatic syndromes of torture? In terms of the evolution of the Protocol, could the experts elaborate on whether it was planned that the Protocol account for technological advances or legal advances?

When asked whether the sentiment, 'things change out in the world; so should we', was uttered in deliberations, a CAT member was quick to retort: 'But they [meaning other members] don't live in the world, do they? […] I would say that a weak part of this Committee is that they haven't been to a closed institution [as it] becomes harder to evaluate if you've never been there.'[133] One expert to have engaged with the CAT was equally scathing of recent members elected: 'you don't really know what you're talking about and you've probably never seen a torture survivor in your life, you have no idea about any of these really intricate aspects, you're just doing this in a kind of very technical, but also superficial and inhumane way'.[134]

One forensic expert with long-standing engagement with the IACtHR offered a tempered account in comparison, explaining that the understanding of suffering within the IACtHR was varied, with some showing a 'deep understanding, showing a lot of interest […] in other cases their attitude has been more superficial'.[135] The same expert saw the exercise not simply entailed judges understanding expertise but as incumbent on the expert

[130] CAT10, member.
[131] CAT20, UN legal officer.
[132] OHCHR, 'Committee Against Torture Discusses Istanbul Protocol' (2 November 2010), www.ohchr.org/en/press-releases/2010/11/committee-against-torture-discusses-istanbul-protocol.
[133] CAT16, member.
[134] IACtHR13, expert.
[135] IACtHR17, expert.

> translating the impact and consequences suffered by the victims into a language, concepts and vision, which can be understood in its profound dimension and evaluated, according to the legal criteria by the Court. I understand the role of an expert as a translator of that suffering that also helps to evaluate the violations [. . .] also often a way of validating the suffering of victims.

This was a version of a recurring explanation, that these institutions were dependent on their social world, for their external actors, to inform them. It was the applicants and their lawyers who had to bring such evidence and present it in a comprehensible and compelling manner. The same expert sought to underscore the temporality of psychosocial impact 'and not just determine a diagnosis [...] as suffering cannot be minimized; it is important to give [judges] keys to understand what can be shown or identified today, but also by making an account of evolution over time, and the relationship of suffering with the facts or with their consequences'. This was unexpected given the general impression exuded by IACtHR judgments that evidence is systematically considered.[136] Yet issues of competence were present, with interviewees admitting to no special training on questions of suffering and a general dependence on external expertise. Similar accounts, as that of the ECtHR, were heard in trusting the process but it was not granted that the nature of suffering was explicitly deliberated in all cases.[137]

Applicant lawyers at the IACtHR for the most part also trusted established evidentiary practices: 'I don't think that there is a particular issue; usually the Court is quite good at carrying out evaluations of which evidence it is going to take in';[138] 'we can't and shouldn't expect, judges, or lawyers in the system to be medical experts or experts in psychology; that's why you have expert witnesses';[139] a psychological report is 'something that we know that has to be present in all the cases'.[140] There was no tension seen in the process; the applicant lawyers and experts did the translation for the judges who were either convinced or not.

Beyond questions of training and translation came time, meaning the time pressures on discussing the nature of suffering in any given case. At the ECtHR,

136 There is normally a stand-alone section claiming to have interpreted the evidence in a particular manner whereas the other two institutions do not always do this.

137 Some cases read as complicated to the untrained eye but find a disposition without too detailed an evidentiary assessment: *Kitiashvili v Georgia* [2018] ECtHR 37747/08; *Teplov v Russia* [2022] ECtHR 69176/17 [7].

138 IACtHR4, former senior IACtHR lawyer.

139 IACtHR9, applicant lawyer.

140 IACtHR2, applicant lawyer.

an initial assessment as to the complexity or clarity of the case vis-à-vis established jurisprudence determined whether the case lands on the desk of a single judge, a committee of three judges, or eventually to the Grand Chamber. This translated to ascending time and resources and closer scrutiny,[141] which directly impacted on the ability to discuss the nature of harms, 'that unless it is a Grand Chamber case there is simply not so much time and effort put into discussing Article 3 cases', and on the consistency of the jurisprudence across different sections, 'there are five sections of the Court and there are five ways of doing things'. The deliberations in the sections, as compared to the Grand Chamber, the lawyer said were 'more pragmatic and less intellectual'.[142] Putting these rather apologetic perspectives together, insiders preferred a pragmatic prioritizing of physical over the psychological.[143]

Time pressures and personnel limitations were also very much present in how interviewees sought to explain the depth of CAT decisions. Each case was allocated two hours[144] or three hours of plenary discussion, with the exceptional controversial cases taking an entire day.[145] CAT members even resisted my description of them as 'decision-makers'. One member said that because of time limitations, they should not be compared to a court, as they could not 'go to the depth necessary to be considered exemplary decision-making'.[146] In rejecting my interview invitation, a member wrote that 'unlike other bodies, we do not operate like a court; we can have photographs which show physical damage but we do not have the opportunity to assess what that does to the heart, as we do not hold hearings; so I don't think I can help you'. There are fewer individuals involved in drafting and deliberating decisions here than at the ECtHR and IACtHR, conceivably amplifying the competence of an expert member or UN lawyer.[147]

[141] ECtHR1, senior registry lawyer.
[142] ECtHR12, senior registry lawyer.
[143] For more on the ECtHR's procedure, see Helen Keller and Corina Heri, 'Deliberation and Drafting: European Court of Human Rights (ECtHR)' (2018) Max Planck Encyclopedia of International Law 23; Cosette D Creamer and Zuzanna Godzimirska, 'Trust in the Court: The Role of the Registry of the European Court of Human Rights' (2019) 30 (2) European Journal of International Law 670.
[144] CAT13, member.
[145] CAT1, former member.
[146] CAT16, member.
[147] For more on the CAT's procedure, see Manfred Nowak and Giuliana Monina, 'United Nations Committee Against Torture' (2018) Max Planck Encyclopedia of International Law; Felicia Gaer, 'Committee Against Torture: Implementing the Prohibition against Torture' in Malcolm D Evans and Jens Modvig (eds), *Research Handbook on Torture: Legal and Medical Perspectives on Prohibition and Prevention* (Elgar 2020) 148. Gaer, a former member who served for twenty years, has characterized the OHCHR support unit as 'very small, which hampers the processing [...] and inhibits the Committee's capacity to decide cases'. Support received from the OHCHR relates to registering individual petitions and drafting decisions. In this regard, the Secretariat saw itself as the CAT's institutional memory and claimed a degree of ownership over its operations. It stayed while members were transient. Yet the

Conclusion

Putting this together depicted three institutions constrained to properly assess scientific expertise, particularly with respect to psychological suffering—sharing common conditions in dealing with evidence, including whether witnesses could be heard or not or otherwise afford much time to deliberate, or more broadly capacitate themselves to apprehend the nature of suffering. Experts here challenged the poor performance of the institutions particularly on their engagement with scientific expertise on psychological suffering. Interviewees revealed that there was no dedicated internal expert competence at any institution to assess psychological suffering. This was explained away as normal by some, who instead relied on its users to provide it with such expertise and translate it in an intelligible manner.

Relatedly, a depth of understanding of psychological suffering on the part of adjudicators and institutional lawyers was rare and depended on years of practical experience gained prior to appointment or through repeated work in the registry on similar cases. Advocates also admitted to a lack of competence, again pointing to their dependence on experts in building a compelling case, particularly if it involved psychological suffering. Some interviewees displayed a sophisticated understanding of psychological suffering but most accepted the difficulty. Despite the principles of equal recognition, physical suffering was prioritized by applicants, advocates, and adjudicators given its visibility and ease of substantiation. Competence also denoted an acknowledgement of disciplinary limitations and in turn a deference to scientific expertise.

Deference

Meaningful engagement with medical and psychological evidence being limited on the face of judgments at all three institutions begged questions of when and to what extent legal actors reached out to and were receptive to scientific expertise, and when, how, and how much circumstantial and contextual aspects were considered sufficient for substantiation. This section now turns to consider questions of what I have referred to as 'deference', meaning how advocates and adjudicators defer to or are respectful of, receptive to, or responsive to scientific expertise. Again, in interviews, I sought to better understand the

decision-making powers, ultimately, were in the hands of the CAT members who did not always align with the views of the Secretariat—which has an interest in jurisprudential coherence.

conditions shaping the discretion here. The discussions started with the assumption, as based on previous research, that evidentiary practices, whether implicitly or explicitly, were likely guided by end-driven considerations—that the desired decision dictated the reasoning.[148] Selectivity of standards and science was used as a point of departure for the interviews. I split the discussion into two, first exploring 'Deference to standards and science' before turning to bring in 'Deference to states'.

Deference to standards and science

Research has identified that the three institutions have not 'uniformly applied'[149] or transparently assessed the scientific expertise where submitted.[150] What I read and heard confirmed this—attributing this rarity and variation to ends-driven reasoning and a lack of deference to established standards and science. Although priding themselves on evidentiary receptivity and innovation, the caselaw reveals that explicit references to the IP have been relatively rare at the ECtHR[151] and the IACtHR.[152] As mentioned, the CAT rejected the claim in *Coppin*, despite overwhelming corroborative evidence including an IP-compliant report, without considering the nature of her suffering. Yet, with official reasoning, or citational practice therein, not necessarily indicative of evidentiary assessments behind closed doors, I relied on interviewees

[148] Freedom from Torture, 'Proving Torture, Demanding the Impossible: Home Office Mistreatment of Expert Medical Evidence' (2016); David Rhys-Jones and Sally Verity Smith, 'Medical Evidence in Asylum and Human Rights Appeals' (2004) 16 (3) International Journal of Refugee Law 396; Rembrandt Aarts and others, 'Expert Medico-Legal Reports: The Relationship between Levels of Consistency and Judicial Outcomes in Asylum Seekers in The Netherlands' (2019) 29 (1) Torture 36; Austin Sarat and others (eds), *How Law Knows* (Stanford 2007) 1–2.

[149] Vincent Iacopino, 'The Istanbul Protocol: Development, Practical Applications, and Future Directions' in Jason Payne-James and others (eds), *Monitoring Detention, Custody, Torture, and Ill-Treatment: A Practical Approach to Prevention and Documentation* (Routledge 2018) 262.

[150] Marcel Reneman, 'Forensic Medical Reports in Asylum Cases: The View of the European Court of Human Rights and the Committee Against Torture' (2020) 38 (3) Netherlands Quarterly of Human Rights 206–28.

[151] IP is only mentioned in: *Arzu v Turkey* [2009] ECtHR 1915/03 [34]; *Balliktas v Turkey* [2010] ECtHR 7070/03 [28]; *Desde v Turkey* [2011] ECtHR 23909/03 [98, 109]; *Ergun v Turkey* [2012] ECtHR 238/06 [41]; *Gazioglu and ors v Turkey* [2011] ECtHR 29835/05 [33]; *Gulbahar and others v Turkey* [2009] ECtHR 5264/03 [53]; *Lunev v Ukraine* [2016] ECtHR 4725/13 [87]; *Yilmaz v Turkey* [2011] ECtHR 27566/06 [54]; *Karademir v Turkey* [2008] ECtHR 30009/03 [54].

[152] *Vargas-Areco v Paraguay* [2006] IACtHR [91] calls the Minnesota Protocol the Istanbul Protocol; *Miguel Castro-Castro Prison v Peru* [2006] IACtHR [326]: 'The expert witness stated, "this method of punishment was [...] collective [and] due to its severity and physical and psychological consequences [is] consistent with torture." In this same sense, the Istanbul Protocol establishes that *falanga* is a form of torture.'

to explain when and to what degree they relied on scientific evidence. Explanations returned to evidentiary discretion.

While evidence was broadly admitted, not all evidence was viewed and weighed equally. How soon the medical evidence was prepared following the acts in question, given how bruises fade and memories fail, served as a similar illustration here. The prompter, fresher, and firmer, the better.[153] Delay in seeking treatment was variably used by respondent governments and the ECtHR in its assessments, either towards finding a lack of substantiation of claims[154] or not attributing to it serious weight.[155] When asked whether the conditions in medical evidence could be discounted or altogether overridden, however, the then President Spano explained that the ECtHR didn't[156]

> act when it comes to expert evidence any differently than any national court […] you have questions of fact, which can only be determined by resorting to expert evidence. As a judge, you really need to have a lot of good reasons if you're going to override or call into question, for example, a medical evaluation […] we have detention of inmates who are mentally unhealthy or mentally disabled, we may have to resort to evidence of psychologists, psychiatrists […] that's part and parcel of being a judge. You learn to do that all the time.

Linking socio-political standards to scientific expertise, the department of the Jurisconsult was viewed as a competent focal point for complex legal and research queries.[157] While access to the Jurisconsult was a given, one judge reflected that 'before you order that research, you will need some sort of impulse to do that; you will be aware that society is changing in this area'.[158] As in the case of *Kurt v Austria*,[159] which raised the question of domestic violence as a social concern, the same judge emphasized the role of external standards and scientific expertise:

[153] *Badalyan v Azerbaijan* [2021] ECtHR 51295/11 [48].
[154] *Dizman v Turkey* [2005] ECtHR 27309/95 [56] where Turkey argued that the applicant had only sought treatment for a broken jaw two days after the incident.
[155] *Balogh v Hungary* [2004] ECtHR 47940/99 did not seek a medical examination until two days after release. *Gurepka v Ukraine* [2005] ECtHR 61406/00 in which the applicant submitted to the Court a medical report, prepared after six days.
[156] University of Copenhagen, iCourts, Interview with President of the European Court of Human Rights Robert Spano by Professor Mikael Rask Madsen, 11 October 2023.
[157] ECtHR1, senior registry lawyer; ECtHR6, senior registry lawyer.
[158] ECtHR24, judge.
[159] *Kurt v Austria* [2021] ECtHR GC 62903/15.

> The Court asks itself is there a standard in another scientific discipline for the correct type of behaviour in a situation like this. In the domestic violence situation, there is criminological research [...] scientific description of the proper type of behaviour. So in order to assess whether the agencies have been acting with sufficient judgment in order to avoid being censored, you compare the behaviour of the agents with the scientific measure. Now, this doesn't happen every day.

If this is the rule, then there have been many exceptions, especially as explained in the caselaw on solitary confinement. Beyond that, an oft-overlooked case relating to hooding (perhaps because it is only available in French) represents a good example. Although the external standards could not have been stronger and clearer as outlined in a dissent opinion, the majority of ECtHR judges summarily dismissed the case.[160] So there were times when this course of action was followed and others when it was not. There was a selection to be made—and adjudicators chose to stay oblivious to prevailing standards.

A former judge explained that, in a case where he presented all the evidence-base around psychologically oriented practices, the majority wanted to disregard it, not hear it, as they did not 'find it absolutely necessary to come up to the result that they wanted', recounting that:[161]

> no one cares about this, no one ever takes it seriously. I made a comparative analysis with contributions from psychological and sociological textbooks [but] people did not really want to go into that. [...] Judges should listen to what the medical experts have to say, they don't, it's very rare that they ask for expert reports. It's very rare that they even mention them when available. [...] So much more good could be done.

For this openly critical judge, practice has often deviated from the principled recognition of evidentiary difficulties—a deviation resulting in downgrading and dismissing allegations of psychological suffering. Taking a similar critical stance in linking competence to deference, one expert took on the CAT:

> Even when they've had medical people there before, they've been medical doctors, Nora Sveaass was the first psychologist. [...] She would probably have told you it didn't carry a lot of weight, except with one or two Committee

[160] *Portmann v Switzerland* [2011] ECtHR 38455/06.
[161] ECtHR19, former judge.

> members. And it's almost as if you're seen as the poor cousin of doctors. So there's a kind of inherent and implicit hierarchy. And I see this, particularly in the legal spheres—that lawyers are seen as the most objective, then doctors, and then sometimes lawyers will defer to doctors, medical doctors, because they think they're God, especially if they're men. And then there's psychologists, and below psychologists, no one counts. Even psychiatrists have more sway even though they cannot comment on many of the things that psychologists can comment on in terms of articulating psychological harm. There's that kind of prejudice and ignorance, the stigma, and avoidance.[162]

A CAT member confirmed as much in arguing that doctors themselves were not infallible, meaning that they stood to be scrutinized.[163] The level of scrutiny could cause internal tensions. Referring to the dissenting opinions in *Coppin*, another member explained that there were 'lengthy discussions on this draft by the Secretariat and the Committee couldn't agree'.[164] The OHCHR draft decision was reportedly reversed. The CAT's ultimate decision to reject the case was a point of consternation among some members, both former and current, as well as some applicant lawyers. One former member assessed the outcome as 'shocking', 'extremely disappointing', 'shameful', lacking 'integrity', and as a regression in how the CAT dealt with issues related to women and a 'stepping back with regard to state responsibility'.[165] An applicant lawyer saw 'very little reasoning [...] confusion to justify those conclusions'.[166] Although 'reluctant to comment', one sitting member explained that the general position of the majority was that of state-deference, asking rhetorically: 'what more can the Irish do?'.[167] Another sitting member characterized the decision as 'technical' in that it was 'evident that the treatment was not in conformity with international law' but that there were technical reasons to reject the case despite what the expert evidence said.[168]

In characterizing such moments of tension between adjudicators and experts as a 'mésalliance', former ECtHR Judge Helen Keller broadly reflected on the use of scientific expertise in the following:[169]

162 IACtHR13, expert.
163 CAT6, former member.
164 CAT1, former member.
165 CAT3, former member.
166 CAT5, applicant lawyer.
167 CAT9, member.
168 CAT10, member.
169 University of Strasbourg, 'Translating Climate Science for the Human Rights Court Room: An Interdisciplinary Encounter between Science and Law', Symposium, Strasbourg, 2 March 2023. This was discussed in the context of climate change cases, but it was worded to apply generally.

> there has been a growing scepticism of science. Science is portrayed as arbitrary and sometimes even denigrated. This tendency also leaves its marks on the courts. The involvement of experts is often considered unnecessary because it prolongs, complicates, and increases the cost of the procedure. Judges often feel overwhelmed by the expertise. That these are sometimes extensive and difficult to understand. Judges often feel that the expertise makes the decision unnecessarily more difficult. They sometimes experience that they know even less what to decide or even more confused than before the expertise, are now confused at higher level. The responsibility in a court case ultimately lies with the judges. This means that the judges do not necessarily want to have even more information for the basis of the decision because they shy away from complexity. Thus a certain blinker mentality of the judges towards the expert becomes apparent.

Broadly confirming Keller's take, for another former judge there were 'a multitude of factors that really contributed to keeping torture very limited', but primarily it was due to judges 'being conservative, not willing to review the concept, according to medical science, not updating the concept according to what the knowledge provided by what a medical expert would say'.[170] Identifiable in these responses were the undertones of deferring to the state over science.

Deference to states

For many, it was not scientific evidence that proved key but a caution not to stand too firmly against a state—instead to point to a lack of evidentiary certainty from which to challenge state practices.[171] Striking such a note of state-deference in referring to a politically sensitive solitary confinement case,[172] one judge explained:

> this is the assessment done by the authorities, that he poses a very serious security risk and we have no basis for second guessing that assessment. That

[170] ECtHR19, former judge.

[171] *Veznedaroglu v Turkey* [2000] ECtHR 32357/96, dissent of Judge Bonello [11], who found 'the standard of proof—beyond reasonable doubt—required by the Court in torture cases to be legally untenable and, in practice, unachievable' and at [17] 'it is difficult to envisage what "proof" the Court expected from the applicant in order to substantiate her claim that she was repeatedly tortured by being forcibly undressed, suspended, threatened with death and rape and deprived of food. These amusements are particularly ungenerous with those tangible signs dear to forensic experts'.

[172] *Hansen v Norway* [2018] ECtHR 48852/17.

> would show us that we are here in a very sensitive area […] it's very clear that everyone realized that this is damaging. It's not because we don't know, simply because we need to make a quite brutal assessment of what risk we can accept. To second-guess that assessment of the domestic authorities […] would put us in a very difficult situation, partly because we simply don't know because we haven't met this person, we haven't heard the evidence, and partly because we are somehow taking the decision of the domestic authorities. The only way for us to say this is not acceptable would be either that the justification is not convincing […] or secondly to say that the Convention does not allow for this kind of balancing exercise.[173]

The limitation in not being a first-instance court, not being able to easily call witnesses and experts, instilled in the ECtHR a sense of deference for domestic processes.[174] Conversely, deference to expert evidence from an applicant could not be readily expected, especially if the case had been assessed at a reliable national instance. Some framed this in terms of evidentiary certainty through proximity. The CAT too saw state authorities as better placed to assess suffering, given that they were 'firsthand in contact with the victim, and they perform an interview, so they know better to assess the weight and the credibility and context'.[175] This could discount or altogether override scientific expertise the victim brought before the CAT. Proximity deserved a premium. One OHCHR lawyer stated that although medical evidence was 'of course taken into account', it did not necessarily

> change anything because most of these asylum seekers come with medical report saying that they suffer from PTSD. […] the problem is that you are not certain that this PTSD was provoked by the alleged fact. Of course, there is the possibility, but you're not certain about this. So you need to corroborate this with other facts. […] it's this uncertainty around the causal link that is very difficult to establish.

Institutional integrity was also at the fore of another member's mind who wanted 'to favour the complainants but we also need to preserve the name, the credibility of CAT', which ran through 'respecting the migration agencies of Sweden, Australia, etc., [considering] that we have half an hour to reach

173 ECtHR14, judge.
174 ECtHR20, judge.
175 CAT8, member.

the decision [without] investigative powers'.[176] In similarly dismissing a case against Norway of solitary confinement (coupled with the lack of access to psychiatric care and police beatings) not to have enough evidence to question and condemn another state, the CAT held that it was unfortunate that the police didn't document her alleged violations.[177] In another case where the complainant attributed a death at sea to Spanish authorities, the CAT accepted that the victim's death amounted to Article 16 but became stuck on the question of intent under Article 1, namely whether Spanish authorities had intentionally punctured the victim's boat. The CAT refrained from ruling on the matter, explaining that 'it is not its task to weigh the evidence or to reassess the statements made regarding the events in question or the credibility of the relevant national authorities'.[178] This was challenged as a 'shocking pronouncement' in a dissenting opinion, which held that weighing evidence was exactly the CAT's job. Beyond this rare internal critique, this case supports the tendency of adjudicators, as argued in research elsewhere, to 'seek more absolute and definitive views in order to come to a final decision'.[179]

What about drawing on standards when faced with difficult questions on the 'minimum level of severity'? Referring to fear as induced by arrest and the law enforcement processes, another judge explained that 'the Court cannot question the basis of these practices'.[180] Standards of what suffering at the hands of the state was necessary was a straightforward case of asking 'why' for one judge. Not all, it has to be said, were so readily accepting of state arguments. Another judge questioned state practices on scientific grounds, claiming to challenge states on occasion:

> What's your basis for making this choice? If it appears to be within reason, what would be considered to be mainstream, is there a scientific basis? [. . .] We would very easily end up in a situation where the Court would not be in the driving seat saying, this is not the way to go. We would rather say you simply have not convinced us that this is justified. Of course, if someone is doing something that is very different from what would be named mainstream, the requirement or justification will be similar.[181]

[176] CAT20, UN legal officer.
[177] CAT-C-63-D-678-2015 [10.2]: 'on the basis of the information before it, the Committee cannot conclude that the complainant suffered inhuman and degrading treatment'.
[178] CAT-C-47-D-368-2008 [10.2].
[179] Tobias Kelly, *This Side of Silence* (Penn Press 2012) 74.
[180] ECtHR22, former senior registry lawyer.
[181] ECtHR14, judge.

A case where a drunk man was thrown on a floor evoked a similar question for another judge: 'why would you throw a person? […] that for me would be the basic: Why? Why?'.[182] If the detainee was stripped because there was a probability of suicide, then that could well be assessed to be necessary, the same judge continued, but the bottom line was that 'you put yourself in the shoes of the victim, perhaps it's more of a particular victim-oriented approach'. Another judge relied on the investigation in assessing the circumstances of necessity, and, where the investigation was lacking, found a procedural violation.[183] This judge concluded, however, on a point of state-deference, that 'you have to be also modest there if the police convincingly tells you but we have to do this, and it is not manifestly unreasonable, then you say, well, then hands off. How are we to say, we are not the ones who lead to criminal investigation; it must be convincing'.

For other judges, the question of necessity brought their assessment disagreeably into the realm of penal policy and beyond the ECtHR's remit despite an established evidence-base. In dissent, one judge even wrote that although 'social science has shown that harsh penal policies do not have the desired effects […] the Court does not have jurisdiction to rule on the rationality of choices made in the field of penal policy'.[184] States were prioritized over scientific standards. Such a note reverberated in *Bouyid* where three dissenting judges wrote that it was 'not for the Court to impose general rules of conduct on law-enforcement officers'.[185]

'Heightened tensions' have been alluded to identify the policing pressures leading to 'excesses'—with what that means for the victim left open for interpretation. A senior registry lawyer defended the ECtHR's acknowledgement of the difficulties states face in law enforcement not because

> it gives the governments an excuse to commit any violation but it is just to acknowledge that we understand the conditions in which the government work. […] it's a way just to reassure governments that we're not trying to hold them up to an impossible standard, right. We just think that this standard should still be upheld in those difficult conditions. This is the message […] like, 'Oh, we're sorry that you have a difficult time' […] but in my mind, in general, we do take seriously all the arguments the government is providing.

182 ECtHR26, judge.
183 ECtHR20, judge.
184 *Rezmives and others v Romania* [2017] ECtHR 61467/12, per Judge Wojtyczek [4].
185 *Bouyid* (n 33), dissent of Judges De Gaetano and others [6].

> So you need to deal with them. Even if you from the very start think they're just ludicrous. You won't write that in a judgment of course.[186]

Revealing a similar register of deference as at the ECtHR, a couple of CAT members explained that cases concerning prevalent state practices required caution and recognized that the infliction of psychological suffering sat at the heart of law enforcement policies. Harsh interrogation practices or even poor detention conditions proved tricky for one member (when the prisoner's 'cell was dark, there was no proper ventilation, not really clean, and so forth, not heated properly'[187]). According to another member, restraints in psychiatry such as 'caged beds' proved tricky, requiring individual assessments. The question became technical:

> Is it a leather bed or a fabric cage? What type is more humane? In the cage bed she was not fixated. What is also important is that whether there were any alternatives. If there were some, then it is closer to a violation. I would also look for whether it was a dedicated room with supervision. This is an assessment of necessity.[188]

Some at the IACtHR connected deference to *science* to deference to the *state*. Legitimacy in the eyes of the states, that is to say, was a constant care and concern, with 'analysis that could be perceived as outliers' a risk to be mindful of and averted.[189] One means of ensuring legitimacy, for this applicant lawyer, was through expertise and amicus briefs. Where the allegation was disputed by the state, the IACmHR and the IACtHR were called upon to provide stricter corroboration and argumentation.[190] This lawyer characterized the IACtHR's reliance on expertise as a 'political consideration', of being 'very conscious' of how states perceived their authority here. In one case where the respondent state did not come to the session as it rejected the Court's competence, the Court wanted to show the state that it was 'objective' through being 'very methodological, asking, "how can you make these conclusions with this small sample?"'[191] An IACmHR lawyer, who worked at the inception of the IACmHR and IACtHR, similarly explained that 'very hard evidence' was seen

186 ECtHR28, senior registry lawyer.
187 CAT4, former member.
188 CAT16, member.
189 IACtHR3, applicant lawyer.
190 IACtHR6, former senior IACmHR lawyer.
191 IACtHR11, expert.

to be a more important foundation for the IACtHR than presumptions,[192] continuing that it was

> very important for us practitioners to fill the record with a lot of very hard evidence. So that if we were to get a good decision by the Court, the Court could feel comfortable that they were not bringing their own kind of impressionistic view on it. But that was then, maybe now it's a little different [. . .] it's important for litigants to gather the evidence that will make courts feel comfortable with saying what you want them to say.

The logic here could be said to mirror the deference to danger-based justifications used to dismiss solitary confinement cases. Deference here and elsewhere meant a deferral to official discretion, to state power. Previous research identifying this has described it as 'the legitimacy loop'—where adjudicators circularly reason that suffering is illegitimate if it crosses the minimum threshold yet 'invokes legitimacy as a criterion based on which a punishment may not be inhuman or degrading'.[193] Far from politically neutral, there is an active decision to defer the decision to the authorities, effectively shielding the suffering away from scrutiny.

Evidentiary practices across the three institutions largely indicated that the measure of deference, through such concepts of certainty as causality, directly determined the institutional reliance on scientific expertise. Although such expertise was never determinative and was subject to the assessments of the judges, there was a discretion to scrutinize it to varying degrees. Deference was revealed, by the interviews, to be dependent on judges' views as to whether a specific situation called for such expertise and whether their inference as to the suffering sufficed or not. In all, two positions were made clear: that either there was no difficulty (or no more so than the usual, per Spano) or that there was a distinct conflict (calling profound ideological and epistemological fault-lines into question, per Keller). Cutting against the unreflected rhetorical push for multi-disciplinarity, this serves to mirror previous research to have urged care and caution[194] or otherwise identified an impossibility for legal actors to genuinely engage with non-legal expertise.[195]

[192] IACtHR7, former senior IACmHR lawyer.
[193] Mavronicola (n 67) 114.
[194] Nimisha Patel and David Pilgrim, 'Psychologists and Torture: Critical Realism as a Resource for Analysis and Training' (2018) 17 (2) Journal of Critical Realism 176.
[195] Kelly (n 70).

Conclusions

There remain important unsettled aspects concerning how scientific expertise is used in substantiating psychological suffering at the three institutions. The institutions have preferred to preserve their discretion to assess freely, and somewhat without full clarity on the face of their judgments, obfuscating how evidence was weighed particularly regarding psychological suffering. Although expertise has been accepted as a principal means for institutions to reach out into their contexts, deference to it remained varied. A range of difficulties arose upon receiving evidence—with principled receptivity to evidence undercut by a preference for pragmatism or scepticism in practice. These were explained away in interviews either as practical in nature (as competence- and resource-related) or as political (admitting state-deference: that a scientific basis for legal reasoning served the persuasiveness of a decision in the eyes of states).

The insistence on causal certainty circumvented the principled recognition that evidence was difficult to produce in psychological suffering cases and that adjudicators had to be flexible in this light regarding evidentiary standards and burdens. Adjudicators' insistence on certainty, therefore, at times overlooked the reality that torture cases are 'often-fragmented'[196] for political or practical imperatives. How expertise, and evidentiary practices more broadly, were understood to work at these institutions impacted directly on how applicants and their advocates approached their argumentation regarding the forms of suffering to prioritize (namely, physical suffering) and how that should be recognized. The variance in practice here pointed to deep-seated epistemological, ideological, and strategic visions,[197] particularly in divergent expectations from expert evidence opening assessments to be self-serving and allowing adjudicators' own views to enter.[198] On this front, and providing an opening to the final theme, interviewees admitted that there were indeed scenarios where they did not feel the need for expert evidence. It was not essential, for instance, when inferential and experiential reasoning was available to them. I examine this interplay in the next chapter on 'sense-centric reasoning'.

[196] Kelly (n 179) 48.

[197] For Sheila Jasanoff, 'Just Evidence: The Limits of Science in the Legal Process' (2006) 34 Journal of Law, Medicine & Ethics 328, 'scientific truths may not be accepted as valid for legal purposes'; Kelly (n 179) 15: 'By entering the legal realm, claims of torture must come up against standards of proof which they often cannot meet. [...] As legal regimes face different ways of knowing, built on different methodological assumptions, theoretical foundations, and political commitments, there can be a clash of epistemologies. In legal forums, though, it is legal actors who come out on top.'

[198] Loran Nordgren and others, 'What Constitutes Torture? Psychological Impediments to an Objective Evaluation of Enhanced Interrogation Tactics' (2011) 22 (5) Psychological Science 689–94.

6

Sense-centric reasoning

> When we say that we just 'know', intuitively, that something amounts to torture, there is probably something of a conflation of two different things taking place: it is not that the existence of pain is necessarily irrelevant, but we can confidently assume that pain of a requisite intensity has been inflicted simply because of the nature of the act—it *has* to have been; how could it not? But I am equally sure that if, for some extraordinary reason, the victim did not actually feel any physical pain, it would not have mattered in the slightest. […] There are some things which just *are* acts of torture.[1]

Not an adjudicator but a prominent 'law and torture' practitioner-academic, Malcolm Evans here captures a sense-centric reasoning that pervades the three institutions. In gesturing beyond textual considerations, to intuition, emotion, and presumption, Evans explains the thinness, variance, and silences concerning evidentiary reasoning in torture-related cases.[2] Given its open texture and complex nature, as an 'interconnected, and interactive system involving the physical, emotional, perceptual, spiritual, and cognitive',[3] suffering resists direct access and articulation. Argumentation and adjudication, therefore, cannot be gauged from a page or heard or understood in its totality. Inference, through instinctive and inductive reasoning, becomes inescapable with the lack of visibility, proximity, or availability of evidence in most cases.[4] Senses and sensibilities are necessarily engaged in gauging what has happened.

[1] Malcolm Evans, *Tackling Torture: Prevention in Practice* (Bristol University Press 2023) 22.

[2] As much has been argued by a senior national judge who characterized the interpretive task here as being 'one of assessment—one not of law or of legal principle, but of evaluation': David Hope, 'Torture' (2004) 53 International and Comparative Law Quarterly 826.

[3] Austin Sarat (ed), *Knowing the Suffering of Others: Legal Perspectives on Pain and Its Meanings* (University of Alabama Press 2014) 2, 37.

[4] Mary-Jo DelVecchio Good (ed), *Pain as Human Experience: An Anthropological Perspective* (UC Press 1994) 139; Ergun Cakal, 'Sensing Suffering: On Common-Sense and Compassion in the Legal Imagination and Recognition of Torture' (2022) 10 (3) London Review of International Law 337–66.

Torture and the Recognition of Psychological Suffering in International Law. Ergün Cakal, Oxford University Press.
 DOI: 10.1093/oso/9780198989493.003.0006

Despite the grounds of objectivity and impulses for reductivity and manageability on which adjudicators premise their denial and foreclosure,[5] the 'senses' have long featured and functioned in legal assessments of suffering, and no less in anti-torture caselaw.[6] Invocations of 'logic', 'common sense', '*sana critica*', and 'must have felt' reasoning, largely left ill-defined and intuitive, are indicative of the complexities here[7]—bringing into view how sense-centric reasoning works in expanding (or restricting) recognition. Adjudicators have, for instance, justified their recognition as *visceral* (that their 'common sense is outraged'),[8] *logical* ('much in an assessment is a matter of logic—and I would say also for other judges'[9]), or *natural* ('we are all humans […] I get the case file with autopsy reports, photos and it does affect you', 'as a normal person, I inherently know what they are; I know what torture is and inhuman and degrading treatment is obvious when you read the case'[10]). Coded into and channelled through such reflections are a panoply of emotive and presumptive modes of reasoning, forged socially, culturally, and politically—which I explore in this chapter.

I take 'sense-centric reasoning' to consist of three intertwined registers: of intuition, emotion, and presumption (see Figure 1.2 in Chapter 1). Although intimately intertwined, I take 'intuition' to generally be the least reflected of the three—and to include gestures to impression, inference, association, gut feeling, guesswork, personal disposition, 'we just know it' reasoning, and *sana critica*. Although much can be included here such as anger, I limit 'emotion' to include empathy, sadness, and the senses (seeing and hearing). The most developed, at least in caselaw and scholarship, is 'presumption', which I take to include 'must have felt' reasoning, common sense (or common knowledge or contextual knowledge), vulnerability, and temporality.

[5] Andrea Bianchi and Anne Saab, 'Fear and International Law-Making: An Exploratory Inquiry' (2019) 32 Leiden Journal of International Law 351, 354.

[6] I respond to recent calls in international law scholarship for its actors (states, individuals, communities, judges, lawyers, activists, media, and public opinion) to 'engage earnestly with emotions' and come to 'acknowledge that emotions are not biases or untruths that need to be weeded out, but rather ought to be understood and embraced as a central component of reasoned decision-making' as they are a part of its 'messy and subjective' reality. See Anne Saab, 'Emotions and International Law' (2021) 10 (3) ESIL Reflections.

[7] Alvaro Paul, 'Sana Critica: The System for Weighing Evidence Utilised by the Inter-American Court of Human Rights' (2012) 18 Buffalo Human Rights Law Review 194: the IACtHR does not define '*sana critica*'.

[8] *Tyrer v UK* [1978] ECtHR 5856/72, Report of public hearings on 17 January 1978, p 71: 'The true test as to whether judicial corporal punishment as described in this case is in breach of the Convention is to ask whether the public of the Isle of Man and common sense is outraged.'

[9] ECtHR9, judge.

[10] ECtHR6, senior registry lawyer.

As in previous chapters, I use the interviews to build on and beyond the scant doctrinal material on these fronts. I drew interviewees on questions around how sense-centric reasoning featured in their work. How was evidence assessed through or even substituted with sense-centric registers of reasoning? What about where there was much less to go on by way of evidence? Was evidence even essential? Without defining them, I asked if 'sense-centric' registers were something they related to. As the material reveals, these registers very much shaped (both expanding but also delimiting) legal recognition of psychological suffering. What was left uncritically or readily accepted suggested how actors actively foregrounded certain suffering as necessarily worthy of attention.

Intuition

Much could take the place of expertise in its absence or for the sake of expedience. As for Evans, intuition or 'gut feeling' was invoked in numerous responses to characterize certain cases that were 'quite obvious'.[11] 'Obvious' cases involved beatings to death where one senior registry lawyer didn't 'need much' and borderline cases were like *Bouyid* which drew in notions of dignity and necessity.[12] A judge explained that they would often point out to other judges that they needed an expert in a specific case, but recognized that 'the flip side is to overuse experts when there is no need; a doctor's report is sometimes not needed'.[13] A registry lawyer similarly challenged the indispensability of evidence in explaining that 'we have to rely on common sense, we usually don't go very technical'.[14] Decades of experience litigating and adjudicating in one area of the law informed working in a 'very intuitive' manner.[15]

Talk of intuition readily slipped into the invocation of experience. While photos could be important, with 'practices that don't serve conducive for photos […] it boils down to how to perceive the world around you'.[16] A CAT member, preferring to call it 'personal predisposition', similarly saw it operating as a guide, which made it 'easier to assess legal issues and to evaluate the impact'.[17] A former member too viewed it as a guide, explaining:

[11] ECtHR20, judge.
[12] ECtHR3, senior registry lawyer.
[13] ECtHR5, judge.
[14] ECtHR28, senior registry lawyer.
[15] ECtHR26, judge.
[16] CAT2, former member.
[17] CAT16, member.

> First you think this person has been treated in a completely acceptable way. And then you look at the definition. Then you say, okay, 'how can we make this fit together?' […] my way of working is you look at the whole case, make an assessment, make your own personal opinion of the case. And this is the right result […] start to apply that insight […] into this decision, which you believe is right, if you can make that decision within the scope of the law.[18]

This connection between common-sense and ends-driven reasoning resonated in a sitting member's account, who explained that 'the conclusion is the priority [in one case, we] focussed on the violation/the conclusion than strong reasoning'.[19]

Others framed intuition in terms of a sensitivity: 'certain backgrounds make us more sensitive to certain human conditions';[20] 'we always say it's the Court, it's an institution, but then there are people behind this institution and I can tell you that the same case probably being treated by one person or another might have a different outcome'.[21] A senior registry lawyer, for instance, accepted that 'the subjective views of the judges play a crucial role' in assessments,[22] and that 'judges act with their own emotions', explaining that 'assessments go something like: for an ordinary human being, does this look like torture?', continuing:[23] 'some are extremely conservative; some people don't like grey zones, and you have those who want to go with reality and with life'. So for this senior registry lawyer, personal and professional experience grounded assessments in 'reality' but could also restrain progressive (or expansive) impulses.

Impressionistic reasoning was also evident when interviewees were asked what for them attracted the specific categorization of torture. Some judges required 'typically a combination of physical and psychological harm of some sort'.[24] For others, torture in the 'classic sense' *necessarily* involved physical suffering.[25] When it came to 'medieval treatments', a judge explained matter-of-factly, 'of course, it is torture'.[26] Torture, for one ECtHR judge, was at its core the loss of control over one's mind and body.[27] While forced nudity on an

[18] CAT1, former member.
[19] CAT8, member.
[20] ECtHR8, judge.
[21] ECtHR28, senior registry lawyer.
[22] ECtHR6, senior registry lawyer.
[23] ECtHR12, senior registry lawyer.
[24] ECtHR8, judge.
[25] ECtHR23, senior registry lawyer.
[26] ECtHR20, judge.
[27] ECtHR10, judge.

island was inhuman or degrading, for the same judge, it wasn't torture because 'they didn't lose their control'. From others I heard, 'there is no clear answer, with each section [of the Court] different, it may be the result of a compromise', pointing to the imperative of consultative assessments.[28]

Sanford Levinson, a prominent torture scholar, relies on pure impression, though offering no elaboration, unlike the judge just quoted. He writes that 'although it is surely "degrading," for example, to be stripped naked before questioning, it is implausible to define this treatment, without more, as "torture"'.[29] His impressionistic reasoning is then turned on sleep deprivation, about which he argues: 'I confess that I do not view, say, 24–36 hours of such deprivation as "torture," even if it is undoubtedly coercive (and, most certainly, "cruel and unusual," if used as a form of punishment rather than as a goad to interrogation)'.[30] Levinson accepts that 'torture' and 'inhuman or degrading' are in effect 'placeholders', 'abstract concepts whose content is to be found in the formulations that are used to fill in the blank or to give meaning to the inkblot'.[31] He ponders, albeit without resolution: 'How, if at all, do we arrive at definitions of these activities? Is this a philosophical enterprise, involving the manipulation of abstract concepts, or are the definitions provided instead by looking at the actual way such terms are used within the general (legal) culture?'. Levinson's impressionistic or intuitive approach, as the interviewees' and Evans', is one that runs deeply in anti-torture work. Related research has also found that adjudicators take an impressionistic approach particularly in counting

> the amount of repeated acts (of the same method) administered to the victim, the number of visible injuries attested by expert medical reports, the effects on the physical health of the victim or the duration and the length of time necessary for the injuries to subside. A search for visible injuries has become a feature of the practice in the field, amounting to a 'we know it when we see it' approach.[32]

[28] ECtHR12, judge.

[29] Sanford Levinson, 'In Quest of a "Common Conscience": Reflections on the Current Debate about Torture' (2005) 1 Journal of National Security Law and Policy 231, 239.

[30] ibid 246.

[31] ibid 242.

[32] Liana Morica Muntean, 'Determining Torture in Interrogation Cases: Comparative Analysis of the Case Law of the European Court of Human Rights, the UN Bodies and the US Courts', Doctor of Juridical Science Thesis, Central European University, Budapest (2017) 89; Michelle Farrell, 'Just How Ill-Treated Were You? An Investigation of Cross-Fertilisation in the Interpretative Approaches to Torture at the European Court of Human Rights and in International Criminal Law' (2015) 84 (3) Nordic Journal of International Law 482, 499.

Linking personal associations to practices of recognition and categorization even more closely, I heard from interviewees that principles such as 'living instrument' were not invoked 'because during the deliberations in the discussion, people would just fit in with their own perceptions'[33] and that, using a slap of a prisoner as an example, a judge claimed that it 'could be very much a personal issue where you draw a line'.[34] In similarly pointing to the inevitability of intuition, one judge spoke of the suffering inflicted through forced sterilisation:

> You can imagine how any person would feel but how do you quantify that? I don't know that there's a medical test for humiliation. You can test whether there is not a medical condition. The realization that you've been treated as less than a human being is not a medical condition. It's something that most of us would find appalling.[35]

Again, such reasons operated on visceral reactions ('imagine', 'feel', 'appalling'), rejecting any notion of rigorous assessment ('quantify' or 'test').

I asked CAT members what practices came to mind when torture was uttered. One member reflected for a moment and came up with: 'EITs [enhanced interrogation techniques], hooding maybe that's a bit more in the middle, loud music, putting people in a coffin, implicit threat to carry pain could also amount to torture'.[36] When asked whether torture was more associated with physical suffering than psychological, the same member answered that all torture had both a physical and psychological element to it. Yet when I posed that torture was primarily associated with physical suffering in the caselaw, the same member explained that it is 'not a rule but a predisposition'. And in that light, while psychological suffering was 'still within the threshold of either ill-treatment or torture, it would be more often considered to be lesser'. For another CAT member, that meant that 'the physical aspect is very inevitable; it's a very essential aspect'.[37] Another member accepted the dominance of physical over psychological suffering ('there's an inclination to rather perceive psychological treatment as a treatment rather than torture'[38]). *Ireland* (1978) too resonated here, with one applicant lawyer using its presumption 'that physical

[33] ECtHR3, senior registry lawyer.
[34] ECtHR26, judge.
[35] ECtHR8, judge.
[36] CAT9, member.
[37] CAT15, member.
[38] CAT2, former member.

suffering, which obviously brings with it mental suffering, is the sort of classic case'.[39]

A former CAT member explained that 'it can be quite often you have to rely on your intuition'.[40] Another member, admitting to not having the benefit of extensive research or the same experience as others, took severity as crucial and recognized that the starting point was 'pretty impressionistic'—meaning 'an assessment is not like seven units of pain etc but physical unit might seem easier to assess. [...] I don't remember the algorithm' (as in there is no algorithm).[41] The member found severity to be an old subjective question ('what seems severe to me might not be for you; [though] it feels obvious, we often seem to ask how much suffering have you experienced, hope that the courts do better than us'). These were not scientific but 'socially constructed' ('what made it severe? God didn't make it, it's the person's perception; forced nudity wasn't always degrading, it is socially constructed'). For instance, this member had come to accept that capital punishment induces psychological suffering but no one asks to prove it scientifically ('like with a wire to the head').

Conclusion

In all, interviewees across institutions readily accepted using intuitive reasoning when dealing with interpretive difficulties, admittedly not completely freely but in a cautious and qualified manner. This was somewhat unexpected given the preponderance of research reporting the doctrinal denial of sense-centric reasoning. With the persistent intuitive association between torture and physical suffering, these accounts indicated, psychological suffering could well be disserved by this register. Intuition, in some responses, came to border on impression, experience, and emotion ('feeling')—the latter of which I now turn to explore.

Emotion

Empathetic reasoning, as with the intuitive, also saw a ready acceptance across all institutions. As it operated without precision in the caselaw, I inquired

[39] CAT21, applicant lawyer.
[40] CAT4, former member.
[41] CAT9, member.

into whether (and if so, how) it played a part in interviewees' work, relating it as closely as possible to the recognition of psychological suffering. As empathy featured in the caselaw more than any other emotion, closely related to vulnerability-oriented reasoning, I framed my questions around empathy and vulnerability. This register of reasoning was self-defined and operated through synonyms. It was viewed as inevitable and instrumental but also very much came with limitations.

As self-defined and synonymized

Empathy was defined as 'putting ourselves in the shoes' of applicants.[42] For another judge, empathy was 'necessary to understand the victim's position to help overcome insurmountable issues for victims to argue'.[43] Referring to a case on access to clean drinking water, a judge reflected: 'try to imagine yourself being a Roma child going to school coming from a household that does not have the minimum sanitary conditions, that will affect everyone, and these children are already stigmatized'.[44] This was an act of imagination.

Another judge said that, while empathy was not used in deliberations, 'we use synonyms', meaning 'quite often that a judge deliberating on the draft will say "I feel sorry for the applicant, it's a very sad story", especially if it involved life loss; so there will be a number of judges who will say that we feel sorry, but still we have to stick to some legal standards'.[45] Another 'synonym' was 'common sense':

> common sense allows you to assess vulnerability or identify these factors in order to dig deeper [...] we have shortcuts saying women are vulnerable, which is again, is not per se correct. It's a situation that makes people vulnerable. Anyone can be vulnerable, [a] young man in good health can be vulnerable in detention [...] But I'm saying it's the common sense of the situation that makes you I don't know maybe put yourself in the shoes of that person and actually think what he or she should have done differently to argue the case better and then you understand there was nothing more to be done.[46]

[42] ECtHR8, judge; ECtHR26, judge.
[43] ECtHR15, judge.
[44] ECtHR8, judge.
[45] ECtHR13, judge.
[46] ECtHR28, senior registry lawyer.

Referring to a case of children in immigration detention, one judge reflected on the nexus between common sense and life trajectories as follows:[47]

> you will be aware having read the facts, how old the person is. You will know subconsciously that we perceive time differently depending upon if we are children or teenagers or if we're I would imagine over seventy and know that we're closer to the end than we were when the journey started. This will impact our perception of time. And so being locked up at seventy is probably mentally dramatic in a different way than at twenty-five but I would not always have the possibility of getting the scientific evidence for this being the case that this will be something that I based on my own life experience. The same goes for children. Whether we discussed it or not, I cannot recall, but it must have gone through our minds when we looked at children in a situation of incarceration. The issue was whether they had something that resembled school, some sort of activity. This also weighed in, whether it was pure incarceration without any attempt to break the lethargy of doing nothing. But if that was based upon a scientific finding or not, I really cannot say and we would have to look at the case again, whether we make any references, I cannot recall that we do. I do, however, know that there must be scientific evidence around that situation.

This judge drew heavily on their own life experience to project it onto the victims before them. Empathy rested on personal or commonsensical knowledge—directing reasoning in significant ways.

As inevitable and instrumental

Almost all responses pointed out that empathy was inevitable and inextricable, with one judge explaining: 'judges say that justice should be blind and emotions should not play a part unless absolutely necessary; even if emotions can't be read in the judgment, it shouldn't mean that it didn't touch the judges' hearts, not at all'.[48] Other judges likewise saw 'nothing wrong with a judge being empathetic; the quality of mercy is part of the judicial process'.[49] Empathy was also central for applicant lawyers ('it's very hard to put your heart and soul into

[47] ECtHR24, judge.
[48] ECtHR15, judge.
[49] ECtHR26, judge.

litigating a case without empathy because you couldn't see that something has gone wrong';[50] for 'judges generally, it's the evidence that persuades them but if you've got a great story, they're going to be more inclined to do that […] you humanize the story. It's just human nature, because you can turn it into a much better narrative, that's always more attractive').[51]

Interviewees were forthcoming with illustrations on this front. A former senior registry lawyer, focussing on the ECmHR proceedings, readily recalled that 'the oral evidence of a witness can of course be very significant' and 'emotionally strong', as illustrated in a case where the mother of a disappeared man came to a hearing and sat behind the lawyers:

> not really knowing what's going on […] she comes across as being such a vulnerable old lady whose son has disappeared. And she's frightened that he's been murdered. And it's very emotional. And I'm sure, when the Commission came to discuss the merits they could not have ignored this, the plight of this old lady crying about her son and wanting him back, but fearing the worst.[52]

Empathy, for this senior lawyer, was 'embedded a little bit in our sense of dignity and human rights'. It drove the development of human rights law, particularly 'positive obligations on governments to create special protection measures for people in vulnerable situations'. Empathy was a motivating factor, for this lawyer, in recognition of suffering as related to the corporal punishment of children and the abolition of the death penalty. Relating other instances of field visits, the same lawyer 'could not help but be sympathetic, empathetic to people who were relatively illiterate, poor, but suffered ill-treatment, properties destroyed, crops destroyed'. Another applicant lawyer from the same era similarly recalled that

> we had opportunities to talk to them informally when the hearings were over. They had a huge amount of empathy for the applicants. I'm sure that did have a bearing on the facts which they found. […] You don't find the same sort of relationship with the judge in Strasbourg, if you're just sitting there, representing the applicant, and they're sort of 100 yards away across the floor in that courtroom.[53]

50 ECtHR32, applicant lawyer.
51 ECtHR31, applicant lawyer.
52 ECtHR22, former senior registry lawyer.
53 ECtHR38, applicant lawyer.

With specific reference to three cases,[54] a senior registry lawyer observed that the Court has often found violations of Article 3 based on psychological suffering 'without documentary evidence' of impact, although 'the events giving rise to the complaints have to be proven'. This was done through empathetic reasoning: 'once they establish that a villager's house had been deliberately burned down, decision-makers then in a way put themselves in the shoes of the applicants, decide with their own thoughts and convictions'.[55] Referring to a case involving terminal illness, a senior registry lawyer said that 'you have to be really insensitive not to feel for these people'.[56] Adjudication and feeling, simply put, went hand in hand.

Given the complexity inhering in the nature of suffering ('we all suffer in our own unique way'), for one senior IACtHR lawyer, what recognition came down to was what he called 'judicial empathy, which is the way in which judges connected with the humanity of the suffering of victims'.[57] Empathy was seen as obvious, indispensable, inevitable, and essential. It allowed 'the victim to tell their story for the first time and be listened to with dignity [...] we don't love cases, we love people';[58] 'you cannot be indifferent to pain and suffering; empathy means that you put yourself in somebody else's shoes'.[59] This pro-victim approach, for one former IACmHR lawyer, 'conditions your mind in terms of thinking from the perspective of the victim [...] to find the most expansive interpretation'.[60] Again, linking suffering and empathy:

> if one really wants to play the victim at the centre of the process, you actually need to open yourself to understanding that the pain that the person is referring [to] is not something abstract. [...] The immediate challenge there is how to ensure continuing our objective appreciation of the facts [...] you don't need to even feel that they're lovely but you need to understand their pain. The moment you do that, there's an inevitability to connect with them on a human level. It's the perception of the humanity in the other.[61]
>
> When it comes to putting yourself in the place of another person to try to understand the experience or the impacts that they were living through during whatever mistreatment was occurring; probably, even though most

[54] *Akkum and ors v Turkey* [2005] ECtHR 21894/93; *Benzer and others v Turkey* [2013] ECtHR 23502/06; *Güvec v Turkey* [2009] ECtHR 70337/01.
[55] ECtHR17, senior registry lawyer.
[56] ECtHR25, senior registry lawyer.
[57] IACtHR4, former senior IACtHR lawyer.
[58] IACtHR5, former senior IACmHR lawyer.
[59] IACtHR7, former senior IACmHR lawyer.
[60] IACtHR5, former senior IACmHR lawyer.
[61] IACtHR4, former senior IACtHR lawyer.

> judges on the Interamerican Court or in any human rights body […] they've never been through a situation like that. They may probably come from a class in society that is not very likely to be arbitrarily detained, and tortured or beaten up at a protest or mistreated in health institution or just whatever context we're talking about, they probably haven't gone through that experience.[62]

As at the ECmHR, live victim testimonies were grounds to engender empathy for the IACtHR. A lawyer recounted 'listening to very vivid descriptions by the survivors of the torture that they suffered […] this gets to the judges, that will have an impact';[63] so much so that, the same lawyer underlined, for judges, 'was the victim convincing?' was the most important question in a hearing. A poor performance could mean that established presumptions around suffering emanating from certain experiences could be questioned (creating 'a huge problem for the case'), and a good performance rendered expertise less important.[64] Empathy was also essential, for one senior lawyer, in determining reparations.[65]

A sitting judge accepted the doctrinal limitations with which the IACtHR was also charged with, for example seeing 'stereotypical' torture as physical,[66] but explained that these were progressively and effectively dismantled through testimonies of those arguing for victimhood[67] based on 'how the case has "touched" judges, such as […] with the victims with a story'.[68] An in-person hearing, used regularly by the IACtHR as compared to the other institutions, was characterized as 'an important event as it's the only opportunity the judges have of direct contact with the proof in the case'. As it was the Court lawyers who processed and summarized the case for the judges, the hearing was an important opportunity for the judges who didn't know much about a case. This might mean that: 'if the judges don't like you [as a victim], this is going to work against you, even though you have a good case with strong evidence' and vice versa—confirming that empathy could be more important than evidence ('empathy is a strong, powerful tool in the Interamerican system'). Such emotional registers impacted, though immeasurably, how much other evidence was needed to persuade the Court in finding a violation.

62 IACtHR9, applicant lawyer.
63 IACtHR5, former senior IACmHR lawyer.
64 IACtHR15, senior IACtHR lawyer.
65 IACtHR14, senior IACtHR lawyer.
66 IACtHR9, applicant lawyer.
67 IACtHR10, judge.
68 IACtHR17, expert.

At the CAT, empathy was also described as used 'inevitably',[69] given that it was 'impossible to be neutral with some victims',[70] and was manifest in pushing harder for gender-based violence victims ('it was my sentimental commitment to human rights [...] that played an important role in pushing this hard [...] it was heart-breaking'[71]). Using common sense was also a means of expedience, with a former member continuing that 'we need that a lot [...] in order to take a decision'.[72] Interviewees at the CAT, beyond confirming the inevitability of empathy, instead focussed heavily on its limitations—a point which I now explore.

As limited by legality

A free admission to empathy's inevitability was quickly followed by its limitations. While the point of departure could be to ask whether 'objectively does this shock me or make me awake and my sense of indignation?', the established caselaw ultimately needed to be followed: 'we cannot change the law itself, the way we apply the rules, so has to be consistent; you cannot have one section saying slapping a guy is all right and the other thing slapping is not'.[73] 'Despite being professionals we are not exempt from compassion', a registry lawyer explained; 'we always try to stay within the framework of legal reasoning [...] and to properly assess and be supported by evidence [...] it cannot be just the fruit of your own assessment'.[74] The dangers of empathetic thinking also had an emotional toll:

> I've been a judge in [X country] for more than [X] years. [...] you see so much suffering and you realize that if you allow yourself to really to open that door, you would not be able to make a good judgment [...] thousands [of] applications from people in prison in [X]. Of course, I felt sorry for all of them. You don't want anyone to be in [X] prison but that was simply not my task because if I were to follow those instincts, I would have allowed all the applicants.[75]

[69] CAT9, member.
[70] CAT10, member.
[71] CAT11, UN legal officer.
[72] CAT4, former member.
[73] ECtHR26, judge.
[74] ECtHR25, senior registry lawyer.
[75] ECtHR14, judge.

While empathy was seen as useful, it did come with limitations. Where the evidence was inadequate, one lawyer recounted, 'you have to go against what you feel but that's okay [...] I feel this way but I can't act on this feeling'.[76] It made a former senior registry lawyer 'look for solutions' and 'make something out of nothing' but it 'doesn't go all the way'.[77] Similarly, 'you have cases that break your heart but, you see, there's nothing you can do about it because either there's no evidence [...] you can't create evidence [...] this is not going to be a magical wand'. For the same lawyer, it was also important to observe that 'even an applicant who doesn't elicit empathy or sympathy has rights which have to be defended [...] terrorists, rapists, or murderers'. And empathy could very much falter with psychological suffering. For an applicant lawyer:[78]

> Even though you don't understand that level of physical pain, you'll understand, oh, my God, this is something that is completely beyond the pale and shouldn't be done to people. And certainly, it's also very easy, just in a kind of factual, logical way to say that this was completely unnecessary. Like, if a state takes you into its custody, for XYZ reason, it's completely unnecessary for them then to inflict this physical suffering, there's no justification, that didn't need to happen. But if you're talking about mental suffering, many judges or people in general who read an account, or are presented in an account, may not have that visceral or immediate empathy or ability to understand the degree of suffering or the degree of coercion that that was causing, because maybe they think, well, if someone said those things to me, let's say that the mental sufferings caused, I could resist, I would know that's not true. And really not appreciating that in the context in which that person was, anything having to do with their own identity and background and the context of what was being said to them.[79]

There was a difficulty but not an impossibility—one that was amplified with psychological suffering given the lack of visibility and the problematic figure of resilience. On this point, the lawyer went on to elaborate that

> it's much easier to blame the victim for mental suffering. If someone is beating you, or cutting you open, it's clearly like, oh, that person is doing that to you. You're the victim and this is not your choice. Like you're bleeding because all

[76] ECtHR25, senior registry lawyer.
[77] ECtHR22, former senior registry lawyer.
[78] ECtHR14, judge.
[79] IACtHR9, applicant lawyer.

> human bodies bleed. It's not your fault. But if it's mental suffering, it's easier to blame the victim. You got really intimidated or emotional because you [are] basically weak-minded [. . .] you could or should have been able to react to that in a different way. You have some sort of particularity inside you that apparently made you feel that you were suffering greatly. That's very much in the range of speculation.

The notion of resilience, therefore, could place responsibility on the victim and away from the perpetrator—that it could be seen as sourced at the psychological weakness of the victim. A similar expectation of resilience also featured in another lawyer's guarded explanation that his supervisor imposed his own experience as a torture survivor as his standard: 'anything that was lower than what he suffered was not torture [. . .] the influential voices sometimes took that approach'.[80] Empathy here was conditioned directly by personal experience, distinctly narrowing its nature and heightening the threshold of recognition in practice.

As at the ECtHR, one CAT member conditioned the power of empathy in explaining: 'if there is a story that looks credible, then of course you empathize with the victim',[81] and that 'empathy is important, but it must be backed up by professional expertise and experience'.[82] This was formulated as a balance between *legality* and *humanity* for another member, who normally viewed cases with 'humanity without going beyond the borders, without harming or undermining legality, in terms of the obligations under the provisions of our Convention'.[83] Again, empathy had its limitations: it could only take you as far as was possible within the 'scope of the law'[84] and, although it helped in 'formulating your own stand to certain issues and evaluating and reevaluating that position, if there is too much empathy then we become like an NGO [. . .] you cannot base your decision on it'.[85] Where the legal grounds were non-existent, the former member felt that:

> I cannot make the decision even though I felt sorry for those complainants [. . .] Because this is not an NGO. This is not a humanitarian organization

[80] IACtHR5, former senior IACmHR lawyer.
[81] CAT20, UN legal officer.
[82] CAT14, member.
[83] CAT11, UN legal officer.
[84] Tobias Kelly, 'Sympathy and Suspicion: Torture, Asylum, and Humanity' (2012) 18 (4) The Journal of the Royal Anthropological Institute 753: referring to a judge who said 'in practice you make a decision first and then write the decision to justify why you have come to that decision'.
[85] CAT16, member.

> […] If we can't do anything, you're going to change the legal frame […] if you start to just act outside the scope of the Convention, we are undermining the system because it's not a legal system anymore. It's not a treaty body. It's just opinion from individuals.[86]

Another former member recounted the experience of an advocacy group that came out quite strong in a meeting with the CAT on intersex genital mutilation:[87]

> At the beginning, I must admit I was somewhat sceptical of whether this would really fall under the Convention. I had probably the perception that there's so much political gain in having your condition recognized as torture that we should be a little bit cautious of not just running in all sorts of directions and other special rapporteurs have sometimes done that, which has probably not been beneficial to the fight against torture. But that's been my view but seeing the results of sex determination operation in photos and listening to the individual stories of people that have been through […] And that is really an example of something where it's a life-long suffering, and it has been induced, perhaps in good faith. I don't know, not intentionally to create suffering that's not the issue. I have also always been against the Committee having too many victims, or appealing for the empathy of the members because it also deviates a bit from the more sound objective evaluation of the situation.

There is much to unpack here of a process of resistance, reception, and progress. The member is first wary of recognizing 'too many victims', wary of acting on 'empathy', but gives way upon being presented with photographic and testimonial evidence. It also accords to the scholarship which characterizes empathy as selective and intersubjectively limited, susceptible to 'bias and stereotype'.[88]

While empathy has been accepted largely as a conduit for heightening judicial receptivity to victims' lived experience and as a 'necessary vehicle for context-engagement',[89] it hasn't always worked in the advantage of the

[86] CAT1, former member.

[87] CAT2, former member.

[88] Emily Kidd White, 'On Emotions and the Politics of Attention in Judicial Reasoning' in Amalia Amaya and Maksymilian Del Mar (eds), *Virtue, Emotion and Imagination in Law and Legal Reasoning* (Bloomsbury 2020) 105.

[89] Corina Heri, *Responsive Human Rights: Vulnerability, Ill-Treatment and the ECtHR* (Hart 2021) 194. Ezgi Yildiz, 'A Court with Many Faces: Institutional Identities and Interpretive Preferences: The Case of the European Court of Human Rights and the Norm against Torture', PhD thesis, IHEID

applicant. State authorities were also seen to deserve it. Returning me to the debate around the *Bouyid* decision, one judge, characterizing it as 'go[ing] very far', focussed on the fact that it 'was a provoked slap' and that the police reacted so because the applicants 'were very arrogant, and that at some point he lost his temper'.[90] Empathy was directed at the police officer, not the children. Empathy, therefore, worked in a complex manner, protected to be selectively used and potentially in the interest of the state.

Conclusion

Despite the scholarship, which assumes adjudicators' propensity to conceal and foreclose discussing empathy, almost all interviewees talked openly and freely.[91] Similarly, empathy did not necessarily lead to expansive recognition but sometimes to caution—countering the preponderance of scholarship promoting its use as a means to genuinely differentiate, ground, and relativize lived experience on a case-by-case basis.[92] Empathetic engagement was a central factor in how interviewees recognized suffering—directive but not determinative. Experience too was a focus, instrumental in directing reasoning towards recognition.

It was difficult to have all interviewees reflect directly on psychological suffering, with some preferring to speak broadly, but those who did offered unique (though somewhat speculative) insights connecting the complexities of psychological suffering to producing even more doubt for adjudicators. Interviewees largely depended on empathetic and experience-informed reasoning in assessing suffering. Importantly, this generally pre-empted the need for evidentiary corroboration and activated adjudicators and institutional lawyers towards recognition, conceivably to do more in difficult cases. Emotional reactions guided adjudicators and senior registry lawyers but had to be presented more convincingly as through the invocation of precedent or similar objectifying means.

Geneva (2016) 219 attributes the expansion in the scope of Article 3 to 'empathizing with the suffering of the victims when identifying violations'.

[90] ECtHR20, judge.

[91] Lynne Hendersen, 'Legality and Empathy' (1987) 85 Michigan Law Review 1576.

[92] For Kidd White (n 88) 110, empathy is 'a facet of attention [...] motivated by an affective respect or concern for the other [and] reinforces the respect owed to the claimant, and cultivates a serious interest in lived experiences under the impugned law'.

Presumption

Suffering, to put all this slightly differently, has largely been presumed (through degrees of speculation) by advocates and adjudicators in submissions and judgments across all three institutions. Adjudicators, for instance, have inferred that a specific experience 'must have felt' a certain way.[93] The ECtHR has in fact held that 'there are circumstances where proof of the actual effect on the person may not be a major factor', alluding to a related presumption of suffering from certain practices.[94] Presumptions have often denoted a universal reaction to certain experiences ('nobody needs to prove the prisoner who was held in horrible conditions suffered mentally; it just follows from establishing the conditions were inhuman').[95] Applicant lawyers too have come to expect adjudicators to not always ask for expertise but rather to simply presume ('I'm not expecting the Court to ask for a report in a case where a child, for example, was expelled in the cold during the winter; you should presume that there should be serious suffering').[96]

Invoking 'rules of logic and based on experience'[97] has similarly led the IACtHR to form presumptions, for instance around disappearances,[98]

[93] Heri (n 89); see, eg, *El-Masri v Macedonia* [2012] ECtHR 39630/09 [202]: 'apprehension as to what would happen to him next and must have caused him emotional and psychological distress'; *Radu v Romania* [2009] ECtHR 34022/05 [48]: 'the constant mental anxiety caused by the threat of physical violence and the anticipation of such […] must have exceeded the unavoidable level inherent in detention'; *Nalbandyan v Armenia* [2015] ECtHR 9935/06 [106]: 'the extremely vulnerable condition that the third applicant must have been in at the material time and the fear and trauma that she must have suffered'; *Wiktoriko v Poland* [2009] ECtHR 14612/02 [55]: 'prolonged immobilisation of the applicant must have caused her great distress and physical discomfort'; *Dimov v Bulgaria* [2015] ECtHR 57123/08 [68]: 'the continuous immobilization of the applicant must have caused him considerable psychological suffering'; *Zherdev v Ukraine* [2017] ECtHR 34015/07 [93]: 'the applicant's placement with adult detainees […] must have contributed to creating in him feelings of fear, anguish, helplessness and inferiority, diminishing his dignity'; *Ostrovenecs v Latvia* [2018] ECtHR 36043/13 [95]: 'the ill-treatment inflicted by the detainee escort officers on the applicant, who was a minor and entirely under their control, must also have caused him considerable mental suffering, diminishing his human dignity'; *Yöyler v Turkey* [2003] 26973/95 [75]: 'the destruction of the applicant's home and possessions, as well as the anguish and distress suffered by members of his family, must have caused him suffering of sufficient severity'; *Yordanov v Bulgaria* [2021] 79709/13 [95]: '[that] the applicant was confined for practically twenty-four hours a day during more than three months to his cell without exposure to natural light and without any possibility for physical and other out-of-cell activities must have caused him considerable suffering'.

[94] *Keenan v UK* [1998] ECtHR 27229/95 [112].

[95] ECtHR27, senior registry lawyer.

[96] ECtHR21, applicant lawyer.

[97] *Cantoral-Benavides v Peru* [2006] IACtHR [48].

[98] *Suárez-Rosero v Ecuador* [1997] [IACtHR] [90–91]: isolation 'produces moral and psychological suffering in any person, places him in a particularly vulnerable position. […] The mere fact that the victim was for 36 days deprived of any communication with the outside world, in particular with his family, allows the Court to conclude [CIDT]'.

massacres,[99] and extrajudicial executions.[100] It has also drawn presumptions against a state where individuals are released from state custody with signs of ill-treatment[101] or if the responding state did not contest certain allegations.[102] This mode of reasoning nevertheless read as vague and varied on the page, unpredictable beyond certain patterns and practices. Although adjudicators unquestionably operate between 'flexibility and legal certainty' in realizing their ends,[103] how and when presumptions were formed, feature, and function in adjudication remained insufficiently explained. In the interviews, I explored how such presumptions arose and what they meant for the assessment of psychological suffering. I group the reflections around context, time, and common sense.

Context as enabling presumption

For interviewees, presumptive reasoning was primarily linked back to the broader context of human rights litigation—confirming the conventional characters of the non-responsive state with a poor record and the evidence-poor victim caught up in a slow process in the pursuit of justice. A senior lawyer explained that many cases

> came from civil wars, dictatorships, not democratic regimes, so extremely difficult to get medical records. The pace of the litigation and everything means that the cases are adjudicated twenty or thirty years after they took place. So concrete evidence was extremely difficult. Because much of the early caselaw

[99] *Mapiripán Massacre v Colombia* [2005] IACtHR [146]: 'no evidence is required to prove the grave impact on the mental and emotional well-being of the next of kin of the victims. Furthermore, the fact that the very circumstances of the case have not allowed the national authorities, as well as this Court, to have more information on other next of kin of the victims, makes it reasonable to presume that all of these, whether identified or not, suffered the extreme circumstances of the massacre or its consequences'.

[100] *Herzog and ors v Brazil* [2018] IACtHR [351]: in 'massacres, forced disappearances, extrajudicial executions or torture, the Court has considered that the Commission or the representatives do not need to prove the violation of personal integrity because a juris tantum presumption exists'; in *Aloeboetoe et al v Suriname* [1993] IACtHR, where victims were forced to dig their own graves, the IACtHR found it 'clear that the victims suffered moral damages, for it is characteristic of human nature that anybody subjected to the aggression and abuse described above will experience moral suffering. The Court considers that no evidence is required to arrive at this conclusion' [52].

[101] *Miguel Castro-Castro Prison v Peru* [2006] IACtHR [273].

[102] IACmHR Rules of Procedure [38–39]; *Bámaca-Velásquez v Guatemala* [2000] IACtHR [100]; *Velásquez-Rodríguez v Honduras* [1988] IACtHR [135].

[103] Francoise Tulkens, 'Judicial Activism v Judicial Restraint: Practical Experience of This (False) Dilemma at the European Court of Human Rights' (2022) 3 European Convention on Human Rights Law Review 293.

> was developed around the cases of enforced disappearances, the presumptions played a very strong role. If the Court was going to require concrete scientific evidence, most of the cases would have been thrown out because it was impossible to have a doctor documenting the situations even after you were released, or things like that. There were no witnesses or anything. There was a pact of silence among the security forces so nobody would dare say anything. So the Court created all sorts of presumptions. The Court never adopted the European Court's standard of 'beyond any reasonable doubt'. Our Court applies *sana critica*, basically the judicial discretion on assessment of evidence. All these factors lead to a very different institutional, cultural approach to evidence.[104]

Others similarly framed their responses with a historical arc. A judge explained that, at its inception, the IACtHR needed to establish an evidence-based understanding of suffering for itself, which it now took for granted through using established presumptions such as 'that impact in certain types of violation that include extrajudicial executions, for disappearances and torture'.[105] Where a practice was not commonly viewed as prohibited, evidence came more into focus; where it attracted a common view as attracting a violation, evidence was less in focus.

Asked when they chose to infer suffering circumstantially or contextually, a senior ECtHR registry lawyer explained: 'as the factors build up, the Court feels free to come closer to making inferences; when there's a hole, there's a jump that needs to be made'.[106] Pointing to the concept of 'administrative practice', another senior lawyer said: 'without mentioning or taking note of the general context and to just examine the case as it just exists in isolation would not be enough to find a violation or no violation—repetition of certain number of events that play a role [often corroborating] official tolerance'.[107] A judge, citing cases on violence against women, characterized this as a contextual assessment where 'the broader social context can play a part in understanding a particular incident'.[108] Another judge, putting this more pithily, urged that: 'we should not strive to individualize the issues in front of us; we are judging systems'.[109]

104 IACtHR5, former senior IACtHR lawyer.
105 IACtHR10, judge.
106 ECtHR28, senior registry lawyer.
107 ECtHR17, senior registry lawyer.
108 ECtHR15, judge.
109 ECtHR24, judge.

That torture was generally understood to prevail in, say, a state like Morocco would likely mean that the CAT would not question too much compared to where the prevalence of torture is rare.[110] Such reference to context also featured in the reflections of a former member who explained that: 'if someone comes and tells you have been severely tortured by the police in Sweden, rather than, for example, China, Vietnam, or Iran, then you really have to explore in much more detail'.[111] General knowledge, country context, and patterns were packed into yet another response: 'If it is Switzerland or Sweden, you feel the need to look harder than if it was Algeria, as based on common sense and the general information.'[112] For another former member, the culmination of patterns and presumptions built over cases similarly helped reach a decision:

> several people have been subjected to the same treatment, or the same place or by the same perpetrators that kind of reasoning. I don't know if you call that common sense. In a way you could say it's actually more sophisticated than common sense because the moment you see patterns, you look for patterns […] You could even expand that to when the CAT links individual communicational to the state party review, to bring that's in concluding observations for the same state party, then who is accused in the individual complaint. […] Because we deduce that from our general knowledge of how conditions are, for instance, for a gay or lesbian person in a detention centre in that country.[113]

Contextual reasoning did not stand unchallenged, however. Presumptions could not, according to one insider, arise from pointing to the general conditions of prison conditions in a country—as not specifying impact meant that it would likely be deemed inadmissible.[114] As with the *Cardenas* case in the final vignette at the book's outset, the reliance on presumptions has engendered the rare dissent at the IACtHR, and, as discussed shortly, at the ECtHR. Reasoning based on precedent and 'common knowledge' eased assessments but it was otherwise admittedly complex.

110 CAT20, UN legal officer.
111 CAT4, former member.
112 CAT13, member.
113 CAT2, former member.
114 IACtHR6, former senior IACmHR lawyer.

Common sense and presumption

A few judges drew links between inferences and common sense, explaining 'that inferences and common sense is drawn upon because context allows for it—that it requires a certain kind of setting—if we as judges weren't using common sense, we wouldn't be in the business'; that 'all judgments are informed by mindset and experience' and 'personal background, values, and experiences of course play an important part'; and that 'weighing evidence is always about common sense, deduce from indications'. This was because, as the judge put it, 'we will always have fragments of cases—like a puzzle with missing pieces'. It was 'common sense which makes you dig deeper or not [which] explains that in the given circumstances you're not in your best fit shape'.[115]

For one interviewee, 'shared values' were channelled through '*sana critica*'.[116] For another interviewee, when 'the normative rule that backs this up' was not found and 'you're just stating something obvious […] then there's this kind of instinctive need to put kind of phrase there, instead of just stating the obvious thing you have to say, "well, because of logic and experience" '.[117] Common sense was readily linked to the concept of '*sana critica*', taken to mean how a judge

> freely examines the evidence incorporated into the case file in accordance with the rules of logic and based on experience, without the probative weight of each of them being predetermined. You could say that's common sense. The idea behind it is to give flexibility to judges at the time of weighing the evidence as a whole.[118]

Commonsensical reasoning, this lawyer qualified, could only be 'appropriate if they are bolstered or supported by science […] it's important to be open to the evolution of international understandings of standards and to how science cooperates in that evolution'. Otherwise, he explained, adjudicators would risk operating on commonsensical attitudes that 'this couldn't have hurt that much'.

While potentially used to understand suffering, 'common knowledge or intuitive estimations of what the public believes could then also be used to argue

[115] ECtHR28, senior registry lawyer.
[116] IACtHR10, judge.
[117] IACtHR9, applicant lawyer.
[118] IACtHR7, former senior IACmHR lawyer.

that psychological ill-treatments are a second-class type of treatment which could never amount to torture'.[119] It remains possible here that:

> far from clarifying our conception of torture, deferring to ordinary usage or common-sense understandings of torture is likely to reinforce such beliefs [as it likely] inhibits recognition of the ways in which such understandings are shaped by and reflect biased assumptions about what counts as suffering and whose suffering counts.[120]

Commonsensical presumptions made between age and vulnerability, for instance, have not been impervious to debate and dissent. In a case concerning immigration detention, a judge questioned the majority's broad-stroke reasoning in one important case on associating age with vulnerability, holding that[121]

> the Court relies on the applicants' age, considering them to be children, and refers to the caselaw that applies special standards of care as regards the conditions of detention of migrant children. However, all the cited cases concern small children [...] In the present case the applicants were about seventeen years old and their age was contested at the time of the detention. I do not consider that caselaw based on the problems of small children is applicable to adolescents.

The focus on specific or heightened vulnerability serves to depict a limited understanding of the harms at play for all concerned and thus invisibilize the general vulnerability of all those who are put in detention and isolation. While on the one hand vulnerability emphasizes recognition, the specific designation 'suggests that some of us are not vulnerable'.[122]

Common sense was also seen to 'connect to what we reasonably expect' in terms of treatment from the state, as illustrated by the Court 'saying it is reasonable to expect that mothers will suffer at the torture of their sons ... we all know that it is logical to expect that our mother suffers'.[123] Another lawyer was more direct about the use of common sense, linking it to presumptions about psychological suffering

[119] Muntean (n 32) 147–48.
[120] Jessica Wolfendale, 'Prison as a Torturous Institution' (2020) 97 (2) Res Philosophica 311.
[121] *Elmi and Abubakar v Malta* [2017] ECtHR 25794/13, concurring opinion of Judge Sajo.
[122] Martha Fineman and Anna Grear (eds), *Vulnerability: Reflections on a New Ethical Foundation for Law and Politics* (Ashgate 2013) 16.
[123] IACtHR4, former senior IACtHR lawyer.

> In general, we do presumptions […] thinking like 'what would a rational person conclude with these elements of proof', more like a rookie guess, I would say. In general, when we don't have expert opinions about that. We make assumptions based on our common sense. We don't require more proof or more opinions. We don't have a scientific rule, or a scientific test, to arrive at this conclusion.[124]

As with the earlier discussion, there was a flexibility in reasoning, allowing for presumptive shortcuts, that led to a lack of methodological rigour. This could also serve to flatten or avoid a deeper consideration of the nature of suffering in question. Such registers could mean that emerging forms of suffering, particularly those psychologically oriented, required more explicit reasoning. Where precedents are established concerning particular practices, reflection and evaluation is replaced with 'principles, presumptions, and benchmarks'[125]—with interpretation reduced to 'sentence plus footnote, sentence plus footnote'.[126] Some suffering, through such reasoning, no longer needs further reflection, 'made relatively swiftly and easily', whereas other forms merit 'a more fulsome exploration':[127]

> As the precedents build up, we replace vague evaluative terms with lists of practices that are prohibited, practices that can then be identified descriptively rather than by evaluative reasoning. In time, the list usurps the standard; the list becomes the effective norm in our application of the provision; the list is what is referred to when an agency is trying to ensure that it is in compliance […] Through its precedents the ECtHR has established a set of principles, presumptions, and benchmarks on various issues relating to the circumstances in which official action might count as inhuman and degrading. […] The standard invites us to reflect upon and argue about whether a given practice is degrading or inhuman. But now we simply consult a list of rules. The result is a decline in the level of the moral argument—I mean the level of abstraction, but perhaps also the quality of moral argument—that the standard seemed to require […] It is not clear how this approach helps when a court is confronted with an unprecedented practice alleged to be inhuman or degrading. How should a court approach the task of establishing a new precedent in this area? How should counsel in such a case frame their

[124] IACtHR15, senior IACtHR lawyer.
[125] Jeremy Waldron, *Torture, Terror and Trade-Offs: Philosophy for the White House* (Oxford University Press 2010) 284–86.
[126] ibid 289.
[127] ibid 35–36.

> arguments? Should they proceed by a process of analogy with the list of practices already condemned as violations of the standard?

This state of affairs has been argued as reducing the quality of moral reflection, especially where emergent practices vie for recognition.[128] Confirming this approach, a former judge characterized the notion of inherent harm as a presumption that 'presumes that there is this harm associated normally associated to these practices […] based on good sense, bad sense […] it's the same more or less the same presumption that leads to the conclusion that rape is a form of torture, but this is not really scientific language, it's very commonsensical'.[129] And, to return to the earlier analysis on time, much commonsensical reasoning has also turned on how suffering has been timed.

Duration and presumption

Assessments of temporal frames (time or duration) for interviewees too allowed presumptions to be made as to the suffering involved; for instance, 'if you have been hung up by your arms for two days; the presumption is that you have experienced physical pain, even though there's no long-lasting disability'.[130] Time was also a central consideration of how the gravity of psychological suffering was assessed. Psychological suffering, for an ECtHR registry lawyer, required repetitiveness to amount to torture (more than 'a single act of terror', 'be of regular character […] of a repetitive nature'[131]), and a judge recounted that: 'when you get a case involving psychological suffering, you must look at vulnerability, how long, and in front of whom'.[132] The variability was wide, attributable to an impressionistic and presumptive reading. For another judge, recognition flowed through 'proxy evidentiary value for assuming mental suffering', explaining:[133]

> solitary confinement as a practice plus a variation in time will sometimes act as a proxy for a degree of mental suffering. That is assumed, yes. We don't really know what happens in the mind of the person who is subjected to this,

128 ibid 289.
129 ECtHR19, former judge.
130 ECtHR22, former senior registry lawyer.
131 ECtHR23, senior registry lawyer.
132 ECtHR9, judge.
133 ECtHR24, judge.

> but through our caseload we have it is a sort of a simple rule to be on the alert for that sort of measure.

Such 'proxy value' was implicit in how a senior registry lawyer questioned whether anything less than one or two months of uncertainty for family of the disappeared reached minimum severity:[134]

> Not just like when you spend a few days just being anxious about what happened. […] It's natural for many people just to find out what happened to their family member and to their dad to, at least, see their bodies so they can pay their respects. It's a normal human desire, right. And when they're deprived of that, and they see this complicity of the authorities […] we'll find a violation where the person was missing for longer than, let's say, one month and then as for the person was missing for just, I don't know, three, four weeks, then the formulation is something like: the Court has no doubt that it must have caused profound suffering; however, it does not attain the minimum level of severity, the threshold.

On suffering arising from retraumatization, a judge similarly reflected that psychological suffering involved a

> typically longer time horizon, it develops over time, that consequences sometimes will take time […] it takes a long time for the impact to be fully visible; whether they have access to people who are able to do proper diagnosis, that's another question. So often, I guess it is fair to say we use shorthand and common sense.

This was 'in the nature of psychological harm' making the Court 'generally more prepared to assume that some kind of treatment will produce psychological harm, as opposed to physical'. After recounting the details of the case, the same judge assessed that

> of course, this has a terrible impact on her but it's not immediately visible because she, apart from the harrowing she had a horrible story, given for adoption, abandoned by a mother, raised in foster homes going through adolescence, and then these terrible things in the sexual abuse. […] it is only

[134] ECtHR29, senior registry lawyer.

> sometime later that, in fact, the full impact of that mistreatment becomes visible and then they figure out that she has full-blown PTSD.[135]

Similar reflections around psychological suffering taking time to become visible were also offered by a senior registry lawyer.[136] Suffering was presumed. The longer it lasted, the easier it became for the purposes of a legal assessment.

Conclusions

Sense-centric reasoning (intuition, emotion, and presumption) featured across all three institutions in how advocates and adjudicators argued and assessed suffering. Such registers operated both for and against recognition of psychological suffering, viewed as means to channel broader associations and values around suffering, to differentiate those deserving and others not, justified on the lack of evidence or time. Advocates and adjudicators admitted to employing these devices to 'screen, categorize, and interpret information; influence [their] evaluations of the intentions or credibility of others; and help [them] decide what is important or valuable'.[137] Although the principled stance was not to require physical, prolonged, or permanent damage, adjudicators continued to take these as central considerations (or 'as a proxy for the intensity of suffering experienced').[138]

Yet, what is unclear here is how much sense-centric reasoning serves to conceal prejudice or predetermination associated with different harms. Reasoning possibly presumes or infers suffering based on preconceived examinations of facts.[139] Adjudicators have unduly overridden expert evidence through applying such preconceptions or the 'invocation of emotional common sense [which] silently privilege their views'.[140] Such generalizations shape sense-centric reasoning, informing empathetic, intuitive, and impressionistic associations—also potentially pre-empting the reference to socio-political standards or scientific expertise. The discretion in opting for, foregrounding,

[135] ECtHR8, judge.

[136] ECtHR7, senior registry lawyer.

[137] Susan A Bandes and Jeremy A Blumenthal, 'Emotion and the Law' (2012) 8 Annual Review of Law and Social Science 161, 165.

[138] Natasa Mavronicola, *Torture, Inhumanity, and Degradation under Article 3 of the ECHR: Absolute Rights and Absolute Wrongs* (Hart 2021) 65.

[139] ibid 96.

[140] Terry Maroney, 'Lay Conceptions in Emotions of Law' in Susan Bandes and others (eds), *Research Handbook on Law and Emotion* (Elgar 2021) 15, 20.

or backgrounding standards, science, or senses was not simply because that was how an adjudicator viewed the best means to dispose of the individual case but were subject to policy and procedural considerations.

Notwithstanding critique, all institutions have depended heavily on inferential or presumptive reasoning, pre-empting a demand for evidentiary corroboration. This was particularly present where adjudicators have resorted to the 'must have felt' or adjacent mode of presumptive reasoning. All interviewees freely admitted to such sense-centric registers but qualified their use through the invocation of precedent or similar objectifying means for a semblance of legitimacy. Such registers could only be indicative—effectively rendering them legally questionable grounds to determine a case. Bringing this back to psychological suffering, the persistent intuitive association between torture and physical suffering raised the possibility that it could limit the due consideration of the nature of suffering generally and inhibit the equal recognition of psychological suffering, as admitted to by numerous interviewees. Psychological suffering, therefore, seemed to require more explicit consideration than physical suffering. That forced nudity, for instance, is generally accepted as degrading without resorting to scientific evidence is a case in point.

7
Conclusions

> The figure of the physical blow cannot describe the full spectrum of violence; indeed, no one figure can.[1]

> [N]ot dealing seriously with all aspects of this kind of suffering, in addition to being against the Convention, ignores the vast existing knowledge on torture and its consequences both on the mind and the body of the individual and on society as a whole.[2]

How well the three institutions have recognized psychological suffering has been varied and cautious. Following initial and immediate recognition in the first international cases on torture, the caselaw reads to raise more questions than resolve those around psychological suffering. While principles as in *Tyrer* and *Selmouni* have promised expansion, this has been realized unpredictably and unreliably. Such expansionism evident in the first cases came coupled with regressive (state-deferential) impulses, particularly with respect to psychological suffering. Recognition on this terrain continues to be contested, conceivably, despite associated harms, as psychologically oriented practices continue to be viewed as crucial to policing and penal practices. Interviewees freely painted a panorama of principled and practical factors that informed their reasoning. Pragmatic and procedural factors included consensus, collegiality, evidentiary caution and certainty, and delay. Reference to *Ireland v UK* (1978) and the historicity of torture enabled the admission that the physical was effectively a prerequisite for some adjudicators, precedentially 'baked into' their interpretive practice. Established problems with *Ireland*, that it fixed a high threshold for torture and that it effectively characterized torture as necessarily physically overt, were not sufficiently reflected upon by adjudicators, who instead sought to emphasize its enduring legacy as a quality not as rigidity.

[1] Judith Butler, *The Force of Nonviolence* (Verso 2020) 138.
[2] Nora Sveaass, 'Destroying Minds: Psychological Pain and the Crime of Torture' (2008) 11 (2) CUNY Law Review 305.

Torture and the Recognition of Psychological Suffering in International Law. Ergün Cakal, Oxford University Press.
 DOI: 10.1093/oso/9780198989493.003.0007

As on other points, most interviewees did not know or initially admit how narrow the torture categorization had proved to be, in terms of how few cases had been categorized as such; some pointed to the non-existence of stand-alone psychological suffering cases but promptly proceeded to rationalize its exceptionality. That the torture categorization remained in principle open to psychologically oriented practices, although none had attained the torture categorization, was sufficient comfort at all three institutions. The exceptionality of the torture categorization was also a matter of preserving the symbolic force of the prohibition—that if it was 'over-inclusive', it would be meaningless. The interpretive discretion afforded was explained, justified, and guarded through multiple modes, with an emphasis placed on procedural pragmatism (judicial consensus and economy), evidentiary certainty, and the possibility for future cases. I end with a summary of six primary conclusions.

Conclusion 1: cases focussing prominently on psychological suffering have been broadly recognized under the respective frameworks of all three institutions—from institutional inception to date

All three institutions have incorporated psychological suffering into their legal and interpretive frameworks, rejecting an *explicit* normative hierarchy between physical and psychological suffering. In fact, this recognition was easily identified in the founding moments of the respective legal frameworks—present in the drafting of respective conventions and in the early cases to be brought before the institutions. At the level of principle, the institutions have accepted that psychological suffering can amount to torture even if it has not yet been found in a particular case. Advocates and adjudicators alike have named psychological suffering in different ways in grasping its essence. They have depended on the words of victims and experts in equipping themselves in this complex exercise. The variability and creativity (and inconsistency) in the caselaw indicated a degree of difficulty in capturing the nature of psychological suffering. Notwithstanding inconsistency, the institutions have also been generally responsive to new cases and to understandings of torturous experiences and practices.

The ECtHR, in sum, loomed large over the adjudication of psychological suffering under torture's prohibition. It has effectively created a path-dependency for the IACtHR and the CAT in closely associating torture with a physical spectacle and rendering psychological suffering as an 'add-on'. This association runs unchecked and unreflected through the practices of all three institutions. As a forerunner, the ECtHR precedent and practice have been largely followed at the three institutions. While not always coherent and consistent, the precedents and practices of all three institutions appeared quite interdependent.

There were also important divergences between the three institutions. Conceptually, the ECtHR was clearly the strongest in relation to psychological suffering. The institutional arrangements (cultural and material) have allowed a relatively deeper discussion of concepts as pertaining to the adjudication of psychological suffering, as compared to the IACtHR and CAT. The question of whether and when these conditions were utilized, however, pointed to wide discretion. Discretion to recognize psychological suffering was individual, as evident through the notable use of dissenting opinions on the matter, as it was institutional, as evident in the explicit mechanisms in place at the ECtHR, namely the Grand Chamber and the Registry. When opportunities have presented, however, to conceptually elaborate on their recognition of psychological suffering, the IACtHR and the CAT have failed to meaningfully do so, preferring instead to generally follow the positions of the ECtHR, particularly in categorization.

The doctrinal material revealed little as to the contestations behind recognition, except where there were dissents. The official positions at all three institutions presented as *delivering* not *delimiting* protection when it came to psychological suffering. This was most clear where the respective institutions expressed their principled recognition that psychological suffering was no less important than physical suffering but effectively dismissed or discounted the former. Precedential rhetoric emphasized expansion, not exclusion, which were in fact both simultaneously afoot. A panoramic reading of the caselaw revealed significant delimitations and conditionalities. Although empirical (and legal realist) scholarship would well have anticipated an explanatory deficiency from doctrine, the doctrinal review was unavoidable in identifying precisely the thinness and silence in the caselaw for more empirical review.

Conclusion 2: recognition has been delimited based on exceptionality, temporality, and necessity

Despite general responsivity, the material presented has demonstrated that how these cases were argued and assessed remains varied (and vague) not just at the terminological level but more importantly in terms of recognition (finding violations or not). As ready as the recognition of psychological suffering reads, there have also been immediate exclusions (as delimitations), as sourced from the distinct association psychological suffering has had with degradation and discomfort rather than with torture. This 'counter-history', of how recognition has been delimited, with arguments made primarily by states against its inclusion, is less emphasized in official accounts at all three institutions. While psychological suffering has had an easier configuration with inhuman and degrading treatment compared to the category of torture, wide contestation in categorization persisted at all three institutions. Much indeed has been excluded, not only from the typical understandings of torture but also as altogether not warranting the protection of the prohibition at all.

Significantly delimiting the recognition of psychological suffering has been argued on the grounds of exceptionality (that the psychological suffering in question was trivial), necessity (that it was inevitable), and temporality (that it was fleeting). Such notions have operated to invisibilize the psychological suffering inflicted by certain psychologically oriented practices. These and related devices rendered forms of psychological suffering as *undesirable* though ultimately *inescapable*, as *overridable* unless *exceptional*, and as legitimated when purported to be rational, proportionate, and thus *necessary* and *indispensable*. More broadly, these logics served to sustain understandings of torture as *physical*, *exceptional*, *direct*, and *visible* as opposed to *psychological*, *routine*, *indirect*, and *invisible*.

Some forms of psychological suffering, primarily that which arose from prevalent state practices as solitary confinement, were excluded with little reflection by adjudicators. That individuals had felt intimidated by state officials, be it judges, police, prison or immigration officers, was often dismissed as inherent or necessary to law enforcement processes. These were boundaries that attracted strong institutional deference, evoking shades of non-justiciability (that it was too political for judicial assessments). It was not up to adjudicators to always second-guess state authorities when states argued that there were no alternatives. While assessments of suffering should be far removed from a consideration of state-centric ends, deference to the state conceivably jeopardized the prohibition. The determination here was a complex threshold- and boundary-drawing exercise with direct implications for the legal configuration of torture (i.e. how it is defined and understood). States demonstrated vested interests in keeping the legality of psychological suffering ambiguous and thus deniable (and non-justiciable to the extent possible) given the degree to which state authorities relied on it. These findings on the doctrinal material, given their ambiguities, then necessitated a closer empirical look at the practices producing recognition.

Conclusion 3: the torture categorization has not been afforded to psychological suffering in all three institutions in individual cases

The variation and caution in the recognition of psychological suffering at all three institutions became particularly manifest when a reading of the doctrinal material moved beyond the general survey of how such suffering was *included* in legal conceptualizations and turned to how it has been *categorized*. Where specific conclusions were reached, all examined decisions fixed a high threshold for torture-specific categorizations. While medico-legal consensus accepted that psychological suffering is no less harmful than physical suffering, the caselaw of all three institutions ultimately fixated on the physical, associating the specific categorization of torture with *physical* suffering. There was a distinct need articulated to preserve the symbolism of the category of torture. These dominated the interviews. Internal comparisons between physical and psychological suffering, rarely surfacing on the face of judgments, took place among judges and registry lawyers. This indicated that severity still served a hierarchal manner of thinking, giving rise to the impetus to reserve torture for the 'worst'.

Politically, the interviewees admitted to cautious consensus-building, reserving the torture category for the most serious cases and preserving its normative weight or requiring a high threshold for the minimum level of severity so as not to open the figurative 'floodgates'. Procedurally, interviewees promptly talked of resource factors in accounting for the lack of depth in their conceptualizations of suffering, instead guided by sense-centric reasoning.

Conclusion 4: despite general acceptance, there was a selective and cautious use of socio-political standards regarding psychological suffering and the categorization of torture specifically

Socio-political standards were generally accepted at the three institutions in both principle and practice, as affecting the recognition of psychological suffering. There was, however, a difficulty in elaborating how this played out in more detail, particularly in the interviews. The practice was left implicit, incremental, and self-evident or as evidenced through cases where interpretation of the prohibition was expanded at all three institutions. That international legal standards were a primary source in this assessment was also not contested. The

social equated to invoking the 'living instrument' or 'consensus'. Responsivity to psychological suffering was apparent in express principles opening the actors up to their social worlds, through social and scientific values. My examination of the caselaw revealed that their application was far from unproblematic. There was a similar spread of those cognizant (or not) of the contests with respect to evidencing. Some unreflectingly based their belief that recognition would accord with the broader realities on these promises of responsivity, self-evident in the expansions over time. Others were less than convinced, pointing to selective and self-serving applications. While most admitted their tasks to be complex, few were far from admitting shortcomings.

Some critical voices inside the three institutions railed against the conservative devices such as consensus and technicalities in slowing down expansive interpretations. Developments were, however, largely deferred to the domestic—where progress needed to happen first for the institution to then react in its recognition. It was also remarkable to hear that applicant lawyers rarely invoked the notion of the living instrument and adjacent concepts of progress or evolution. The analysis on offer in the interviews remained broad, rendering it difficult to pinpoint social perceptions around psychological suffering with a desirable (transparent, consistent, operationalizable) degree of precision. That irreducible life sentences and prolonged solitary confinement had not met stronger and sustained recognition was attributed to more institutional (procedural and political) considerations than social. Responsivity to socio-political standards, and in turn to psychological suffering, was a means to ensure that decisions were convincing to institutional users, especially states.

Conclusion 5: all institutions recognized the importance of scientific evidence in principle but were limited due to a lack of competence to assess and an undue emphasis on causal certainty partly out of state-deference, leading to potentially downgrading or dismissing psychological suffering

The discussion also trained its attention on how institutions dealt with scientific expertise. The pertinent questions were: how did law interact with scientific expertise in the recognition of torture? What types of knowledge and evidence counted? What types were effaced and rendered inadmissible? Expert evidence was readily accepted as a means of how legal actors reach out into the world where torture is inflicted—informed by a more empirically and scientifically grounded language of suffering. Advocates and adjudicators understood the significant role played by evidence, in principle, particularly when it came to psychological suffering—but could not all precisely explain how they went about using it. Without evidence, their hands were tied but exceptions abounded where precedent and presumptions were available. The emerging discretion signalled profound contest. Packing the potential to give expertise the short shrift, these were revealed to be points at which where psychological suffering failed to be adequately recognized.

Simultaneously, adjudicators demanded certainty. There was a sleight of hand here, to appear to be receptive to scientific expertise and, in turn, interpretive control, but not completely so. The determination was ultimately preserved to be a legal one. While this was expected, a greater degree of deference to scientific expertise was also expected given the evidentiary difficulties pertaining to psychological suffering. This brought into focus how the demands for multi-disciplinary collaboration (particularly through relying on medico-legal documentation) have been treated by advocates and adjudicators—revealing a rudimentary appreciation of scientific expertise. A distinct aspect of this was when legal actors did not feel the need for expertise, instead drawing on their own knowledge and feelings in assessments. These devices of evaluating and interpreting, such as *sana critica* and 'logic and experience', were taken for granted. It was difficult to conclude whether expert evidence featured more prominently than common knowledge. Expert evidence was never determinative; at times it was prioritized and at others side-lined.

Conclusion 6: sense-centric reasoning predominated in creating and preserving associations with certain experiences; the physical spectacle with torture and prolonged psychological suffering with 'lesser' categories

Some interviewees did not admit to having reflected in much depth on questions posed, instead holding that precedent on the recognition of psychological suffering was firm. Some pointed to their precedents as framing their possibilities, while others read them as duly flexing with circumstances. One aspect not codified was the use of sense-centric reasoning, which was generally confirmed by interviewees as not only present but prominent in their work and was defended as a means of grounding judgement in the social context (making judgments faster and more convincing) or as assisting in dealing with the difficulties of adjudicating torture cases. In this vein, sense-centric reasoning, through evocation of precedents, presumptions, 'logic and experience', empathy, and *sana critica*, allowed adjudicators to deal with evidentiary difficulties. The dangers associated were also recognized—with interviewees openly admitting to ends-driven reasoning in this vein. The implications for psychological suffering for the most part remained open to speculation, that these devices served suffering which already was generally understood to be recognition worthy. Sense-centric reasoning competed directly with expert knowledge. When adjudicators considered sense-centric reasoning sufficient, it determined dispositions. As decisions, however, were always made without total knowledge, common knowledge was introduced pragmatically. Sense-centric reasoning came to count as precedent, which then was reified as common knowledge—circulated as currency to be used unreflectively.

Drawing together the three thematic discussions on socio-political standards, scientific expertise, and sense-centric reasoning has provided critical insights into the practice of recognition at the three institutions. There are strong indications, for instance, that the nature of psychological suffering is disserved by how the three institutions perform on these three grounds. How these connect to each other is also significant. Scientific expertise informs and shifts socio-political standards. The necessity and utility of scientific expertise, in specific cases, are then determined by socio-politically established and ingrained understandings around suffering.

A final note

This has been an exercise in adding nuance to the narrative of the legal recognition of psychological suffering, towards more fully acknowledging the totality of victim-survivors' experiences. The dominant position regarding the recognition of psychological suffering at the institutions has also been one of caution and requiring consensus, and as conditioned by the high thresholds argued by the states and adopted by the institutions. Despite judicial authority and extensive precedent, the foregoing material indicated that thresholds and categories remain inherently unstable. Perhaps with one exception: that torture be physical and a spectacle, as protected through the enduring notion of 'special stigma'. In all, this was simultaneously concealing and revealing: that distinction did not matter but then again it did, and then dependent on various factors—difficult to pin down. The institutions have not always enhanced the recognition of psychological suffering as expected, constructing torture as an archetype and essentially a physical and exceptional spectacle. Certain practices and experiences, evoking visceral reactions, have been privileged over others. To be clear, the point here is not that practices already recognized (particularly as torture) should not be understood as torture (as, in most cases, it is not difficult to accept that they inflict severe suffering). The point, rather, is that in typifying torture, and associating it with such practices, it privileges them in the hierarchical juridical imaginary, affording them easier access than other practices and experiences equally as harmful.

What does any of it mean for the anti-torture field more broadly? For research, four directions are identified: (1) there is a need to explore beyond doctrinal brackets; (2) there is a need to problematize progressive impulses; (3) there is a need to question assumptions around multi-disciplinarity; and (4) there is a need to better connect the body–mind in pain to society. For practice, two directions are identified: (1) there is a need to redirect resources and manage expectations from adjudicatory institutions; and (2) there is a need to invoke higher reflections on naming practices. There is also a broader shift that is required—for suffering not to be seen to stop inviting serious doubt and dismissal. There is no book, report, or paper which can singlehandedly achieve this. This is not a change to be expected overnight.

ANNEX 1

List of interviews

ECtHR

ECtHR1	Senior registry lawyer	February 2023
ECtHR2	Judge	February 2023
ECtHR3	Senior registry lawyer	February 2023
ECtHR4	Judge	February 2023
ECtHR5	Judge	February 2023
ECtHR6	Senior registry lawyer	February 2023
ECtHR7	Senior registry lawyer	February 2023
ECtHR8	Judge	February 2023
ECtHR9	Judge	February 2023
ECtHR10	Judge	February 2023
ECtHR11	Judge	February 2023
ECtHR12	Senior registry lawyer	February 2023
ECtHR13	Judge	February 2023
ECtHR14	Judge	February 2023
ECtHR15	Judge	February 2023
ECtHR16	Former senior registry lawyer	February 2023
ECtHR17	Senior registry lawyer	February 2023
ECtHR18	Senior registry lawyer	February 2023
ECtHR19	Former judge	February 2023
ECtHR20	Judge	February 2023
ECtHR21	Applicant lawyer	March 2023
ECtHR22	Former senior registry lawyer	March 2023
ECtHR23	Senior registry lawyer	March 2023
ECtHR24	Judge	March 2023
ECtHR25	Senior registry lawyer	March 2023
ECtHR26	Judge	March 2023
ECtHR27	Senior registry lawyer	March 2023
ECtHR28	Senior registry lawyer	March 2023
ECtHR29	Senior registry lawyer	March 2023
ECtHR30	Applicant lawyer	March 2023
ECtHR31	Applicant lawyer	March 2023
ECtHR32	Applicant lawyer	March 2023
ECtHR33	Applicant lawyer	March 2023
ECtHR34	Applicant lawyer	March 2023
ECtHR35	Applicant lawyer	March 2023
ECtHR36	Applicant lawyer	March 2023
ECtHR37	Applicant lawyer	April 2023
ECtHR38	Applicant lawyer	April 2023
ECtHR39	Applicant lawyer	April 2023
ECtHR40	Applicant lawyer	April 2023

CAT

CAT1	Former member	January 2023
CAT2	Former member	February 2023
CAT3	Former member	March 2023
CAT4	Former member	March 2023
CAT5	Applicant lawyer	April 2023
CAT6	Former member	April 2023
CAT7	Applicant lawyer	April 2023
CAT8	Member	April 2023
CAT9	Member	April 2023
CAT10	Member	April 2023
CAT11	UN legal officer	April 2023
CAT12	Member	April 2023
CAT13	Member	April 2023
CAT14	Member	April 2023
CAT15	Member	April 2023
CAT16	Member	April 2023
CAT17	Expert	May 2023
CAT18	Applicant lawyer	May 2023
CAT19	Applicant lawyer	May 2023
CAT20	UN legal officer	June 2023
CAT21	Applicant lawyer	June 2023

IACtHR

IACtHR1	Applicant lawyer	April 2023
IACtHR2	Applicant lawyer	April 2023
IACtHR3	Applicant lawyer	May 2023
IACtHR4	Former senior IACtHR lawyer	May 2023
IACtHR5	Former senior IACmHR lawyer	May 2023
IACtHR6	Former senior IACmHR lawyer	May 2023
IACtHR7	Former senior IACmHR lawyer	May 2023
IACtHR8	Applicant lawyer	May 2023
IACtHR9	Applicant lawyer	June 2023
IACtHR10	Judge	June 2023
IACtHR11	Expert	June 2023
IACtHR12	Former senior IACtHR lawyer	June 2023
IACtHR13	Expert	June 2023
IACtHR14	Senior IACtHR lawyer	July 2023
IACtHR15	Senior IACtHR lawyer	August 2023
IACtHR16	Senior IACtHR lawyer	August 2023
IACtHR17	Expert	August 2023

ANNEX 2

Sample interview guide

These are presented as examples of the questions adapted for each interview. Not every question was asked of all interview participants, particularly if topics were discussed unprompted.

- What practices or experiences do you clearly associate with the specific categorization of torture?
- What practices or experiences do you clearly associate with the specific categorization of inhuman and degrading treatment?
- What clearly falls below the minimum level of severity for you? Or: what informs your assessment of 'incidental', 'inherent', 'unavoidable', or necessary harm? Or: what are lawful sanctions?
- What type of cases argued under the prohibition are rejected on the merits by the filtering mechanism (single-judge cases)?
- Why has there been no torture-specific violation found in prohibition-related cases relating to solitary confinement (or any other case where psychological suffering was most prominent)? Why are the UN Nelson Mandela Rules rarely referred to?
- Does the assessment of psychological suffering under the prohibition pose any conceptual challenges for you? If so, how?
- What explains the terminological plurality in the Court's reference to the phenomenon of psychological suffering?
- How are you influenced by broader social and scientific changes? What informs your assessment of 'present-day conditions' or, to put it more broadly, changes in social values? How does this feature, if at all, in judicial deliberations?
- Under what conditions should the prohibition be expanded?
- How often is expert evidence provided to support torture-related cases?
- How well placed/equipped are you to assess expert evidence?
- Are there scenarios in prohibition-related cases which require little or less evidentiary support to lead to a violation?
- Does the articulation/assessment of psychological suffering under the prohibition pose any evidentiary challenges for you? If so, how?
- When are adjudicators more receptive to look up from the individual instance and be informed by a pattern of related cases?
- Would you say common sense plays a part in your articulation/assessments under the prohibition? If so, how?
- Would you say empathy plays a part in your articulation/assessments under the prohibition? If so, how?

ANNEX 3

Review of 'minimum level of severity' (ECtHR)

Practices which straddle the threshold: strip-searches;[1] restraints;[2] forceful arrests (including handcuffing);[3] lengthy prison sentences;[4] mental impact of court and related official/administrative processes;[5] adequacy of medical assistance;[6] surveillance;[7] less than

[1] *Wieser v Austria* [2007] 2293/03 (strip-search at home met minimum); *Frerot v France* [2007] 70204/01 (strip-search necessary but minimum when arbitrary); *Pawel Pavlak v Poland* [2013] 13421/03 (strip-search of 'dangerous' detainee met minimum); *Iwanczuk v Poland* [2002] 25196/94 (search and insults met minimum); *Swiderski v Poland* [2016] 5532/10 (daily strip-search accumulated stress).

[2] *Aggerholm v Denmark* [2020] 45439/18 (restraint met minimum); *Henaf v France* [2004] 65436/01 (restraint met minimum); *MS v Croatia (No 2)* [2015] 75450/12 ([102] restraint of fifteen hours met minimum); *Lavorgna v Italy* [2024] 8436/21 ([115] mechanical restraint for eight days not minimum).

[3] See *Koval and others v Russia* [2021] 29627/10 [210] (offers a good summary of handcuffing and minimum level); *Douglas-Williams v UK* [2002] 56413/00 (forceful arrest not minimum); *Erdogan Yagiz v Turkey* [2007] 27473/02 (handcuffed in public and taken home met minimum); *Kaverzin v Ukraine* [2012] 23893/03 (handcuffing during family visits met minimum); *Kuzmenko v Russia* [2011] 18541/04 (handcuffing not minimum); *Zamfirachi v Romania* [2014] 70719/10 (handcuffs during transfers not minimum); *Kucheruk v Ukraine* [2007] 2570/04 (handcuffing of mentally ill met minimum); *Kleuver v Norway* [2002] 45837/99 (handcuffs in clinic not minimum); *Borodin v Russia* [2013] 41867/04 (use of truncheon during search met minimum); *Berlinski v Poland* [2002] 27715/95 (dangerous athletic arrest not minimum); *Güler and Öngel v Turkey* [2012] 29612/05 and 30668/05 (use of force in well-defined circumstances not minimum); *Heikkinen v Finland* [2011] 22102/09 (arrest went wrong but couldn't be better planned so no minimum); *Iliev v Bulgaria* [2007] 53121/99 (physical arrest not minimum); *Popandoulo v Russia* [2011] 4512/09 (physical force to stop unruly behaviour not minimum); *Ivan Vasilev v Bulgaria* [2007] 48130/99 (physical force legitimate if indispensable); *Oya Ataman v Turkey* [2007] 74552/01 (pepper-spray during protest not minimum); *Y v Latvia* [2015] 61183/08 (arm hurt by police lasted six days not minimum); *Yusiv v Lithuania* [2017] 55894/13 (at least eighteen blows by police met minimum).

[4] *Bullivant v the UK* [2000] 45738/99 (long sentence not minimum); *Sehmi v UK* [2000] 43470/98 (long sentence not minimum); *Aswat v UK* [2013] 17299/12 (high threshold to show sentence is disproportionate, not minimum); *Maricak v Slovakia* [2011] 26621/10 (irreducible life sentence not minimum); *Harkins and Edwards v UK* [2012] 9146/07 (life not inevitable).

[5] *EK v Netherlands* [2017] 72586/11 (court process resulting in frustration, uncertainty, and anxiety but not minimum); *Beck, Copp and Bazeley v UK* [2003] 48535/99 (criminal process distressing but not minimum); *V v UK* [1999] 24888/94 (trial pressures not minimum); *Diamante and Pelliccioni v San Marino* [2012] 32250/08 (legal process stressed but not minimum); *Masneva v Ukraine* [2012] 5952/07 (mental suffering from investigation not minimum); *Danielsson v Sweden* [1995] ECmHR 16115/90 (council proceedings not minimum); *JS and others v Netherlands* [1995] ECmHR 14561/89 (dispute with authorities not minimum); *Paruszewska v Poland* [1998] ECmHR 33770/96 (dispute with authorities not minimum); *Gusinskiy v Russia* [2002] 70276/01 (strong feelings aroused by criminal process but not minimum); *Mattheopoulos v Greece* [1994] ECmHR 20415/92 (excessive length of proceedings not minimum).

[6] *Mouisel v France* [2003] 67263/01; *VS v Estonia* [2018] 8685/15 [36]; *Mechenkov v Russia* [2008] 35421/05 (lack of hepatitis C treatment met minimum); *Rozhkov v Russia* [2007] 64140/00 (eye surgery refused but not minimum); *Novak v Croatia* [2007] 8883/04 (lack of PTSD treatment not minimum). This is only a selection of cases on this point.

[7] *Moiseyev v Russia* [2004] 62936/00 (surveillance stressful but not minimum); *Van der Graaf v the Netherlands* [2004] 8704/03 (on camera not minimum).

six hours of sleep deprivation;[8] forcible examinations and searches;[9] uncertainty and fear caused by state authorities;[10] psychologically pressured interrogation techniques;[11] therapeutic intervention;[12] isolation, segregation, and special security regimes;[13] suspension of driving licence;[14] insufficient social security payments;[15] limited access to toilet while detained;[16] homelessness, eviction, and dispossession;[17] witnessing injuries on others;[18] immigration detention;[19] low age of criminal responsibility;[20] public display of criminal

[8] *Sadretdinov v Russia* [2016] 19222/09; *Bagel v Russia* [2008] 37810/03.

[9] *Schmidt v Germany* [2006] 32352/02 (blood saliva sample not minimum); *Skawinska v Poland* [2001] 42096/98 (psychiatric exam not minimum); *Devrim Turan v Turkey* [2006] 879/02 (gynaecological exam not minimum); *GD v Germany* [1998] 27425/95 (intrusive search not minimum); *Julin v Estonia* [2012] 16563/08 (distressing search but not minimum); *Iliya Stefanov v Bulgaria* [2008] 65755/01 (search hurt reputation but not minimum); *Atici v Turkey* [2007] 19735/02 (strip anal search not minimum); *Young v the UK* [2005] 60682/00 (observation of drug test not minimum).

[10] *Starovoitovs v Latvia* [2012] 27343/05 (mere fear not minimum); *LCB v the UK* [1996] ECmHR 23413/94 (mere uncertainty not minimum); *Garabayev v Russia* [2008] 38411/02 (uncertainty and fear met minimum); *Khan v the UK* [1996] ECmHR 28021/95 (uncertainty in detention not minimum); *Cakici v Turkey* [1998] ECmHR 23657/94 (uncertainty, doubt, and apprehension met minimum); *Kurt v Turkey* [1996] ECmHR 24276/94 (uncertainty of son's whereabouts long enough to meet minimum); *DF v Latvia* [2014] 11160/07 (protracted fear and anguish of the imminent risk met minimum); *Özdemir v the Netherlands* [1998] ECmHR 35758/97 (mere possibility of ill-treatment is not minimum); *TM and CM v Moldova* [2014] 26608/11 (fear of further assaults met minimum); *Cyprus v Turkey* [1999] ECmHR 25781/94 (uncertainty, doubt, and apprehension of relatives as inhuman).

[11] *Ebbinge v Netherlands* [2000] 47240/99 (Zaanse verhoormethode); *Jager v the Netherlands* [2000] 39195/98 (Zaanse verhoormethode); *M and others v Italy and Bulgaria* [2012] 40020/03 (threat of imprisonment not unlawful threat); *Foka v Turkey* [2009] 28940/95 (some police intimidation not minimum); *Nechiporuk and Yonkalo v Ukraine* [2011] 42310/04 (stress from threats and humiliation not minimum); *Bogulak v Poland* [2001] 33866/96 (threatening and abusive treatment by police not minimum); *Kositsyn v Russia* [2006] 69535/01 (pressure from interrogation techniques not minimum).

[12] *Persson v Sweden* [1993] ECmHR 14451/88; *Buckley v the UK* [1997] ECmHR 28323/95; *Frommelt v Liechtenstein* [2003] 49158/99.

[13] *Valasinas v Lithuania* [2001] 44558/98 (fifteen days' solitary not minimum); *Toth v Croatia* [2002] 64674/01 (twenty-one days' solitary not minimum): *Renolde v France* [2009] 5608/05 (forty-five days' segregation not minimum); *Lorse and others v Netherlands* [2003] 52750/99 (detention in high security not minimum); *Yurttas v Turkey* [2004] 25143/94 (incommunicado for eleven days no violation); *Feilazoo v Malta* [2021] 6865/19 (isolated with COVID risk not minimum); *JL v Finland* [2000] 32526/96 (isolation and medication not minimum); *Bastone v Italy (dec)* [2005] 59638/00 (special regime not minimum); *Messina v Italy* [1999] 25498/94 (special regime not minimum); *Schummer v Germany (No 1)* [2011] 27360/04 (prolonged preventive detention ten years not minimum); *Keenan v UK* [1998] 27229/95 (segregation not minimum); *Haidn v Germany* [2011] 6587/04 (detained post-sentence indefinite with two-year reviews not minimum).

[14] *Kholodov v Ukraine* [2016] 64953/14.

[15] *Öz v Turkey* [2017] 56995/10 (low social security payments after son's death not minimum); *Trickovic v Slovenia* [1998] ECmHR 39914/98 (pension not minimum); *Bodo and Horgos v Hungary* [2017] 29180/16 (financial hardship not minimum).

[16] *Price v UK* [2001] 33394/96.

[17] *Meads and others v UK* [2001] 69471/01 (eviction not minimum); *Gerasimova v Russia* [2004] 24077/02 (eviction, stressful but not minimum); *O'Rourke v UK* [2001] 39022/97 (eviction and homelessness not minimum); *Balci v Turkey* [2007] 60202/00 (forced dispossession of land not minimum); *Dzharageti v Russia* [2006] 8459/03 (housing issue not minimum); *X v UK* [1982] ECmHR 9261/81.

[18] *Cangöz and ors v Turkey* [2016] 7469/06 (witnessing dead bodies not minimum); *Süleyman Demir and Hasan Demir v Turkey* [2015] 19222/09 (witnessing father's injuries not minimum).

[19] *Slivenko and others v Latvia* [2003] 48321/99 (immigration detention not minimum by nature); *Rusu v Austria* [2006] 34082/02 (deportation not minimum by nature); *Singh v UK* [1996] ECmHR 28022/95 (immigration detention not minimum); *Cicek v Netherlands* [2001] (immigration detention not minimum); *Gourkis v Sweden* [1994] ECmHR 21839/93 (denial of residency).

[20] *T v UK* [1999] 24724/94 (conviction of child not minimum).

conviction;[21] defamation;[22] forced to travel for an abortion;[23] military discharge;[24] storage of dead bodies;[25] number written by pen on the hands of applicants in the process of being expelled;[26] lack of window in detention cell;[27] destruction of property;[28] difficulty in obtaining gender reassignment surgery;[29] imprisonment of blind man;[30] threatened with criminal sanction for wearing a burqa;[31] threatened with deportation;[32] vaginal examination.[33]

[21] *Lhermitte v Belgium* [2015] 34238/09 (public display of criminal conviction not minimum); *Baydar v Turkey* [2018] 25632/13 (normal element of humiliation from conviction not minimum); *Cardenas v Norway* [2006] 12148/03 (psycho-social problems of sex offender not minimum).

[22] *Alinak v Turkey* [2000] 30514/96.

[23] *A, B and C v Ireland* [2010] 25579/05.

[24] *Celikates and others v Turkey* [2000] 45824/99.

[25] *Sabanchiyeva and others v Russia* [2013] 38450/05.

[26] *Čonka and Ligue des droits de l'homme v Belgium* [2001] 51564/99.

[27] *Von Hoffen v Liechtenstein* [2006] ECtHR 5010/04 [57].

[28] *Keser and others v Turkey* [2006] ECtHR 33238/96.

[29] *L v Lithuania* [2007] ECtHR 27527/03 [47].

[30] *Laniauskas v Lithuania* [2022] ECtHR 48309/19 (no violation).

[31] *SAS v France* [2014] ECtHR [GC] 43835/11 [69–71].

[32] *OM and DS v Ukraine* [2022] ECtHR 18603/12.

[33] *Turan v Turkey* [2006] ECtHR 879/02 [20]: 'The Court notes that being taken to the hospital for a gynaecological examination might have caused distress to the applicant.'

ANNEX 4

Review of torture-specific findings (ECtHR)

Abdulkadyrov and Dakhtayev v Russia (2018) 35061/04
Akkoc v Turkey (2000) 22947/93
Aksoy v Turkey (1996) 21987/93
Aktaş v Turkey (2003) 24351/94
Aleksakhin v Ukraine (2012) 31939/06
Artyomov v Russia (2010) 14146/02
Ateşoğlu v Turkey (2015) 53645/10
Aydin v Turkey (1997) 23178/94
Ayrapetyan v Russia (2010) 75472/01
Azzolina and others v Italy (2017) 28923/09
Bambayev v Russia (2017) 19816/09
Baran and Hun v Turkey (2010) 30685/05
Bati and others v Turkey (2004) 33097/96
Bekirski v Bulgaria (2010) 71420/01
Belousov v Russia (2008) 1748/02
Belousov v Ukraine (2013) 4494/07
Bulgaru v Moldova (2014) 35840/09
Buntov v Russia (2012) 27026/10
Bursuc v Romania (2004) 42066/98
Çakici v Turkey (1999) 23657/94
Carabulea v Romania (2010) 45661/99
Blair and others v Italy (2017) 1442/14
Cestaro v Italy (2015) 6884/11
Chitayev v Russia (2007) 59334/00
Ciorap v Moldova (2007) 12066/02
Cirino and Renne v Italy (2017) 2539/13
Corsacov v Moldova (2006) 18944/02
Daubekov and others v Russia (2022) 60844/11
Devyatkin v Russia (2017) 40384/06
Dikme v Turkey (2000) 20869/92
El-Masri v Macedonia (2012) 39630/09
Elçi and others v Turkey (2003) 23145/93
Eren v Turkey (2015) 36617/07
Gallo and others v Italy (2017) 12131/13
Georgia v Russia (II) (2021) 38263/08
Gisayev v Russia (2011) 14811/04
Grigoryev v Ukraine (2012) 51671/07
Hajrulahu v Macedonia (2015) 37537/07
Ilaşcu and ors v Moldova and Russia (2004) 48787/99
Ilhan v Turkey (2000) 22277/93
Ismoilov and others v Russia (2008) 2947/06
Israilov v Russia (2023) 21882/09

Ivanov v Russia (2018) 14416/06
Ivanov and others v Russia (2022) 50942/08
Kaçiu and Kotorri v Albania (2013) 33192/07
Karabet and others v Ukraine (2013) 38906/07
Karakaş and Yeşilirmak v Turkey (2005) 43925/98
Karayiğit v Turkey (2004) 63181/00
Kaverzin v Ukraine (2012) 23893/03
Khashiyev and Akayeva v Russia (2005) 57942/00
Khojoyan and Vardazaryan v Azerbaijan (2021) 62161/14
Kozinets v Ukraine (2007) 75520/01
Kudayev and others v Russia (2022) 4261/06
Kulish v Ukraine (2012) 35093/07
Kutayev v Russia (2023) 17912/15
Lapunov v Russia (2023) 28834/19
Lenev v Bulgaria (2012) 41452/07
Levinta v Moldova (2008) 17332/03
Lolayev v Russia (2015) 58040/08
Lutsenko and Verbytskyy v Ukraine (2021) 12482/14
Lyapin v Russia (2014) 46956/09
Lykova v Russia (2015) 68736/11
Makhashevy v Russia (2012) 20546/07
Mammadov (Jalaloglu) v Azerbaijan (2007) 34445/04
Maslova and Nalbandov v Russia (2008) 839/02
Meliksetyan v Ukraine (2022) 40057/11
Menesheva v Russia (2006) 59261/00
Mikheyev v Russia (2006) 77617/01
Mindadze and Nemsitsveridze v Georgia (2017) 21571/05
Mukayev v Russia (2017) 22495/08
Myumyun v Bulgaria (2015) 67258/13
Nasr and Ghali v Italy (2016) 44883/09
Nechiporuk and Yonkalo v Ukraine (2011) 42310/04
Nevmerzhitsky v Ukraine (2005) 54825/00
Novoselov v Russia (2013) 33954/05
Ochigava v Georgia (2023) 14142/15
Öktem v Turkey (2006) 74306/01
Öner and others v Turkey (2006) 73792/01
Olisov and others v Russia (2017) 10825/09
Ovakimyan v Russia (2017) 52796/08
Paduret v Moldova (2010) 33134/03
Polonskiy v Russia (2009) 30033/05
Pomilyayko v Ukraine (2016) 60426/11
Razzakov v Russia (2015) 57519/09
Salman v Turkey (2000) 21986/93
Samoylov v Russia (2008) 64398/01
Saribekyan and Balyan v Azerbaijan (2020) 35746/11
Satybalova and others v Russia (2020) 79947/12
Savin v Ukraine (2012) 34725/08
Savitskyy v Ukraine (2012) 38773/05
Selami and others v Macedonia (2018) 78241/13

Selmouni v France (1999) 25803/94
Shchokin v Ukraine (2013) 4299/03
Shestopalov v Russia (2017) 46248/07
Shmorgunov and others v Ukraine (2021) 15367/14
Stoykov v Bulgaria (2015) 38152/11
Teslenko v Ukraine (2011) 55528/08
Tsakoyevy v Russia (2018) 16397/07
Türkmen v Turkey (2006) 43124/98
Valyayev v Russia (2012) 22150/04
Virabyan v Armenia (2012) 40094/05
Vladimir Romanov v Russia (2008) 41461/02
Yaman v Turkey (2004) 32446/96
Yavuz v Turkey (2006) 67137/01
Zakharin and others v Russia (2015) 22458/04
Zhyzitskyy v Ukraine (2015) 57980/11
Zolotorev v Russia (2017) 13408/07
Zontul v Greece (2012) 12294/07
Zyakun v Ukraine (2016) 34006/06

Bibliography

a. Articles

Aarts, Rembrandt and others, 'Expert Medico-Legal Reports: The Relationship between Levels of Consistency and Judicial Outcomes in Asylum Seekers in The Netherlands' (2019) 29 (1) Torture 36–46

Asad, Talal, 'Agency and Pain: An Exploration' (2000) 1 (1) Culture and Religion 43

Bandes, Susan A, and Jeremy A Blumenthal, 'Emotion and the Law' (2012) 8 Annual Review of Law and Social Science 161

Başoğlu, Metin, Maria Livanou, and Cvetana Crnobarić, 'Torture vs Other Cruel, Inhuman, and Degrading Treatment: Is the Distinction Real or Apparent?' (2007) 64 Archives of General Psychiatry 277

Bernhardt, Rudolph, 'Evolutive Treaty Interpretation, Especially of the European Convention on Human' (2000) 1999 German Yearbook of International Law 11–25

Bianchi, Andrea, and Anne Saab, 'Fear and International Law-Making: An Exploratory Inquiry' (2019) 32 Leiden Journal of International Law 351

Bossuyt, Marc, 'Belgium Condemned for Inhuman or Degrading Treatment Due to Violations by Greece of EU Asylum Law, M.S.S. v. Belgium and Greece, Grand Chamber, European Court of Human Rights' (2011) European Human Rights Law Review 581–96

Bratza, Nicholas, 'Living Instrument or Dead Letter: The Future of the European Convention on Human Rights' (2014) 2 European Human Rights Law Review 120

Cakal, Ergun, 'Assessing (and Making Sense of) Severity: Conceptualising and Contextualising Torture's Core' (2022) 91 (2) Nordic Journal of International Law 284–309

Cakal, Ergun, 'Befogging Reason, Undermining Will: Understanding Sleep Deprivation as Torture and Other Ill-Treatment in International Law' (2019) 29 (2) Torture 11–22

Cakal, Ergun, 'Debility, Dependency and Dread: On the Conceptual and Evidentiary Dimensions of Psychological Torture' (2018) 28 (2) Torture 15–37

Cakal, Ergun, 'Law and Torture: Contemporary Legal Scholarship on Torture, from the Doctrinal to the Critical' (2023) 25 (5) International Community Law Review 397--425

Cakal, Ergun, 'Perception, Practice and Proximity: Qualifying Threats as Psychological Torture in International Law' (2021) 31 (1) Torture 19–36

Cakal, Ergun, 'Registering Time in Recognising Torturous Harm: Figuring the Single, Plural and Historical in Torture's Adjudication' (2024) 33 (2) Social & Legal Studies 276–96

Cakal, Ergun, 'Sensing Suffering: On Common-Sense and Compassion in the Legal Imagination and Recognition of Torture' (2022) 10 (3) London Review of International Law 337–66

Cassese, Antonio, 'Can the Notion of Inhuman and Degrading Treatment Be Applied to Socio-economic Conditions?' (1991) 2 European Journal of International Law 144

Cavanaugh, Kathleen, 'On Torture: The Case of the "Hooded Men"' (2020) 42 Human Rights Quarterly 519

Chowdhury, Tanzil, 'Time Frames and Legal Indeterminacy' (2017) 1 Canadian Journal of Law & Jurisprudence 57–76

Coracini, Celso Eduardo Faria, 'The Lawful Sanctions Clause in the State Reporting Procedure before the Committee Against Torture' (2006) 24 (2) Netherlands Quarterly of Human Rights 305–18

Davidson, Natalie, 'Everyday Lawmaking in International Human Rights Law: Insights from the Inclusion of Domestic Violence in the Prohibition of Torture' (2022) 47 Law & Social Inquiry 205

Davis, Michael, 'Torture and the Inhumane' (2007) Criminal Justice Ethics 29–43
Dembour, Marie-Bénédicte, 'Beyond Reasonable Doubt at Its Worst—But Also at Its Potential Best: Dissecting *Ireland v the United Kingdom*'s No-Torture Finding' (2023) 4 European Convention on Human Rights Law Review 375–425
Dembour, Marie-Bénédicte, 'Introduction: The Evidentiary System of the European Court of Human Rights in Critical Perspective' (2023) 4 European Convention on Human Rights Law Review 363–74
Dzehtsiarou, Kanstantsin, 'European Consensus and the Evolutive Interpretation of the European Convention on Human Rights' (2011) 12 German Law Journal 1730
Dzehtsiarou, Kanstantsin, and Conor O'Mahony, 'Evolutive Interpretation of Rights Provisions: A Comparison of the European Court of Human Rights and the U.S. Supreme Court' (2013) 44 Columbia Human Rights Law Review 390
Echeverria, Gabriella and others, 'Panel IV: Challenges to Proving Cases of Torture before the Committee Against Torture' (2013) 4 (5) Human Rights Brief 20
Erdal, Ugur, 'Burden and Standard of Proof in Proceedings under the European Convention' (2001) 26 (1) European Law Review Human Rights Survey 68–84
Evans, Malcolm, 'Getting to Grips with Torture' (2002) 51 International and Comparative Law Quarterly 365
Farrell, Michelle, 'Just How Ill-Treated Were You? An Investigation of Cross-Fertilisation in the Interpretative Approaches to Torture at the European Court of Human Rights and in International Criminal Law' (2015) 84 (3) Nordic Journal of International Law 482
Farrell, Michelle, 'The Marks of Civilisation: The Special Stigma of Torture' (2022) 22 (1) Human Rights Law Review 1
Hendersen, Lynne, 'Legality and Empathy' (1987) 85 Michigan Law Review 1576
Hope, David, 'Torture' (2004) 53 ICLQ 826
Ingelse, Chris, 'The Committee Against Torture: One Step Forward, One Step Back' (2000) 18 Netherlands Quarterly of Human Rights 307
Jasanoff, Sheila, 'Just Evidence: The Limits of Science in the Legal Process' (2006) 34 Journal of Law, Medicine & Ethics 328
Karapetyan, Anna, 'A Recurring Phenomenon: The Lawful Sanctions Clause in the Definition of Torture and the Question of Judicial Corporal Punishment under International Human Rights Law' (2016) 36 Polish Yearbook of International Law 137
Kelly, Tobias, 'Sympathy and Suspicion: Torture, Asylum, and Humanity' (2012) 18 (4) The Journal of the Royal Anthropological Institute 753
Kelly, Tobias, 'The UN Committee Against Torture: Human Rights Monitoring and the Legal Recognition of Cruelty' (2009) 31 Human Rights Quarterly 777
Madrigal-Borloz, Victor, 'Damage and Redress in the Jurisprudence of the Inter-American Court of Human Rights (1979–2001)' (2001) 7 Human Rights in Development Yearbook 211
Maia, Taína Garcia, 'External Sources and Inter-American Court of Human Rights' (2023) 72 International and Comparative Law Quarterly 977
Marchesi, Antonio, 'Implementing the UN Convention Definition of Torture in National Law' (2008) 6 Journal of International Criminal Justice 195–214
McNeilly, Kathryn, 'Are Rights Out of Time? International Human Rights Law, Temporality, and Radical Social Change' (2019) 28 Social & Legal Studies 817
McQuigg, Ronagh, 'How Effective Is the United Nations Committee Against Torture?' (2011) 22 (3) European Journal of International Law 813–28
Mowbray, Alistair, 'The Creativity of the European Court of Human Rights' (2005) 5 Human Rights Law Review 57
Neuman, Gerald, 'Import, Export, and Regional Consent in the Inter-American Court of Human Rights' (2008) 19 European Journal of International Law 101
Nordgren, Loran F and others, 'What Constitutes Torture? Psychological Impediments to an Objective Evaluation of Enhanced Interrogation Tactics' (2011) 22 (5) Psychological Science 689–94
Nowak, Manfred, 'What Practices Constitute Torture? US and UN Standards' (2006) 28 (4) Human Rights Quarterly 809–41

Nowak, Manfred, and Elizabeth McArthur, 'The Distinction between Torture and Cruel, Inhuman or Degrading Treatment' (2006) 16 (3) Torture 147–51

Nowak, Manfred, and Giuliana Monina, 'United Nations Committee Against Torture' (2018) Max Planck Encyclopedia of International Law

Parry, John, '"Just for Fun": Understanding Torture and Understanding Abu Ghraib' (2005) 1 Journal of National Security Law & Policy 253

Patel, Nimisha, 'Psychological Torture' (2020) 29 Torture 79

Patel, Nimisha, and David Pilgrim, 'Psychologists and Torture: Critical Realism as a Resource for Analysis and Training' (2018) 17 (2) Journal of Critical Realism 176

Paul, Alvaro, 'Decision-Making Process of the Inter-American Court: An Analysis Prompted by the "In Vitro Fertilization" Case' (2014) 21 (1) ILSA Journal of International & Comparative Law 87–130

Paul, Alvaro, 'Sana Critica: The System for Weighing Evidence Utilised by the Inter-American Court of Human Rights' (2012) 18 Buffalo Human Rights Law Review 194

Peirce, Jennifer, 'Making the Mandela Rules: Evidence, Expertise, and Politics in the Development of Soft Law International Prison Standards' (2018) 43 (2) Queen's Law Journal 263

Petersen, Hans Draminsky, and Peter Jacobsen, 'Life-Threatening Torture without Visible Marks' (1985) 13 Scandinavian Journal of Social Medicine 87

Pilcher, Jeremy, 'Listening for Silence' (2021) 33 Law & Literature 461

Quiroga, Cecilia, 'The Inter-American Court of Human Rights 35 Years' (2015) 33 (2) Netherlands Quarterly of Human Rights 118–22

Rejali, Darius, 'Modern Torture as a Civic Marker: Solving a Global Anxiety with a New Political Technology' (2003) 2 (2) Journal of Human Rights 153–71

Reneman, Marcel, 'Forensic Medical Reports in Asylum Cases: The View of the European Court of Human Rights and the Committee against Torture' (2020) 38 (3) Netherlands Quarterly of Human Rights 206–28

Reyes, Hernan, 'The Worst Scars Are in the Mind: Psychological Torture' (2007) 89 (867) International Review of the Red Cross 591

Rhys-Jones, David, and Sally Verity Smith, 'Medical Evidence in Asylum and Human Rights Appeals' (2004) 16 (3) International Journal of Refugee Law 381–410

Roberts, Anthea and others, 'Comparative International Law: Framing the Field' (2015) 109 American Journal of International Law 467

Rodley, Nigel, 'Reflections on Committee Against Torture General Comment No. 2' (2008) 11 (2) New York City Law Review 353–58

Rodley, Nigel, 'The Definition(s) of Torture in International Law' (2002) 55 Current Legal Problems 467–93

Saab, Anne, 'Emotions and International Law' (2021) 10 (3) ESIL Reflections

Shaffer, Gregory, and Tom Ginsburg, 'The Empirical Turn in International Legal Scholarship' (2012) 106 American Journal of International Law 1

Shir, Efrat, 'How Do You Say Istanbul Protocol in Hebrew? The Curious Case of Mr Firas Tbeish' (2019) 29 (2) Torture 90–95

Sørensen, Max, 'Do the Rights and Freedoms Set Forth in the European Convention on Human Rights in 1950 Have the Same Significance in 1975?' (1975)

Sullivan, Mark, 'Finding Pain between Minds and Bodies' (2001) 17 (2) The Clinical Journal of Pain 146–56

Sveaass, Nora, 'Destroying Minds: Psychological Pain and the Crime of Torture' (2008) 11 (2) CUNY Law Review 315

Tardu, Maxime E, 'The United Nations Convention Against Torture and Other Cruel, Inhuman or Degrading Treatment or Punishment' (1987) 56 Nordic Journal of International Law 303

Tulkens, Francoise, 'Judicial Activism v Judicial Restraint: Practical Experience of This (False) Dilemma at the European Court of Human Rights' (2022) 3 European Convention on Human Rights Law Review 293

Vannier, Marion, 'Normalizing Extreme Imprisonment: The Case of Life without Parole in California (1972–2012)' (2019) Theoretical Criminology 519–39

Vedsted-Hansen, Jens, and Ida Koch, 'International Human Rights and National Legislatures: Conflict or Balance?' (2006) 75 Nordic Journal of International Law 3
Viterbo, Hedi, 'Seeing Torture Anew: A Transnational Reconceptualization of State Torture and Visual Evidence' (2014) 50 (2) Stanford Journal of International Law 281–317
Vorhaus, John, 'On Degradation Part Two: Degrading Treatment and Punishment' (2003) 31 Common Law World Review 65
Winter, Yves, 'Violence and Visibility' (2012) 34 (2) New Political Science 195–202
Wolfendale, Jessica, 'Prison as a Torturous Institution' (2020) 97 (2) Res Philosophica 297–324
Yildiz, Ezgi, 'A Court with Many Faces: Judicial Characters and Modes of Norm Development in the European Court of Human Rights' (2020) 31 European Journal of International Law 73
Yildiz, Ezgi, 'A Norm in Flux: The Development of the Norm against Torture under the European Convention from a Macro Perspective' (2016) iCourts Working Paper No 45

b. Books

Abi-Saab, Georges and others (eds), *Evolutionary Interpretation and International Law* (Hart 2019)
Amnesty International, *Report on Torture* (Duckworth 1973)
Amnesty International, *Torture in the Eighties* (Amnesty International Publications1984)
Bates, Ed, *The Evolution of the European Convention on Human Rights: From Its Inception to the Creation of a Permanent Court of Human Rights* (OUP 2010)
Bloom, Anne, David M Engel, and Michael McCann (eds), *Injury and Injustice: The Cultural Politics of Harm and Redress* (CUP 2018)
Boddice, Rob, *Pain and Emotion in Modern History* (Palgrave 2014)
Boddice, Rob, *Pain: A Very Short Introduction* (OUP 2017)
Boulesbaa, Ahcene, *The UN Convention on Torture and the Prospects for Enforcement* (Brill 1999)
Brinkmann, Svend, and Steinar Kvale, *InterViews: Learning the Craft of Qualitative Research Interviewing* (3rd edn, Sage 2014)
Bronner, Stephen, *Critical Theory: A Very Short Introduction* (OUP 2011)
Burgers, J Herman, and Hans Danelius, *The United Nations Convention against Torture: A Handbook on the Convention Against Torture and Other Cruel, Inhuman, or Degrading Treatment or Punishment* (Nijhoff 1988)
Burgorgue-Larsen, Laurence, and Amaya Úbeda de Torres, *The Inter-American Court of Human Rights: Case-Law and Commentary* (OUP 2011)
Butler, Judith, *The Force of Nonviolence* (Verso 2020)
Canning, Victoria, *Torture and Torturous Violence* (Bristol University Press 2022)
Carcano, Andrea, and Tullio Scovazzi, *Upholding the Prohibition of Torture: The Contribution of the European Court of Human Rights* (Brill 2023)
Cassese, Antonio, *Inhuman States: Imprisonment, Detention and Torture in Europe Today* (Polity 1996)
Cohen, Stanley, *States of Denial: Knowing about Atrocities and Suffering* (Polity 2001)
Daems, Tom, and Luc Robert (eds), *Europe in Prisons: Assessing the Impact of European Institutions on National Prison Systems* (Springer 2017)
Dayan, Colin, *Law Is a White Dog: How Legal Rituals Make and Unmake Persons* (Princeton 2011)
De Weck, Fanny, *Non-Refoulement under the European Convention on Human Rights and the UN Convention Against Torture: The Assessment of Individual Complaints by the European Court of Human Rights under Article 3 ECHR and the United Nations Committee against Torture under Article 3 CAT* (Brill 2016)
DelVecchio Good, Mary-Jo (ed), *Pain as Human Experience: An Anthropological Perspective* (UC Press 1994)
duBois, Page, *Torture and Truth* (Routledge Revivals 1991/2018)
Dzehtsiarou, Kanstantsin, *Can the European Court of Human Rights Shape European Public Order?* (CUP 2022)
Fassin, Didier, and Richard Rechtman, *The Empire of Trauma: An Inquiry into the Condition of Victimhood* (Princeton University Press 2009)

Fineman, Martha, and Anna Grear (eds), *Vulnerability: Reflections on a New Ethical Foundation for Law and Politics* (Ashgate 2013)
Forowicz, Magdalena, *The Reception of International Law in the European Court of Human Rights* (OUP 2010)
Foucault, Michel, *Discipline and Punish: The Birth of the Prison* (Vintage 1979)
Garland, David, *Punishment and Modern Society: A Study in Social Theory* (Clarendon Press 1993)
Hennebel, Ludovic, and Hélène Tigroudja, *The American Convention on Human Rights: A Commentary* (OUP 2021)
Heri, Corina, *Responsive Human Rights: Vulnerability, Ill-Treatment and the ECtHR* (Hart 2021)
Hirsch, Mosche, *Invitation to the Sociology of International Law* (OUP 2017)
Ingelse, Chris, *United Nations Committee Against Torture: An Assessment* (Nijhoff 2001)
Kelly, Tobias, *This Side of Silence* (Penn Press 2012)
Mason, Jennifer, *Qualitative Researching* (3rd edn, Sage 2017)
Mavronicola, Natasa, *Torture, Inhumanity, and Degradation under Article 3 of the ECHR: Absolute Rights and Absolute Wrongs* (Hart 2021)
Medina Quiroga, Cecilia, *The American Convention on Human Rights: Crucial Rights and Their Theory and Practice* (2nd edn, Intersentia, 2016)
Morgan, Rod, and Malcolm Evans, *Combating Torture in Europe: The Work and Standards of the European Committee for the Prevention of Torture* (Council of Europe 2001)
Moscoso, Javier, *Pain: A Cultural History* (Palgrave 2012)
Nolte, Georg (ed), *Treaties and Subsequent Practice* (OUP 2013)
Nowak, Manfred, and Elizabeth McArthur, *The United Nations Convention Against Torture: A Commentary* (OUP 2008)
Nowak, Manfred and others (eds), *The United Nations Convention Against Torture and Its Optional Protocol: A Commentary* (2nd edn, OUP 2019)
Oette, Lutz, *The Transformation of the Prohibition of Torture in International Law* (OUP 2024)
Pérez-Sales, Pau, *Psychological Torture: Definition, Evaluation and Measurement* (Routledge 2016)
Rejali, Darius, *Torture and Democracy* (Princeton University Press 2007)
Rodley, Nigel, and Matt Pollard, *The Treatment of Prisoners under International Law* (3rd edn, OUP 2011)
Sarat, Austin (ed), *Knowing the Suffering of Others: Legal Perspectives on Pain and Its Meanings* (University of Alabama Press 2014)
Sarat, Austin and others (eds), *How Law Knows* (Stanford 2007)
Silverman, Lisa, *Tortured Subjects: Pain, Truth, and the Body in Early Modern France* (University of Chicago Press 2001)
Spierenburg, Peter, *The Spectacle of Suffering: Executions and the Evolution of Repression:From a Preindustrial Metropolis to the European Experience* (CUP 1984)
Teff, Harvey, *Causing Psychiatric and Emotional Harm: Reshaping the Boundaries of Legal Liability* (Bloomsbury 2008)
Waldron, Jeremy, *Torture, Terror and Trade-Offs: Philosophy for the White House* (Oxford University Press 2010)
Wilkinson, Iain, *Suffering: A Sociological Introduction* (Polity 2005)
Williams, Simon J, and Gillian Bendelow, *The Lived Body: Sociological Themes, Embodied Issues* (Routledge 1998)
Yildiz, Ezgi, *Between Forbearance and Audacity: The European Court of Human Rights and the Norm against Torture* (CUP 2023)
Zyl Smit, Dirk V, and Catherine Appleton, *Life Imprisonment: A Global Human Rights Analysis* (Harvard University Press 2019)

c. Book chapters

Asad, Talal, 'On Torture, or Cruel, Inhuman, and Degrading Treatment' in Arthur Kleinman, Veena Das, and Margaret Lock (eds), *Social Suffering* (University of California Press 1997) 285–308

Bandes, Susan A and others, 'Introduction' in Susan Bandes and others (eds), *Research Handbook on Law and Emotion* (Elgar 2021) 1–14

Bianchi, Andrea, and Moshe Hirsch, *International Law's Invisible Frames* (OUP 2021)

Cassese, Antonio, 'Prohibition of Torture and Inhuman or Degrading Treatment or Punishment' in Paola Gaeta and Salvatore Zappalà (eds), *The Human Dimension of International Law* (OUP 2008) 296–331

De Pauw, Marijke, 'The Inter-American Court of Human Rights and the Interpretative Method of External Referencing' in Yves Haeck and others (eds), *The Inter-American Court of Human Rights: Theory and Practice, Present and Future* (Intersentia 2015) 3–24

Iacopino, Vincent, 'The Istanbul Protocol: Development, Practical Applications, and Future Directions' in Jason Payne-James and others (eds), *Monitoring Detention, Custody, Torture, and Ill-Treatment: A Practical Approach to Prevention and Documentation* (Routledge 2018) 249–66

Kelly, Tobias, 'Recognizing Torture: Credibility and the Unstable Codification of Victimhood' in Steffen Jensen and Henrik Rønsbo (eds), *Histories of Victimhood* (University of Pennsylvania Press 2014) 144–60

Kelly, Tobias, 'The Causes of Torture: Law, Medicine and the Assessment of Suffering in British Asylum Claims' in Ian Harper and others (eds), *The Clinic and the Court: Law, Medicine and Anthropology* (CUP 2015) 72–95

Kidd White, Emily, 'On Emotions and the Politics of Attention in Judicial Reasoning' in Amalia Amaya and Maksymilian Del Mar (eds), *Virtue, Emotion and Imagination in Law and Legal Reasoning* (Bloomsbury 2020) 101–120

Lieblich, Eliav, 'Beyond Life and Limb: Exploring Incidental Mental Harm under International Humanitarian Law' in Derek Jink and others (eds), *Applying International Humanitarian Law in Judicial and Quasi-Judicial Bodies* (Asser Press 2014) 185–218

Maroney, Terry, 'Lay Conceptions in Emotions of Law' in Susan Bandes and others (eds), *Research Handbook on Law and Emotion* (Elgar 2021) 15–25

Méndez, Juan, and Andra Nicolescu, 'Evolving Standards for Torture in International Law' in Metin Başoğlu (ed), *The Definition of Torture in International Law* (OUP 2017) 215–45

Moeckli, Daniel, and Nigel White, 'Treaties as "Living Instruments"' in Dino Kritsiotis and Michael Bowman (eds), *Conceptual and Contextual Perspectives on the Modern Law of Treaties* (CUP 2018) 136–71

Patel, Nimisha, 'The Psychologization of Torture' in Mark Rapley, Joanna Moncrieff, and Jacqui Dillon (eds), *De-medicalizing Misery* (Palgrave 2011) 239–55

Waldock, Humphrey, 'The Evolution of Human Rights Concepts and the Application of the European Convention on Human Rights' in P Reuter (ed), *Mélanges offerts à Paul Reuter: Le droit international: Unité Et diversité* (Padone 1981)

Yildiz, Ezgi, 'Interpretative Evolution of the Norm Prohibiting Torture and Inhuman or Degrading Treatment under the European Convention' in Anne-Lise Kjær and Joanna Lam (eds), *Language and Legal Interpretation in International Law* (OUP 2022) 295314

d. Other

CoE, *European Convention for the Protection of Human Rights and Fundamental Freedoms*, as amended by Protocol Nos 11 and 14, 4 November 1950, ETS 5

CoE and CPT, 'Solitary Confinement of Prisoners', CPT/Inf(2011)28-part2

Crew Against Torture (Russia), 'Prohibited Methods of Psychological Influence: Analysis of Russian and International Law' (2022)

ECmHR, 'Preparatory Work on Article 3 of the European Convention of Human Rights' (CoE 1956) DH (56) 6

ECtHR, 'Dialogue between Judges: What Are the Limits to the Evolutive Interpretation of the Convention?' (2011)

ECtHR, 'Guide on Article 3 of the European Convention on Human Rights: Prohibition of Torture' (August 2023)

ECtHR, 'Key Theme, Article 3: The Minimum Level of Severity Test in Light of *Bouyid v. Belgium*' (2022)
Enright, Máiréad, '*Coppin v. Ireland*: Depressing Conservatism from the UN Committee Against Torture', 12 February 2023, *Opinio Juris*
Freedom from Torture, 'Proving Torture, Demanding the Impossible: Home Office Mistreatment of Expert Medical Evidence' (2016)
Mavronicola, Natasa, 'Cruel Legacies: The CAT's Decision in *Coppin v Ireland*', 12 February 2023, *Opinio Juris*
Muntean, Liana Morica, 'Determining Torture in Interrogation Cases: Comparative Analysis of the Case Law of the European Court of Human Rights, the UN Bodies and the US Courts', Doctor of Juridical Science thesis, Central European University, Budapest (2017)
OAS, 'Report of the Committee on Juridical and Political Affairs on the Draft Convention Defining Torture as an International Crime', OEA/SerG CP/doc1524/84, 1984
OAS and American Convention on Human Rights, 'Pact of San Jose', Costa Rica, 22 November 1969
OAS and Inter-American Convention to Prevent and Punish Torture, 9 December 1985, Treaty Series, no 67
OHCHR, 'Committee Against Torture Discusses Istanbul Protocol', 2 November 2010, www.ohchr.org/en/press-releases/2010/11/committee-against-torture-discusses-istanbul-protocol
OMCT (Hasan Bakirci and Ugur Erdal), *Article 3 of the European Convention on Human Rights: A Practitioner's Handbook* (OMCT 2006)
Public Committee Against Torture in Israel (PCATI), 'Torture in Israel 2019: Situation Report'
Søndergaard, Elna and others (eds), *Three Protocols for the Medico-Legal Documentation of Psychological Torture* (DIGNITY 2024)
UN Body of Principles for the Protection of All Persons under Any Form of Detention or Imprisonment, GA res 43/173, 9 December 1988
UN Commission on Human Rights Draft Convention Against Torture and Other Cruel, Inhuman or Degrading Treatment or Punishment, 'Report of the Working Group' E/CN.4/11367 (5 March 1980), International Legal Materials, May 1980, 19 (3), 647–67
UN Commission on Human Rights, Situation of Detainees at Guantánamo Bay E/CN4/2006/120 (2006)
UN General Assembly, Convention Against Torture and Other Cruel, Inhuman or Degrading Treatment or Punishment, 10 December 1984, UN Treaty Series, 1465, 85
UN Istanbul Protocol I (1999)
UN Istanbul Protocol II (2022)
UN Nelson Mandela Rules (2015) (A/RES/70/175)
UN SRT, Report (1997) E/CN4/1997/7
UN SRT, Report (2010) A/56/156
UN SRT, Report (2016) A/71/298
UN SRT, Report (2020) A/HRC/43/49
University of Copenhagen, iCourts, Interview with President of the European Court of Human Rights Robert Spano by Professor Mikael Rask Madsen, 11 October 2023
University of Copenhagen, iCourts, President Judge Robert Spano, Talk, 'What Role for Human Duties, Obligations and Responsibilities in Our European Human Rights Discourse?', 2 December 2021
University of Strasbourg, 'Translating Climate Science for the Human Rights Court Room: An Interdisciplinary Encounter between Science and Law', Symposium, Strasbourg, 2 March 2023
Yildiz, Ezgi, 'A Court with Many Faces: Institutional Identities and Interpretive Preferences—The Case of the European Court of Human Rights and the Norm against Torture', PhD thesis, IHEID Geneva (2016)

Index

For the benefit of digital users, indexed terms that span two pages (e.g., 52–53) may, on occasion, appear on only one of those pages.